PROOF OF THE *Afterlife* 2

The Conversation Continues

+

June 20, 2017

May God bless
you as you read!

+ Bro.
Craig

PROOF OF THE *Afterlife* 2

The Conversation Continues

MERCY BOOKS
SERVANTS OF THE FATHER OF MERCY, INC., LOS ANGELES

BRO. GARY JOSEPH

PROOF OF THE AFTERLIFE
THE CONVERSATION CONTINUES
BROTHER GARY JOSEPH

Copyright © 2010-2017
All rights reserved.
Mercy Books, Servants of the Father of Mercy, Inc.
Printed in the United States of America

This book may not be reproduced in whole or in part, in any form, by Photostat, microfilm, or any other means, or incorporated into any informational retrieval system, electronic or mechanical without written permission of the copyright holder.

Published by *Mercy Books*, Servants of the Father of Mercy, Inc.
P. O. Box 42001, Los Angeles, CA 90042

First *Mercy Books* edition published November 2010 and Second Edition October 1, 2017 by special arrangement with the author

Cover design and interior layout by
Exodus Design Studios www.exodusdesign.com

Library of Congress Cataloging-in-Publication Data
Joseph, Gary Bro.
Proof of the Afterlife 2 – *The Conversation Continues*
1. Spiritual life – Catholic Church 2. Christianity

ISBN 978-0-9833816-2-4
U.S. $24.95
Softcover
Published October 1, 2017

10 9 8 7 6 5 4 3 2 1

Dedication

Proof of the Afterlife 2 – *The Conversation Continues* is enthusiastically and gratefully dedicated to Fr. Frank D., Fr. Jim C., Fr. John N., Monsignor Liam K. and Fr. Paul H., insightful Spiritual Directors, guides and dear friends.

Note of Thanks

On July 30, 2010, this book's manuscript was sent to the archbishop of the Archdiocese of Los Angeles, Cardinal Roger Mahony for theological review three months in advance of its publication. I offer many thanks to Cardinal Mahony, his priest assistants and theological team for having received the manuscript and for perusing its content.

Also, I send many prayers and blessings to Fr. Frank D. and Fr. John N. my Spiritual Directors for the time they took to offer feedback and in some cases read the manuscript in the nascent stages of the book's creation to present.

Last but not least, *Proof of the Afterlife – The Conversation Continues* first edition was lovingly evaluated and edited by Pam, Angela and Anita and her mom Mildred. God bless each of you for all your time, insights, passion and effort.

The second edition was wonderfully edited by Rick Cotterman with input from his wife, Kris Cotterman, the owner of *Exodus Design* in Apple Valley, MN and who is also the creator of both the first and second editions' awesome book covers and artwork.

May the Lord bless the more than 10,000 readers of the first edition who have made *"Proof of the Afterlife"* a huge publishing success!

Book 1

Table of Contents

Prologue

The Bilheimer Cabin

As I write the first book, *Proof of the Afterlife – The Conversation Continues,* I'm holed up for many days in a mountain cabin that a friend so generously provided. It's in the high desert of the San Gabriel Mountains, and although no one is here, one can't help but to hear the conversation that is going on all around.

Right now it is springtime. Nature seems to have a unique dialogue with itself and with the visitors that come here this time of year, very different from summer, fall and winter I would imagine. For instance, there are a plethora of birds and their new born little ones that congregate around the cabin, mostly in the morning at sunrise. Some sing, some chirp, squawk, squeal and yet others even seem to talk. I thought only humans did that! The chipmunks, baby rabbits, jack rabbits and the ground squirrels all play in the moment and somehow everyone seems to get along, surprisingly, really well.

Up here, around five thousand feet above the Pacific Ocean, the wind seems to howl with mysterious utterances too, especially in the springtime. You can never see the wind – from where it comes or where it goes, but it's always a surprise when a forceful gust coaxes the car off a mountain road, like a dry leaf aimlessly flopping about in the desert below. It's times like this that the wind seems to tell everyone that it's in charge in this neck of the woods. When I first arrived, the winds were calm and balmy. Last night they had a mind of their own and they were frigid – powerfully gusting particles of desert sand and pinecones all the way to Kansas! That particular exchange told me to stay inside, build a fire and snuggle up because it's going to be a long boisterous night. It was.

Living in the desert has taught me to be obedient to the sun when it talks – in these parts, the sun rules. In the springtime, that ninety-three-million-mile-away fireball wakes up pretty darn early. At about 5:30am, the first rays of soft blue and orange light ever so gently begin to bathe the front kitchen window, which incidentally has no curtain on it. It's a cabin with a view, so while doing the dishes dialoguing with the twinkling valley lights at sunset, or grey stormy clouds below in the morning, one needs to be ready and waiting with no hindrances, like a drape obstructing the chatter. But let's get back to the 5:30am first soft rays of dawn's early light. By 6:00am, the blaring luminous streams of sunbeams burst into the cabin vociferously crying out, *"Wake up; it's time to get up!"* There's no escaping that conversation, no matter how tired you are or how hard you try. It's just time to obey, crawl out of bed and make a nice freshly brewed cup of hot coffee.

The mountains and hills all around have a wonderful babble, too. These are majestic old mounts that in the parching hundred-degree desert heat of summer, might say, *"Go away, there's nothing to look at right now,"* but not so in the spring. At the moment, lush green wilderness cactus blossom everywhere with delicate white and pink blooms. The neighboring shrubs and ground cover sprout royal purple, white and deep yellow flora. All of it seems to create a symphony of voices that croon, *"Look at us. Look at the mountains and hills. We've gotten ready for your visit. Resurrection has come. Rejoice!"*

What's most remarkable is how much of the discussion here goes on in silence. Yes, the silence speaks volumes. Far from the distractions of urban life like idle chatter, whining, complaining, going to the store for this-or-that, meetings and phone calls – life here is so very silent, so purged of fast food and other modern addictions that its emptiness tells the conversation within to speak out. That's frightening sometimes. Possibly it's easier in the city where one does not have to wrestle with the silence. But here you do. It's all good though. In the end, I'm thankful I stuck out my many days in solitude on this mountain. The hush gave birth to the voice of this book, *Proof of the Afterlife – The Conversation Continues*. How remarkable and extraordinary to enter into the silence to write a book about dialogue. Only God could orchestrate that anomaly!

Lastly, the cabin itself is a conversation. How so you may

ask? Well, the Bilheimer family has been coming to this mountain retreat for more than fifty years, long before there were any civil roads to get here. Back then, the trip from the coast took hours and provided for a lot of the folks time to just chat in the car on the way up. On the walls, there are pictures of grandpa Bilheimer posing with '40s politicians – that tells a story too. Other old photographs of the children, grandchildren and great-grandchildren are hung up on what looks like aged California redwood paneling. According to the clothing of the time, some of the photos look as though they were taken straight from a 60s television shoot of *"Father Knows Best"* or *"Leave it to Beaver."* Also, not far from the charred, stone fireplace, are inviting pictures of snowy winter days, an Indian-themed Thanksgiving fiesta and lots of plain ol' black and white family shots. All of which seem to say that here are relatives who know how to pursue and enjoy engaging conversations with each other. Hopefully, now that everyone has read this prologue, we'll all go out and be stirred to do more of the same. Thank you DJ, Susan and family for the cabin, the inspiration and the conversation. Thank you to Pam and Joel for making the connection.

Chapter One

Introduction to the Conversation

In the early hours of the morning of September 27th, I had awoken at 1:00am feeling energetic and unable to sleep. After a few minutes, I got up and stood in the living room with some pillows, a blanket and the television's remote control in hand, somewhat expecting that a round or two of late-night shows might help me to fall back asleep. As I glanced at the DVD player, it was now 1:15am. What happens next is recorded as the first entry in a journal that would eventually chronicle five years of repeated encounters with the Other Side. Here is what I wrote that startling night at two o'clock in the morning.

Tuesday, September 27, 2005 – It is 2:00am in the morning and I will try to put into words the gift of "seeing" and experiencing the presence of God, the Father Almighty and his son, the Lord Jesus Christ. At 1:00am this morning, I awoke after just a couple of hours of sleep and was going to watch television with a pillow and blanket on the living room floor. Instead, in the darkness, while the television clock read 1:15am, I decided to try and fall asleep on the floor and get some additional rest. Just as I began to turn over to fall asleep, I was overcome by an enormous Presence that came into the room and filled the atmosphere all around me. Initially, I did not know Who or What this Presence was, but I was terrified.

Physically weakened, by the shock of an overwhelming supernatural Power densely saturating the room, I grasped the edge of the dining room table in hopes to give my legs strength to run and hide. I attempted to run away three times. However, I was completely overcome and could not stand on my own ability. I was only able to make it to my knees, but then I had to surrender to this Almighty Power and fell to the floor yielding to its Presence and control. At this point, I was fearful, yet I felt strangely safe giving in to this Power. My heart raced and beat out of my chest. My body felt as though it would burst from His Presence. My hands and feet felt as though they would explode.

After I collapsed on the floor, I had a sense that I had died. My heart stopped, it became extremely quiet and all the energy – an intense electrical tingling sensation exited out of my hands and feet. Next, in the solitude, I hovered over my body for a brief moment and saw myself, my body collapsed on the floor. Immediately I left the living room and I was facing the front of a gray screen. I was powerfully aware that I was now in the presence of God the Father Almighty. The gray screen was shielding me from His pure white rays of radiant and piercing glory. Some pieces of brilliant light escaped and passed through small holes in the screen, but God chose to shield me from His complete presence. Spontaneously, I said over and over to Him, *"Glory to God in the highest and peace to His people on earth."*

He identified Himself as the God of the Bible, the God of Abraham, Isaac and Jacob. He did not speak the way we do; his communication seemed absorbed, like a crashing tsunami wave soaking into a dry sandy beach.

Next, I asked if I could see Him. He responded to me with a simple but emphatic, *"No!"* He said, *"No, you cannot see me or you will be dead."* He revealed to me that He cannot expose me to His complete glory, that I could not survive such an experience. He made known to me many lifetimes of Biblical and theological studies in what seemed like seconds. He spoke of His character, He is my Father and He created me. He revealed His Fatherhood qualities are composed of duty, righteousness, honor, high expectations, labor, love, steadfastness and judgment. He communicated not in linear thoughts, but by instant absorption, transmitting millions of messages that flooded my soul in a brief moment.

Then I was taken from His presence and began to drift aimlessly in total blackness, as if I was in some remote part of outer space. At first, I was terrified of the dark and the void. Yet, the thought occurred to me that I had just been with God the Father, there is nothing to fear. I began to have faith. At the moment of having faith, my feet landed on solid ground and I felt more secure in the darkness. As I looked around, I was transfixed on a small speck of light way out in the black universe. I watched as it came closer to the planet. It appeared to be my only hope in the vast darkness. The light, so it turns out, was actually a great, magnificent, luminous white cross radiating powerful beams, piercing the blackness and slicing through the void in an indescribable way – unlike any illumination we have here on earth. It powerfully cut through the blackness of the night. Instantly, I realized that this light is Christ, as it grew in radiance above me. I recognized Jesus in his *"sign of the cross."* Upon realizing that it was Jesus, He immediately came from the cross, flooded me with love, mercy and hugs that exceed millions of times more than any earthly love and hugs a child could ever receive from a mother or father. As he caressed me with His love and presence, I said to him over and over, *"A day in your presence, Lord, is better than thousands elsewhere."* I wanted to stay right there in His arms forever.

However, in those very moments while I was being embraced by Christ, I was sent back to my body. I awoke on the living room floor and saw that the clock in front of me now said 1:45am. I had been like a dead man, immersed in this encounter for exactly thirty minutes. My heart had restarted again and it was pounding out of my chest. With every beat, the chest lifted high from my body and I felt as though my heart and my chest would explode. It seemed as though my body could not sustain the soul's direct encounter with God.

Not at any time did I ever feel as though this was a medical emergency and never did I think about calling for help. To the contrary, I recalled over and over in my mind the events that had just occurred. I had just "seen" God! I was completely overcome, dazed and confused as to what it all meant. I lay there some minutes, hoping to gain strength and the ability to walk again after absorbing the complete impact and shock of the event. At 2:00am I stood up, weak and trembling and wrote in my computer this account of what had just happened.

As a footnote to this momentous encounter, that same day, weak and still overcome by a collision with God's presence, I somehow mustered up the ability to go to work as usual and then attended the daily 5:30pm Mass that I had begun going to the past couple of months. After receiving Communion, I spoke with Fr. Ed in the church parking lot about the extraordinary event that had just taken place. Shaken, overwhelmed and feeling internally corrupt to the core because I had been exposed to the purity of God, I went to Confession for the first time in decades. I remarked to Fr. Ed that no human should be allowed to be in the presence of God, especially me! I was both doomed and cleansed by the illuminating presence of God granting me full knowledge of my worthlessness. I was unworthy to have been there and repeatedly asked myself, *"Why me?"* After what happened today, I feel like I can relate in a very small way and also eerily echo the words of Isaiah the prophet, who after having been caught up into heaven and seeing the presence of God, he wrote: *"Woe is me! For I am lost; for I am a man of unclean lips; and I dwell in the midst of a people of unclean lips; for my eyes have seen the King, the Lord of hosts."* (Isaiah 6:5)

Reading this incredible account, some might feel that one extraordinary encounter would be enough of a conversation with God to convince anyone to believe in him and reform their ways. However, this book is not about one meeting with Eternity. After the events of September 27th, a cascade of supernatural meetings began to take place, surprising me, my spiritual director, mother, family and friends at every turn. I will share their details throughout the book, just as recorded when they happened.

In hindsight, now I realize that God was having a conversation with me all my life. I suspect not only me, but he is having it with every person he has ever created. For this reason, it became apparent to me to share with others my on-going dialogue with the other side. Those willing to read the entire book, may it awaken within each, the ability to hear the voice of God speaking in our lives today.

So what is this conversation all about? Our English word *"conversation"*, prior to its use in Middle English and French, came to us in ancient times. Its root is from the Latin word *'conversari'* which means *"to associate with."* Nowadays, we primarily think of the word *"conversation"* to mean *"a discussion or an exchange of thoughts and ideas."* It is refreshing to add the Latin root *'conversari'* to the mix. It is here, in this added dimension that this book uses the word *"conversation."* Meaning, it is not simply a discussion or an exchange of ideas between family, friends or colleagues. At its very core, *"conversation"* is first and foremost an intimate and life-giving *'association'* with others. In that light, let us begin.

The whole world is a conversation isn't it? When we are newborn babies, we struggle to enter into that conversation. After months of incoherent sounds, one day and completely unexpectedly, babies suddenly explode with first words like, *Da Da* or a hearty, *Ma Ma*! Next, we spend most of our childhood going to school where we learn the alphabet and then on to history, science, languages and math, so we can grow up and competently participate in the entire conversation around us.

Ever plan a trip to a foreign country? The first thing to do is get a crash course in their language. It's very important to engage in the conversation once you arrive there isn't it? Conversing with the locals is no doubt rooted in the desire to associate with others around us – the people in airports, cafes, bars, restaurants, shops and museums. Dialoguing at every turn is at the very core of what we will do each and every minute while visiting that country.

Our desire to have conversation and association with others is so strong, that most people would like to believe that the conversation we are having now with our loved ones, somehow even continues after their death. This desire is so innate in the human experience, that long before Christianity reached ancient cultures in the Americas, the Mayans, the Aztecs and other Indian tribes had firmly established beliefs in the afterlife. Our celebration of Halloween, in fact, has gained popularity around the world beyond the U.S. in recent years. The fall celebration provides many a chance to think about and even have fun with the notion of souls being fully alive in the hereafter. Acknowledging life after death and having contact with these souls, is at the core of most cultures and peoples' experience.

Although some may struggle with the idea of life after death, still others firmly believe that it is also possible to even converse with God himself. According to very ancient records of the Bible, Abraham spoke with God and Moses did too. Many saints and modern mystics have been said to have conversed with God as well. As recent as the mid-1900s, right prior to World War II, a small unassuming nun in the country of Poland, by the name of Faustina Kowalska, experienced frequent and direct conversations with God. Her astonishing mystical encounters are meticulously detailed in a six-hundred-page journal titled, *Diary of Maria Faustina Kowalska,* available at most bookstores.

Thus, taking all things into consideration throughout the ages, it seems as though the conversation in our lives is actually a lot bigger than possibly could be imagined – spanning both heaven and earth. The cosmic dialogue that is going on around us is much grander than all our cell phone calls, texting and emails combined! However, the caveat is that one can't even hear or participate, if belief in God is rejected. God's conversation is reserved only for people of Faith, those who are humbly searching for truth and who hunger and thirst for righteousness.

Not only has God been having a conversation and association with the world since its inception, but we too have been experiencing the same with each other. Our families, friends, nations and even foes have also been striving to be in conversation with each other since the beginning of civilization. Life itself – living here on this earth, is one big exchange with each other and with God.

Most people attend religious services at one time or another because of our inborn desire to speak with God and in hope that he speaks back to us. But also with our family and friends, our lives are centered on this sort of grand chatter going on all around us. For instance, we take meals together, we sit and have coffee together, we go out for a drink, we go for a walk together and what do we do? We chat, and we chat, and we chat! That is why when a friend or loved one dies, our immediate reaction is to miss calling them, to miss visiting them, going out together and ultimately, we miss conversing with them. And where do we eventually end up when we have anxieties about these matters? We head back to church and in our "cloud of unknowing" we try to initiate a dialogue with God.

Of course, most know, on some interior level, that the Bible – the Holy Scriptures are a key chunk of God's conversation with all of us here on earth. The Bible is the number one bestselling book of all time. The Book has sold in the billions of copies since the invention of the printing press. No other book has ever or will ever come close to this literary sales record. It is unbeatable, and for good reason. In it, God himself has a discussion with us about our individual and collective human condition. The Scriptures are authoritative and we can count on them to frame what God has to say to us about being in association with him, going to heaven and enjoying eternal life.

Through this collection of ancient manuscripts, written primarily in Hebrew and Greek, and assembled over thousands of years of history (no other book in the records of the world has ever been compiled in this way), God converses with us individually and corporately. He shows us that illness, suffering and death are not what he had planned for us. We discover that humans, at one point in ancient time, cut ties with God and quit effectively conversing with him and with each other. When we decided to go it alone, our association with each other also suffered gravely. Shortly after the first sin, the "Big Screw Up" in the Garden of Eden, as the story goes, Cain kills Abel and the first of millions of murders takes place in human history. Now, today in hindsight, we all know what the Garden's first sin of human pride, arrogance and declaration of independence from God has gotten us – wars, violence, crime, murder, injustice, inequity and the like.

But God is merciful and has steadfastly conversed with us over the ages, with the goal to put each one of us, all of humankind back on track – to reorder our lives, to reorder our passions so that we can enter into peace and eternal life. It has been his goal to create cosmos out of chaos, which God is infinitely good at according to the "Big Bang Theory." His aim has been to take our "disconnect" and re-establish the connection, no matter what the personal cost is to him or us.

However, God's conversation with us does not end at the close of the last book of the Bible. In every age, he also speaks to each one of us through nature as well as through our hearts, minds and souls – right within the context of our daily lives. He is no doubt having a dialogue with each of his children at this very moment. But some are so busy with an iPhone or don't even care, that they are not listening. Many obsess with their worldly pursuits that unequivocally silence the voice of God. As a result, many believe that God does not exist or doubt that he exists because they are deaf to his conversation.

Each of us here, on the earth today, is just as special to him as the Biblical characters and writers he once directly inspired – Isaiah, Esther, Jeremiah, Ruth, Peter, James or John. His conversation continues with each of us just as it did in the days of old. It is a common mistake to think that God's "words" and "mighty deeds" are told only in

Scripture. Every person's heart and life is etched with God's "words." We are imprinted with his creative expression of art, goodness, compassion and love that interiorly speak to each one of us loud and clear in our daily lives. God talks first and foremost in our hearts, minds and conscience. But he also speaks through friends, events in our lives, situations we find ourselves in, family, nature and the spiritual writings of the saints.

However, what is most remarkable, God also piques our interest in his words of life through "supernatural" means. Many call it "supernatural", but I like to think of it as "natural." Through his "natural" ways, God speaks to us in dreams, our personal prayer times, church services and even provides some with visions, bi-locations (Padre Pio) and various types of auditory and interior locutions (cf. Teresa of Avila and John of the Cross). The point of the matter is that God cares and he *is* speaking – even today, this very minute! Some may have not taken the time or the effort to stay in touch, so they think he doesn't care or worse yet, *"God is dead!"*

Having a book like this, to validate that the conversation is on and hotly engaging, is very encouraging for many. That is why I am writing the manuscript. As I stated in the Prologue, I have taken some weeks off work to be holed up in this mountain cabin to do one thing, to carve hope out of human hearts – some made of flesh and yet others of stone. To give encouragement to the many that struggle to know about the marvelous winds of God's Spirit aggressively at work, dusting off our lives and blowing new life into our hearts today.

If you are like me, possibly you have never known or met someone that has had visions, locutions and conversations with God or with souls from the other side. Frankly, I am the first person I have ever known or met in this regard. Now, I am learning of many others as I share my story. Since completing the study of undergraduate and graduate-level theology in 1978, I've been experiencing "natural" phenomena from the other side from time-to-time. However, since my near-death-experience (NDE) in 2005, and then recent theological studies at St. John's Seminary, the encounters have increased significantly and I have been gifted with sometimes two – three events a week. I imagine many of these gifts are not for me, but to share for the building up of Faith in others like you. Many miraculous interventions recorded in my journal I will share in the following chapters of this book in order that you may have hope in God – hope for your life, as well as hope for your family and friends' lives; that you may also have peace and have it abundantly.

At this point, there may be more questions raised than answers. Of course, it is only the introduction, so give time for the following pages to make known my story and I will also try to address your concerns. So what are the many questions one may have and that people might be asking about the possibility of having authentic conversations with God and the souls on the other side? Will the obvious questions be covered in this book?

Yes, *Proof of the Afterlife – The Conversation Continues,* will shed light on the following: How do we hear from God? How do we enter into a conversation with him? Just as importantly, how do we enter into life-giving conversations with each other in the midst of being preoccupied with our work, commuting, household responsibilities and the like? Does the conversation with a loved one end at their death? Does the conversation end with God upon our own death? What happens to us when we die? How do we enter into conversation with family and friends who have crossed over to the other side? Can they hear us? Can we hear them? What is the ultimate purpose of this cosmic dialogue when we actually tune into it? What happens at a person's funeral – are they there – can they see and hear us? Does God continue conversing with souls who have departed? Do they receive more chances to "get it right"? Can we help them? Can they help us? Is this a book just about the dead? How will the evidence in this book help the living? Will it help me to live a better life? What are the lessons to be learned here?

Wow, that's a lot of questions! But you probably have dozens more. After all, we are talking about the very nature of eternity here – that's an endless bundle of information. However, I suspect that by the time you finish reading *Proof of the Afterlife – The Conversation Continues,* you will have a sense that many of your questions will have been addressed and possibly even resolved. But how will you know that? That's a good question too. Don't take my word for it. The proof is in the peace! There will be a growing peace in your heart and mind as you read. There will arise, deep within, a sense that you are tapping into the very nature, the very truth of who *God Is*. (He tells Moses, [my name is], *"I am."*) The proof is in the peace that will saturate your soul, like fresh bread dunked in a wonderful coffee or tea, but millions of times more satisfying!

Okay, let's be real. There may be even more proof for some readers. What do I mean by that? Well, I suspect that what God has done for me, by opening up the flood gates of conversation on all sides, he wants to do the same for the many who are reading this book; mainly because of your sincere desire to seek after him. God wants to have ongoing dialogue with you as well as with your loved ones, no doubt. There may be a need for souls on the other side to "speak" with you, especially if there is the unfinished business of love and forgiveness to be worked out. All it takes on your part is a humble heart, daily prayer, charity and an open mind to accept all that the limitless Lord God has to offer. It is more about coming to God in poverty, acknowledging our sinfulness and emptiness than it is about knowing, wanting to know, pride or wealth.

If you sincerely wish to have merciful and compassionate relationships with your family and friends, whether dead or alive, God wants to open up the dialogue for you here on earth and with the other side. If you have a sincere desire to forgive others, to be patient, kind and compassionate as God has done for you, God wants to hook you up to where all the chatter is. However, if you are stuck in unforgiveness, hate, anger, unbelief and other negative emotions – it is important to know that the gifts of heaven are reserved only for those who have faith, forgive and pray blessings for one's enemies. Now would be a good time to begin to pray for those who have hurt you and whom you have hurt, and make a decision to become merciful toward them – whether they are dead or alive. Just as God is being merciful toward us in our failures, sins and shortcomings – so must we be that way with others. The more heroically merciful that you are, the more likely it is that God will be gracious toward you and open the flood gates of heavenly conversation with him and with others.

For those who have a Catholic heritage or would like to have one, the Sacraments of the Church can help big time to facilitate this dialogue with God and with each other. To this point, here is an entry from my journal just a few weeks after my near-death-experience:

Friday, October 14, 2005 – Attending daily Mass and Communion has become for me the sign and symbol and the reality that all through my life, Jesus Christ has longed to have an on-going Communion, a constant dialogue with me. Minute-by-minute he wishes to talk with me and to walk with me. Second-by-second He wishes to reveal his presence to me. Going to daily Mass and Communion brings me into an eternal perpetual conversation with Christ, very God himself. Daily Communion fills me with a constant moment-by-moment presence of God in my life, as initially revealed in the encounter of September 27, 2005, when right prior to it, for two months I had begun to go to daily Mass and Communion.

Going forward, as the story unravels; you will discover that this book's chapters are named after my family associations, all leading to the point that the conversation does indeed continue with loved ones, dead or alive. Ranging from a chapter starting with myself, to chapters about how the conversation has played out with loved ones such as my brother, father, mother, cousin as well as other family and friends.

Chapter Two
Me

I planned, for a while now, to open up this chapter with a particular clip from my journal, because its reflection gives hope to all those who see themselves as weak, lost, broken and a sinner. I am a first-hand witness to the fact that a loser is exactly the kind of person that God loves in a special way and wants to talk to. Yes, I am a contemporary "eyewitness" to God, but that is only because I am a sinner like everyone else on the planet. It would be inaccurate for anyone to think that I am anything "special" because of the enormous gift I have received by directly encountering God. My eyewitness account should not make anyone feel envious or slighted, but to the contrary, it should make us all feel strengthened and filled with hope that God goes after the "ordinary" as well as those who are empty and broken. Almost two years after my near-death-experience, I wrote the following in my journal in this regard:

Wednesday, July 18, 2007 – In a vision this morning, I was standing in a large hall filled with many people. I got up and addressed the crowd and said to them, *"It is significant for you that a sinner like me has encountered the Lord. Although you were not there* [at my Paul-like, NDE] *you accept my testimony. It is a message of hope, that God likewise is revealing himself to you. He loves you and wants to have a relationship with you."*

Now, here's a little bit of my story . . . In the summer of 2005, I was suddenly diagnosed with a tumor – a large growth about the size of a golf ball attached to the thyroid. In April, I had been examined for two days by one of the top hospitals in the country and it was their professional opinion that the on-again, off-again rapid heart arrhythmias and sensations of suffocation I had been experiencing for a few years were psychological and they recommended Prozac. I refused to take it. However, it was in June that a medical student accidentally picked out my x-rays for class work and discovered a golf-ball-size tumor growing interiorly in my throat, compressing on the airway. The doctor in charge called me apologetically and said to come in immediately; he suspected, given the size, it was going to test positive for cancer.

About that very same time, my cousin Kim (who was a childhood favorite and adult business partner too), living 3,000 miles away, was about to go on a scuba diving expedition. After a routine checkup on a Monday, on the following Friday, what she thought would be a regular day of receiving normal test results, turned out to be the doctor telling her that she had extensive lung cancer and was being given about 6-9 months to live.

Although I had been very "busy" for the past twenty-one years as a writer and business consultant and had made very little time for God, I knew that had to immediately change. In July of 2005, though working 9-5 at the time, I had made a decision to attend daily Mass and Communion for the special intention of my cousin Kim, her well-being and for myself and my own health woes. The Mass was at 5:30pm and that meant I had no ability to work overtime and be a workaholic like I had done for decades. Establishing a dialogue and a relationship with God was now a top priority.

Up until the middle of August, when inpatient surgery was scheduled, the medical professionals were thinking "cancer" because two different biopsies came back inconclusive. However, the day the surgery was performed, afterwards in O.R., the tumor was immediately tested by frozen section and it miraculously came back negative! After some weeks of daily prayer and Mass, a miracle had taken place. Likewise, my cousin Kim had begun aggressive cancer treatments at a hospital in Houston, Texas, and was commuting by air 2,000 miles a week. Through the advancements of modern medicine, and I believe various miracles from God, Kim out-lived her prognosis (by one-and-a-half years) and had a much fuller life than expected. One miracle that stands out in my mind was the day Kim, had succumb to undiagnosed fluid building up around her heart. "Coincidentally," she was walking into the hospital for a regularly scheduled check-up when she went into cardiac arrest. The professional and timely treatment she received, added many more quality months to her life. She died on May 30, 2007. Kim was 49 years old.

I recovered well after my surgery. Within 24 hours I was

sent home from the hospital and within two weeks I was back to work and had begun attending daily Mass and Communion again. But in August, my thoughts were turning more contemplative than before and not as self-centered as I normally was in life. In my college years, I had dedicated myself to completing a Bachelor of Theology degree and a Masters in Biblical Studies and quite actively served God. Since that time, I had drifted away from my conversation with God – that is up until now.

In August of 2005, I had returned to reading the Scriptures once again. In the first moment that I had flipped open my old tattered Bible dating back to the '70s, I accidentally and quite randomly turned to this first sentence after twenty-one years away, *"This I have against you, you have lost your first love."* (Revelations 2:4) Whoa! There was no doubt in my mind that God was having a conversation with me and it was spanning the length and breadth of my lifetime.

In that August, I was also thinking a lot about my dad as I was resting, healing and getting stronger from the surgery. He had passed away in July of 2003. He was a harsh man in many ways and in today's terms he would be called "abusive." He was tough with almost everyone – his wife, children and co-workers – no one was exempt. Confusingly, at times he could also be very charming and cordial too. However, what bothered me the most in this relationship was his cavalier ability to behave belligerently and somehow justify it all in the name of religion. I guess that would be called a type of "hypocrisy." For decades, it was tough to forgive all that had happened to so many of us at his hands.

But suddenly, I was coming to a more accurate realization about myself and frequently saying interiorly, *"Hey, you're a loser! You're a sinner too. Your sin is just different from his."* That insight helped me to muster up the mercy and compassion necessary to genuinely forgive him. It felt good when it all came together in my mind in those weeks right after surgery. It seemed as though the conversation was opening up, but I had no idea at this point how huge it was going to get.

A few weeks after the near-death-experience, I saw my family physician for a regular follow-up visit and he diagnosed the event as a heart attack caused by a rapid arrhythmia which was set off by a thyroid that was healing (from where the growth was removed). The thyroid had momentarily become hyperactive. He and his nursing staff gathered and listened intently as I shared the details of the NDE. The doctor, convinced that what had happened to me was real, said candidly, *"Dude, you've been somewhere where few people ever return from. I have had a few other patients over the years that have described very similar after death experiences."*

In the days and weeks that followed this enormous God-encounter, I began to journal. To this very day, almost five years later, I keep record of many reflections, illuminations, thoughts, visions and locutions. I will be sharing various entries from my journal in the chapters that follow.

There is no doubt that when God reveals himself in such an amazing manner, that the revelation is a complete gift. Everything is a gift – our salvation, sanctification, faith and even being connected to God himself. I realize that I bring nothing to the table. It is all grace; it is all a gift. I have done nothing to deserve anything. I am the very least to have received such an enormous prize!

In hindsight, I have begun to realize that not just these mountain top revelations of God are a gift, but also his pursuit of us over the total years of our life is a gift too. It is apparent to me now, that God comes after us in a way that he allows the gifts of suffering, afflictions and illness in order to bring us to himself. It is very similar to the athlete, who suffers greatly while in training, just to win an Olympic Games competition. While preparing, the coach allows his protégé to feel the pain, knowing the value of the great prize to be won. Thus, suffering truly is a gift. It can help us to become perfected into a peaceful state of quietude, by divesting one from the daily internal noise of self-seeking activities that crowd out God's voice.

Ultimately, how does suffering work its magic? It has the unique ability to temporarily suspend – arrest one's free will by creating a type of Purgatory here on earth. Thereby, the way is paved for the soul to become wonderfully tranquil; thus giving the person the phenomenal ability to be directly united in conversation with very God himself.

Chapter Three
Brother, Jimmy

In the fall of 1989, I had not heard from my older brother Jimmy for many years. At this time, he was now thirty-seven years old. In fact, my two older sisters and my parents had not heard from him either. On my part, there was no lost love here in this relationship to even want to go and search for him. I can remember being only five or six years old, and as some older brothers notoriously do, he would beat up on me for no apparent reason. When the day was done, in many instances, what he instigated got blamed on me and more often than not, I was the one put in the dog house. There was no justice! That early-on pouncing was basically the dynamic of our relationship that lasted until he moved away from the house at the age of eighteen. In 1989 he was out of sight and therefore the pain of it all was out of mind. But that was about to change.

On a Wednesday night in October of 1989, I was fast asleep, when all of a sudden I had a terrifying dream about my brother. It was so horrible; it moved me to feel compassion for him. Something I don't ever recall having before for this angry soul. In the dream, I saw my brother in an empty and very dimly lit room. Of all places, he was lying on the floor. He had no bed and no possessions. Instantly, I became acutely aware that he was suffering greatly, that he was dying and most terrifying of all, he was dying alone. In the dream, I was aware that he had no friends, no family and no one to come to his aid.

As we all do, upon awakening, I dismissed this dream as something connected to the crazy world of nocturnal imaginings. I blocked out its content and went on my merry way of work and activities for the day. *"No one believes that God converses this way - do they?"* I thought to myself. Well, that denial did not last for long.

It was now the very next night, Thursday, and while I was fast asleep, it was if I had gone to a movie theater and the entire vision from the night before was played over again in its entirety. I saw the same stark, dimly lit room, and my brother lying on the floor. Again, I was acutely aware that he was suffering so, but had no one to assist him or even care about him.

Upon awakening, I had a sense that God was talking to me and I needed to listen. The first thing I did was to contemplate the "what if." What if the two consecutive nights of dreams are true? Would I be willing to step in and be his friend? Would I be willing to be forgiving and compassionate, putting aside our differences? Out of nowhere, and in very little time, I had made the decision to help someone who at one time was considered the "enemy." Interiorly, it just seemed like the right thing to do. But how would I find him to see if everything was okay?

Immediately that same day, I telephoned an older sister who was living in Colorado at the time. I shared with her the content of the dream. She concurred that it would be a good idea to research this more. She thought of a friend in New York City that just may know something about Jimmy's whereabouts. Within a few days, she had received word that her friend had found our brother in Saint Francis hospital with a very critical condition – pneumonia for the third time in six months. Wow! God was talking and he was using amazing means to associate with our family and to help us. Although the news was not good at all, it was encouraging to know that God had used a series of dreams to speak out and send help for a dying soul. More importantly, he did it in a way that it became *"my idea"* to help my brother, and not a command where I was boxed in and I had no choice in the matter. God always suggests through inspiration and in that process completely respects our free will. He is a *perfect* gentleman.

My sister flew to New York in December, helped close out Jimmy's apartment and he boarded a flight for Miami, where he would be closer to me and I could facilitate his care. Because of my willingness to help him, my brother told others that the sun sort of rose and set on me. That was embarrassing because I knew that I was nothing special. Our life-long antagonistic relationship was instantly set aright by a combination of my simple act of charity and a lot of suffering on his part. As I said earlier, God does not send suffering, but he uses it as needed to establish dialogue with us and each other here on earth.

It was at a Miami hospital in January of 1990 that my mother and father appeared there to meet their prodigal son for the first time in years. It was also here that he was diagnosed as being H.I.V. positive. In the hallway, outside the door of Jimmy's hospital room, hostilely my father said to me, *"Well, what do you expect? That is what God does to gay people like him."* At that point, it became clear to me; my brother was being hated and rejected by his very own father.

Unfortunately, my mother was trained to follow the "party" line, so although she had a strong devotion to God, and of course a mother's instinct is to never forsake her child, she was afraid to disagree and suffer dad's wrath. When I had asked for their financial help with his care, they refused. When asking for some of their personal time, they refused as well, on the grounds that, *"our church friends would not understand."* My poor brother was being despised and rejected by those closest to him, his own mother and father. But in my mind, to a certain extent that was okay – Jesus suffered rejection by some closest to him, so Jimmy was in good company.

It was astonishing for my dad, of all people, however, to behave this way when he himself was apparently hiding severe skeletons in his own closet that, oddly enough, he did not feel were that bad. In hindsight, all severe sin is bad and one type is no better and no worse than another – they just have different names. That should cause each of us to be honest with ourselves about our sinfulness and be compassionate towards others in their struggles, contradictions and brokenness.

Being alerted by God to care for my brother, to offer him charity, compassion and mercy may have repaired that relationship in eternity, but the conversation obviously got worse withy my mother and father. It seemed evident to me that here are two people that say they love God, go to church every Sunday, but in the big picture have their own blatant sins of power, being judgmental, hate and hypocrisy still dominating our familial relationships. The injustice of it all tugged at every fabric of my moral sensibility to forgive and forget. In their case, it took years before that could ever completely happen.

God's compassion and powerful conversation with me and my brother was astonishing. It became very clear to me one of the messages that God was sending, through Jimmy's life story, is that he loves all of his children equally, no matter if they are straight, gay, black, brown, adulterer, atheist or saint. In my brother's case, I was overwhelmed by the personal responsibility of God as he delivered on his word in the Bible where the Psalmist David wrote, *"For he will deliver the needy who cry out, the afflicted who have no one to help. He will take pity on the weak and the needy and save the dying when they're alone. He will rescue them from oppression and violence, for precious is their blood in his sight."* (Psalm 72:12-14)

My brother died peacefully in his sleep in July of 1990. When he was buried, by my prompting, he had these words placed on his grave stone: *"Jesus said . . . 'Let us rejoice and be glad, because this brother of yours who was dead and is now alive again; he was lost and now is found.'"*

About two months after his death, in September of 1990, I can recall a vision where God permitted me, for the first time, the opportunity to visit my brother in the afterlife. What we shared together at that time was significant. In it, I was transported in spirit to the backyard of the large three story redbrick home that Jimmy and I grew up in as children. Immediately, I recognized my brother having a party at a picnic table under the shade of a grand old elm tree that our family loved. Spunky, he looked and acted as if he was fourteen. He and a few friends (who were deceased too) were having a good time talking, eating and playing in the yard as if they were teenagers again. I asked him if he was okay, he said *"Yes!"* and that he was very happy. With that, I was satisfied that he was doing well, I turned around, left him and returned back to my body.

After pondering the vision on and off for many years, it occurred to me that the place we refer to as "Purgatory" may have many and various levels, as well as many and different purposes for developing a soul before it can enter into heaven. In my brother's case, he was given an opportunity to grow and mature through some years of his life that he missed out on. The intensity of childhood abuse that was present in our family, especially from my father, had robbed him of some key formative years. Now, through the love and mercy of God, he was being given a chance to mature through what was lost through no fault of his own. God is enormously responsible for the abuses that occur within his creation. He was calling my brother to be his son and he was providing for him an afterlife dialogue and an association that would mature him and prepare him for heaven. God is amazing, and he is doing these astonishing things in our lives that very few people believe and will give him credit for; namely his steadfast love, mercy and compassion that unites us to himself as his conversation continues with each of us, no matter what – even after death!

In 2008, almost three years after my NDE, I had an encounter with my brother for a second time in the afterlife. This time, instead of it being a vision, he came directly to me while I was asleep and spoke with me initially in the form of an interior locution. A locution is a word, or two, or a phrase that a person may receive, establishing a conversation with God, saints or from others in the afterlife that are in heaven or purgatory. In the 1500s, Saint Teresa of Avila received many, and said there are three types of locutions; the hearing of a voice speaking interiorly, hearing a voice speaking audibly, or having a sudden but profound thought. Here is what I wrote in my journal about this second encounter with my brother in the afterlife:

Wednesday, May 28, 2008 – This morning, while I was asleep, I received an interior locution where in it my brother began conversing with me about my acoustical guitar playing at church. He said, *"I like it when you sing the song, 'To you Yahweh, I lift up my Soul, O my God.'"* Right then and there, I sang the song for him, passing a few minutes together. He listened intently and then I was given the gift to also see him visually and the great happiness and joy the serenade brought.

After this time together, I was not clear in my own mind as to whether my brother was as of yet to arrive in heaven. But one thing was for sure, he had matured greatly from where he was in 1990, just three months after his death. Now, in 2008 he was no longer a teenager. Because of his interest in heavenly songs and worship, I surmised that he was on the right track and definitely on his way to heaven. That would soon be confirmed in what happens next.

In the early morning hours of Wednesday, September 9, 2009 (9/9/9), my brother's birthday, I recorded this in my journal: Lord God, this morning, [not even realizing it was Jimmy's birthday until later in the day] you came to me and spoke ... *"I took your brother to heaven today because there was one time in his life when he was merciful to someone."* Next, you interiorly showed me how my brother, one day, went to a small New York neighborhood grocery store on Bleeker Street to buy food and water and then delivered it all compassionately to someone who really needed it. As a result of that one act of mercy, you also had mercy on him and took him to heaven.

My brother was not much known for his selflessness. Usually what we fought most about growing up was the fact that he would disappear when there were chores to be done around the house. Later, once he moved out of the house, he apparently got wrapped up, as so many do, into an *"it's all about me"* lifestyle, which included many parties, alcohol and drugs. While growing up, it was highly unusual for Jimmy to remember Mother's Day with a card or a family member's birthday. But of course he sure appreciated when we remembered his!

I share all of this not to make fun of his shortcomings, but to illustrate how big and how great God's mercy is toward each one of us. Jesus said, *"Blessed are the merciful, they shall obtain mercy."* (Matthew 5:7) Apparently, Jimmy's one and only selfless act of mercy toward another, paved the way for him to be welcomed into heaven after nearly twenty years in Purgatory. God's mercy is so much more extensive and vast than the way we see mercy and justice here on earth.

Some who have previewed this book before it went into print have read the story of my brother and have found it troubling – disconcerting. It seems implausible to some as to how a guy who had led a troubled, party and gay lifestyle in New York City winds up in heaven. However, it should not seem that unbelievable based on Jesus' parable of the "Laborers in the Vineyard." Here is the story, as it illustrates the unfathomable and bottomless mercy of God. Jesus turns conventional wisdom of justice upside down!

"For the kingdom of heaven is like a landowner who went out early in the morning to hire men to work in his vineyard. He agreed to pay them a denarius for the day and sent them into his vineyard. About the third hour he went out and saw others standing in the marketplace doing nothing. He told them, *'You also go and work in my vineyard, and I will pay you whatever is right.'* So they went. He went out again about the sixth hour and the ninth hour and did the same thing. About the eleventh hour he went out and found still others standing around. He asked them, *'Why have you been standing here all day long doing nothing?' 'Because no one has hired us,'* they answered. He said to them, *'You also go and work in my vineyard.'* When evening came, the owner of the vineyard said to his foreman, *'Call the workers and pay them their wages, beginning with the last ones hired and going on to the first.'* The workers who were hired about the eleventh hour came and each received a denarius. So when those came who were hired first, they expected to receive more. But each one of them also received a denarius. When they received it, they began to grumble against the landowner. *'These men who were hired last worked only one hour,'* they said, *'and you have made them equal to us who have borne the burden of the work and the heat of the day.'* But he answered one of them, *'Friend, I am not being unfair to you. Didn't you agree to work for a denarius? Take your pay and go. I want to give the man who was hired last the same as I gave you. Don't I have the right to do what I want with my own money? Or are you envious because I am generous?'* So the last will be first, and the first will be last." (Matthew 20:1-16)

There is a case similar to my brother's in a book called *"Get Us Out Of Here!"* The book is about an Austrian mystic by the name of Maria Simma who recently passed away at the age of eight-nine on March 16, 2004. By the time of her death, Maria had conversed with hundreds of souls from Purgatory since 1940 when the visitors first began to call on her at the age of twenty-five. One soul in particular appeared to Maria Simma asking for prayers that might help her to go to heaven one day. Simma offered to pray for her and then asked her to share a bit about herself. The woman explained that she almost wound up in hell because of the awful self-centered life she had lived. However, last minute, God was merciful to her because of *one* act of kindness that she genuinely had performed.

As the story goes . . . One day, while leaving the front door of her home and going off on her way to work, she looked at the house next door and remembered that an elderly sick woman lived there. So, she knocked on the door and offered to go to the store and to help out the old woman. As a result of that one act of mercy and compassion, upon her death, she was given mercy in her own hour of need and at the very last minute. She won herself a spot in Purgatory with the hope of one day going to heaven.

Shortly before her death, Maria Simma was asked in an interview for Canadian-based *Michael* magazine, *"Maria, why does one go to Purgatory? What are the sins which most lead to Purgatory?"* She replied, *"Sins against charity, against the love of one's neighbor, hardness of heart, hostility, slandering, and calumny* [lies] — *all these things."* Our sins against charity are all our rejections of certain people we do not like, our refusals to make peace, our refusals to forgive, and all the bitterness we store inside.

Yes, the conversation is going on all around us. Ultimately, it is God's good will and good pleasure to upright all wrongs, and to bring about reconciliation by establishing a dialogue with him and healthy relationships with each other; whether a person is dead or alive, it doesn't matter.

Reconciliation is not an easy thing to do. You have to be God to unravel, and untangle all the wrongs that are going on around us and in us; in the past, present and future. All the evil and all the bad that have ever been done; God has a silent but profound plan to reconcile all things harmoniously back into himself. As Isaiah once wrote . . . *"Comfort, comfort my people, says your God. Speak tenderly to Jerusalem, and proclaim to her that her hard service has been completed, that her sin has been paid for, that she has received from the Lord's hand double for all her sins. A voice of one calling: 'In the desert prepare the way for the Lord make straight in the wilderness a highway for our God. Every valley shall be raised up, every mountain and hill made low; the rough ground shall become level, the rugged places a plain. And the glory of the Lord will be revealed, and all mankind together will see it. For the mouth of the Lord has spoken.'"* (Isaiah 40:1-5)

Chapter Four
Father, Jim

In August of 1999, I had written a *"can we talk"* letter to my father, Jim Sr. (my brother was known as "Jimmy" or Jim Jr.) and I sent a copy of the letter to my mother as well. She never received it because my dad, who got the mail each day, pulled a "KGB" and was monitoring what she read. The letter was in response to a recent phone conversation with my mom where she aired her tearful concerns that in their latter retirement years, he was still very angry and verbally aggressive toward her and for no apparent reason. Some hardened people soften in their old age, but at this juncture, at the age of eighty-two, not my dad! In one phone call in particular, mom was lamenting that a simple change of the house thermostat setting to higher or lower, would set him off in an argumentative rage.

When I sent my letter to him in the blazing heat of August, I suggested that a life-time of belligerent behavior had to stop. In opening, I quoted from a letter his youngest daughter had written him a few weeks earlier, which my sister had shared with me. In it she said, *"This principle of 'know it all' – 'superiority' – 'right at any price' permeates so many areas of your mind.* [It permeates] *your daily ways of functioning and responding to everything that there is no single answer* [for your unreasonable and ill behavior toward others]. Her point was well made and I concurred with her assessment and frustration.

As my letter progressed, I defended my mother and said many of the things that she found difficult to say. Especially, because for her it would have been a politically bad move to confront him (or so she thought) for fear she would wind up out on the street unable to fend for herself in her old age. In part, this is what I said, *"Although mom is extremely unhappy in her present day marital situation with you, she feels that your anger, rudeness, belligerent attitude, and at times violent shouting matches, is related to your prescription medication. In some respects she feels obligated to be a victim of spouse abuse because of your health problems and she feels that your medications are further driving your ill behavior."*

After recapping a long history of other severe abuses, I assured him that the intention of my letter was not to belittle him, but to offer love and forgiveness – but he must fess up and make an effort to change. About midway through, I said: *"Your horrible behavior continued well into my teens and twenties* [with no letting up]. *I have forgiven you and love you. I am only saddened that you continue to behave poorly toward the only person left in the house, your wife – to this very day."* My one sister, (the younger of the two) was not as forgiving or understanding, and still may not be to this very day, and for good reason. She had been badly hurt by him and my mother's denial of the damage he was causing.

Lastly, the letter had a call to conversion; to choose life and to offer him final assurances of love and forgiveness. I closed with the following words . . .

"[Dad] *if you are ready to do some things differently starting today – then let us all be friends. If you are willing to forgive as we have forgiven you, then begin today to live in the spirit of friendship, equality and family. Shed your anger and abuse and choose peace.*

"My hope is that you will choose life, the Spirit, forgiveness and happiness over the darkness and the argumentative behavior that you have perpetrated and has shrouded your marriage and family for years. It's never too late to blossom. Spring always comes. Let a decision to personally change and be a kinder and gentler man bring renewal and create something wonderfully beautiful to take with you into your next life.

"We your children wouldn't mind an apology, but we're not waiting for one. More importantly mom is waiting for something she said you have never said – 'I'm sorry.' You have never said that to her! She said those two simple words up to now have not been in your vocabulary. Please make a determination now to become a kinder person and a better listener . . . You will always be loved and forgiven by Christ's example. (Signed) . . . *Your Loving Son."*

Of course this is a book about conversation. Sometimes the conversation may be uncomfortable, difficult and even painful to engage in, as it was here. As life gets more entangled and goes awry, people are less likely to have dialogue for that very reason. Forgiveness, kindness, mercy and compassion are the keys that open up the dialogue door in tough times and in difficult situations like these, but not always instantly. However, many cannot see how charitable qualities are productive, so they run from kindness and compassion and things only get worse. Then they become angrier, spiteful, unkind and unforgiving. In August of 1999 when I spoke to a parish priest about my letter and the fact that it was ill received, he said, *"Your problem is that you and your sisters waited entirely too long to have this conversation."*

Yes, the letter was ill received. In short, my father denied everything and permanently cut off contact with all three of his remaining children. My mom never saw the letter so she only heard his side of the story. Ultimately backing him up, she became a temporary accomplice in his divisive tactic to sever dialogue with us and followed him into denial and silence. That would later change when a few months after his death God supernaturally descended upon my mother and showed her everything my father had done, and then some. Her eyes were opened and she grieved for years after. I will share more about that in Chapter 5 titled, *Mother*. Dad died in my mother's arms four years after my letter. He passed from a sudden burst of an aneurism shortly after 8:00am on the morning of July 14, 2003.

At his death, I stuck by my letter of forgiveness and that made it possible for me to attend his funeral and wish him well. However, just saying *"I forgive"* is one thing, but really knowing-that-you-know you have forgiven is another. It is here that God stepped in and energized the conversation just about two years after my father's death.

As I said in Chapter 2, by September of 2005, I had been attending daily Mass and Communion for a few weeks and had also begun to daily read the Scriptures once again. Over this time period, I became more contemplative. Thoughts began to occur to me that a complete interior forgiveness of my father was absolutely possible just by recognizing the fact, *"I am a sinner too!" "My failures and shortcomings are just different from his,"* I surmised. Everyone's particular brand of sins may have different names but the same end – self-destruction. That realization within my own heart motivated me to revisit forgiveness and make it complete once and for all.

With that said, the contradictions and hypocrisy going on with my dad and mom, I later had the ability to constructively frame and explain this way . . . It seems to me that it does not much matter whether one's severe, unrepented sin, is as big as the gash in the haul of the Titanic or a hole the size of a baseball, in either case that person is going down with the ship (hell). It also seems, now more than ever, many well-meaning religious people find it easy to take judgmental pot shots at minorities like drug addicts, homeless, alcoholics, prostitutes, obese and gay people to mention a few – all the while, many who are married are cheating at one time or another (about 80%) on their own spouses, because it's more septic as long as one does not get caught, and thanks be to God, it's considered "straight sex." Yet, even still, others are secretly stealing from employers, lusting in their hearts (adultery) and turning their homes and cars into consuming money pits (idolatry), all of which are violations of the Ten Commandments. In America today, for some reason, these "majority-type sinners," apparently, do not see the log that is in their own eye. All the while they hate "minority-type sinners"– individuals who are struggling with their own, very unique brand of addictions, sins, problems and issues. "Majority-type sinners" seem to be concerned about removing the spec from others' eyes, while ignoring their own contradictions and brokenness.

Jesus, undeniably, condemns religious hypocritical behavior of this sort and frequently speaks out against it in the Gospels.

Henri Nouwen, in his acclaimed book, *The Return of the Prodigal Son,* asks the question, *"Which offense is more identifiable to sinners, lust or self-righteousness?"* In chapter six, Nouwen asserts that in Jesus' parable of the Prodigal Son, the younger son is swept away by lust, greed and is wickedly wasteful. The elder son, although he is obedient and dutiful, he is swept away by the darkness of selfishness, pride and bitter arrogance.

Recently, www.HomelessInAmerica.BlogSpot.com bloggers, were polled a poignant question inspired by Nouwen. They were asked, *"In your opinion, which sin is more readily identifiable and easily repented for, lust or self-righteousness?"* According to the readers, it appears as though the lustfully poor, the broken and the morally bankrupt seem to have an intuitive clarity that their lust is sin. However, the wealthy-powerful-self-righteous, in the opinion of the readers, may have an absence of right moral judgment about themselves and their sin. The vast majority of our bloggers - 95% felt that the offense of lust is most easily identified by sinners. Only a miniscule group - 5% felt that the sin of self-righteousness is most easily identified and repented for.

The Apostle Paul was no stranger to the evil of self-righteousness and hypocrisy. Paul confronted it when he said, *"You, then, who teach others, do you not teach yourself? You who preach against stealing, do you steal? You who say that people should not commit adultery, do you commit adultery?"* Romans

2:21-22 If Paul were alive today, possibly he would add . . . *"You who condemn others that have sex addictions, or who are dependent on drugs and alcohol; are you yourself cheating on your spouse, being a workaholic or shopaholic, abusing prescription medications or do you have another weakness or sin that you hide from others?"*

Ultimately, this type of judgmental behavior by church members comes at a cost and it comes with a warning from Paul. He wrote, *"You, therefore, have no excuse, you who pass judgment on someone else, for at whatever point you judge the other, you are condemning yourself, because you who pass judgment do the same things. Now we know that God's judgment against those who do such things is based on truth. So when you, a mere man, pass judgment on them and yet do the same things, do you think you will escape God's judgment?"* Romans 2:1-4

But, I digress. Let's get back to the story about my father. Because of this complete forgiveness of my dad that had interiorly taken place, in the days leading up to my NDE of September 27th, I was beginning to experience waves of intense peace and joy that would flood my inner being. At strange moments in time – for instance while driving the car or taking a walk, I would all of a sudden become "drunk" with laughter and joy. I was learned enough in Holy Scripture to know that I was experiencing the fruits of the Holy Spirit. God was all over me.

The conversation is getting ready to intensify. In November of 2005, just a few weeks after the NDE I was fast asleep for the night when all of a sudden at 4:00am I was overcome by a strange event. Here is what I noted in my journal:

Friday, November 18, 2005 – In the early hours of yesterday morning, startled, I suddenly awoke at 4:00am. While having been solidly asleep, I heard a loud voice crying out like a broadcast over a megaphone's loudspeaker. The voice said, *"Your father is very proud of you and your mother!"* Instantly awake, I sat up in bed and saw a figure, one resembling my father, standing right in front of me. It was him, but hardly recognizable because he was shrouded in black. He was wearing black pants and a black shirt. His arms and skin were black too. For a few seconds, he looked intently at me but was unable to speak. Next, I had an interior locution that he was proud of me and my mom because of our Faith as well as our daily commitment to Mass and Communion. To my astonishment, early Friday morning (today) while I was fast asleep, the scenario happened all over a second time.

In a phone call today, I shared with my mother the two back-to-back visions and locutions. I was hesitant at first. What would she think? However once shared, they echoed as being authentic to her because she said that dad had never once mentioned he was proud of her or the children in all the 63 years they were married. She had a strong reaction of emotion and tears hearing the words spoken possibly by a Guardian Angel on his behalf, *"Your father is very proud of you and your mother."* As she profusely sobbed, she said, *"He finally gets it after all these years, after he is dead and gone!"*

For days after, I contemplated the meaning of all of this and then the thought occurred to me, *"My dad must be in Purgatory!"* It seemed to make sense because he was shrouded in black as well as the fact that he could not speak for himself. Apparently his Guardian Angel or another angel had to do the speaking for him. At any rate, shrouded in black, and mute silence could not be good and it was evidence enough that he needed our prayers. I consulted with my Spiritual Director, Fr. F. and he recommended that my mom and I begin to offer prayers and Masses for him. But there was much more that God had in store as the healing; the forgiveness and the conversation of our family ensued.

Inspired by an interior waking locution from the Lord in late November of 2005, I quickly set my sights on becoming a volunteer to serve the homeless. In Los Angeles at that time, there were more than 90,000 homeless men, women, children and teens living under bridges, in alleyways and on the streets of the city. But I did not know how to "break into the business" of caring for poor homeless souls. A few days later, on a Saturday morning while on a day retreat at my church, a woman sitting right next to me was of all things, vice-president of one of the largest homeless agencies in downtown. It was just three blocks from where I lived. What are the chances? Within a few days, she had me scheduled for an interview with one of the managers of the organization by the name of Angelina. The interview went well and I was accepted as a volunteer job placement counselor. I received my own office and began to work twenty hours a week from 8:00am to 12:00 noon, Monday through Friday. However, Angelina was not your "normal" supervisor.

After only a couple days of work at the homeless center, Angelina stopped by my office, she looked up to the center of the room and alarmingly shouted, *"Jim, Jim!"* Not even looking at me, abruptly, she left as fast as she came in with no explanation. She repeated that same scenario again, later that same morning. *"Jim, Jim!"* she shouted for yet a second time.

The next morning upon arriving back to work, she poked her head through my office door and asked me to immediately come see her at her desk. She shut the door of her office and explained that she is a Christian mystic and that yesterday she saw a spirit in my office – twice in fact. *"His name is Jim,"* Angelina blurted out without hesitation. She called out to *"Jim"* hoping to distract the invasion because she thought he might be disturbing me. "So, *who's dead in your family by the name of Jim?"* she said authoritatively. Speechless, I stuttered for words. *"Oh, well uh, my brother who passed away in 1990 is Jim and my father who died in 2003 is Jim as well. Both have the name of Jim,"* I replied. *"He wasn't young!"* she emphatically said. Angelina continued, *"It was an older man and therefore it had to be your father."* From what she witnessed, he was intently watching me – curious about my work with the poor and seemed to want to get to know me – something he had not done very well while here on earth.

Well, the conversation was heating up and now I had hard evidence – even a manager and co-worker had become a neutral and credible eyewitness to what God was doing in our family's lives. Obviously, Angelina had no way of knowing about my dad because we had just met two days earlier and purely by way of a professional interview. It would have been impossible for her to know about the auditory locution and appearance of my dad just a few weeks earlier. That was private information and no one knew about it but me and my mother at that early stage. But there is way more to this story. God had much more to do connecting the disconnected!

In the early morning hours of July 20, 2006, just about eight months after the experience I had with Angelina, another significant event took place. Here is how I recorded the morning in my journal:

Thursday, July 20, 2006 – I just awoke with my heart pounding as if I had run a race. First, I remember suddenly leaving my body, exiting through a penthouse apartment bedroom window and then having a birds-eye view high above downtown and the skyscrapers. Next, I began to pass through many small rooms deep in the earth constructed of very thick cement walls. The well-built construction of each reminded me of rooms having been fashioned in the style of bomb shelters. After being transported in spirit through a few rooms with great difficulty, I became fearful that I would become stuck and never would be able to return back to my body. At that thought, I turned back around and began to leave. Next, the same Jesus that held me at the time of my NDE came ever so gently along side of me. He said, *"You can do it if you have faith."* Yes, I had faith, I knew I did and immediately I became stronger. By trusting in Christ, I was able to descend swiftly and smoothly through many more layers of rooms constructed of these thick cement walls, but this time it was as if they were made of thin air. I had no more fear of them, especially knowing that the Lord was there. When I arrived however, I was alone. The room was very small, dimly lit, foggy and desolate. Immediately I saw my father who had died three years earlier, almost to the day, seated at a very small café table. Quite naturally, taking him by the hand, I made an invitation to him and said, *"Come, stand aside so we could talk."* My conversation with him was centered on the questions, *"Had Christ come to console you since your death? Had he appeared to you yet?"* I said. He shook his head, *"No."* He looked very introspective and despondent.

While I was still speaking with my father, a gentle man entered the room from around a dimly lit corner in front of me and to my left. He was like an angel, a soft low light glowed from his face and he appeared peaceful and confident. He gave me a nod of calm assurance. Possibly he was my father's Guardian Angel; he appeared to be an attendant from the Lord who was there to help my dad, myself and our family. I looked at the angel and said, *"The peace of Christ be with you."* Without speaking, it seemed as though we were both there on a similar mission – to console my father. Having the assurance that my dad was in good hands, I immediately turned around and felt the liberty to return through the very same solid walls from which I had come. I arrived in my bedroom and instantly awoke. My heart was pounding as if I had run a marathon.

After some reflection this morning, it is safe to say my father is in Purgatory and in an aspect of it that is very isolating – similar to solitary confinement. The rooms found in this part of Purgatory are very small, constricting, devoid of comforts and intimacy. The intensely thick walls and imprisonment leaves one feeling captive and desolate. Without the soul having had charity and a living Faith in God while on earth, one may lack the power to call on Christ and to be freed from the darkness that overwhelms them here. The darkness and isolation is suffocating. (Purgatory appears to be designed so that one's conversation with God somehow continues on his terms, and with his methods, to purge us of our faithlessness, as well as our unmerciful, unforgiving and selfish ways.)

Not long after this, I remember Fr. F. posing a question that I had not thought much about. He said, *"Do you think God will let you know when your dad finally gets out of Purgatory?"* That was a great question, but I never really thought much more about it until February of 2008. Here is what I recorded one afternoon in my journal:

Saturday February 2, 2008 – On this day at 1:30pm, what I thought would be a short afternoon nap, immediately the power of you O God, fell upon me. God the Father, your powerful and loving presence mightily overshadowed me in my room. You weighed heavily upon me as I remained crushed and immobilized by your awesome and Holy Presence. Then, you brought into the room and presented my own father. He was incredibly strong and radiantly different from when I had seen him in Purgatory, on July 20, 2006. Today I saw him as he is now in heaven, and how you intend each of us to be – whole, complete, happy, smiling and joyful and in perfect unity with you. Next, I remember Jesus entering through the door of my room and then coming from behind me. He placed his arm around me and my father, as if to say, *"Everything is fine now, I have reconciled you and your father and all things in your life. Peace be with you."* Coming out of a suspended state, I came to after the apparition had ended, filled with tears of happiness for my father. I was overflowing with joy to see his completeness. I rejoiced to see the mercy that was shown my father by you, God my Father.

Left to Right (Back) Louis, Tony, My Father, Jim and Mike
(Front) Eleanor, Florence, Marie, Rose, Clara, and Lena,
Photo Taken in 1994 of Jim Sr., and His Brothers & Sisters

Chapter Five
Mother, Paula

As my mother Paula tells her story, in October of 2003, just about three months after my father's death, she had arrived home as usual at eleven o'clock in the morning after having attended daily Mass, Communion and sharing coffee and freshly baked bread rolls with the "church ladies" at a local café. This was her daily habit for the past fifty years. Since the 1960s, when I was in grade school, I can remember her going to morning Mass, and then crossing the nearby railroad tracks to volunteer as a substitute teacher at my elementary school. However, on one tranquil and mild fall day in 2003, there was nothing serene about what would happen next.

Upon walking in the house and placing her car keys down on the kitchen counter, she was instantly overcome by an interior revelation powered by the Holy Spirit, as she tells it, illuminating her conscience and mind. It seemed as though all her years of going to daily Mass, and praying the rosary, had placed her on God's radar to receive special graces and help. What she learned next, was going to be one of those profound days, that in hindsight, although turbulent, it would become a valuable gift from the Lord.

In a very brief moment of time, she became intensely aware that all the accusations floating around the family regarding her husband were true, and then some. Simultaneously she received a locution and the words, *"He did it all."* In an instant, she was enlightened like a dry desert soaking up the springtime rains. Believe me, for my mother to be able to face the truth had to be the work of God. To admit any flaws went against the "white picket fence" image she and my father desperately tried to keep up over the years. Together, they held the fundamental world view, *"the world is wrong, but we're right."* It's akin to the transactional analysis expert, Thomas Harris' book, *I'm OK, You're OK,* and his profound identification of the disorder, *"I'm OK, you're not OK,"* world view.

As sweet as my mom was, and yet with her head in the sand most of the time, my mother was a person who frequented church, tuned out everyone else, and strangely, indulged in playing Bingo and gambling trips to Las Vegas, all the while believing everything her husband told her, never questioning a word he said. Jokingly, family and friends often said they were the original "Edith" and "Archie" from the television sitcom, *"All in the Family."* None of us children would have ever thought in a million years that she would escape her narrow-minded world of self-denial and self-centeredness, except by an act of God. And an act of God it was. The conversation was heating up for her.

She immediately picked up the phone and called my eldest sister. Surprisingly, for the first time in her life, she was able to verbalize and discuss some of the abuse my dad perpetrated and covered up over the lifetime of our family. Also, she became acutely aware that some trips to Las Vegas with my dad were not just innocent or petty gambling vacations – especially because there were times that he disappeared from the hotel and gave no explanation or apology for his hours of mysterious absence. A simple, two-plus-two, made a solid four, and boy was she fuming, raging mad in fact and feeling betrayed! But knowing the truth is the first step to embracing forgiveness isn't it? God wanted to give her a heavy dose of the truth. Most importantly, he wanted the truth to be known in order to challenge her ability to grant forgiveness as Jesus forgave his executioners on the Cross.

Even on the telephone, I knew she was extremely upset by the tone of her voice. Because, on call after call, she repeatedly and angrily vented to me about dad over these past six years, leading up to her recent death a few months ago. Just when I thought mom had resolved everything, six months later, she would rehash the same wounds and unforgiveness toward dad. Her profuse crying made it clear that she was hurt, abused and feeling deceived. In fact, just a few weeks ago, after a one-year battle with breast cancer, upon her death, I noticed something odd about some of the family photos in the house. In picture after picture she had ripped off the part with my dad standing next to her. She had been crazy mad, and for good reason. But could she forgive?

Heaven is only for people that know how to forgive, and because of her bout with terminal cancer in 2009-2010, she had to make some fast decisions about such matters before passing on to the next life. To facilitate her forgiveness of my dad, God granted her an additional miracle about one year before her death. Because God knows the future – he knew the soon coming date of her death. He also had decided to step up the conversation in order to get her ready for heaven. Here is what I wrote in my journal:

Thursday, April 3, 2009 – Lord, in your mercy, last night you granted my mother and me back-to-back companion visions with my father appearing from the afterlife in order to bring about some forgiveness on her part that may be long overdue. In the encounter, my father came to me and lamented, *"Your mother is still mad at me and she is still complaining about me after all these years."* He asked for my help. My candid response to him was, *"Dad, don't worry, that is just the way she is, she doesn't mean anything by it. Besides, you know how women are; sometimes they may hold a grudge for a long while. Give her time, she will get over it."* (Now, if you are a woman reading this, please do not hold this dialogue against me. I am only journaling what I spontaneously constructed within the context of an afterlife conversation.)

Now, today, while speaking with my mother by phone about a different matter (I was not planning to discuss the above encounter with her) she excitedly quipped, *"Oh, by-the-way, I had a dream about your father last night."* I responded, *"I did too! Tell me all about yours first and then I'll tell you mine."* *"Well,"* she said, *"As soon as I saw him, I began complaining to him about all the things he did to me in our marriage of over sixty some years and I was very mad at him. I told him get the hell out of here!"*

After mom finished, I said to her again, *"I had a dream about dad last night too!"* Her response was, *"Okay, tell me about it."* Then I proceeded to share with her the content of what I wrote above. It was obvious, the whole situation was now adding up to each of us having had a direct encounter with my father in the hereafter. My meeting with him obviously took place right after he had just visited with my mother. She was silent and dumbfounded by it all, but God was speaking.

And so, Lord, as a result of the companion back-to-back dreams, it opened up dialogue with my mom about your mercy and how we are obligated to share your mercy with others. We discussed how God often gives certain individuals longer lives on this earth, in order for them to freely choose complete forgiveness, compassion, mercy and understanding of those who have hurt them in this life. Every day we wake up, it's one more additional day on earth that we have to make a decision to be forgiving of others and to make right and bring to order our relationships.

With all that said, I have to back up a little. Being kindhearted to the poor and the broken was historically difficult for my mother practically her entire life. Now, all of a sudden seeing her very own husband whom she naively held up for sixty-three years as a wealthy "superstar," he was now "poor" and broken too. It was not going to be easy to be merciful to him or anyone else in this pitiable condition. She had little experience being sympathetic to the poor. Her faith in God gave her a lot of practice praying and seeking after him, but somehow she missed out on many of the pastors' homilies and Gospel lessons of forgiveness, compassion and mercy, to her own recent admission just weeks before her death. However, we know that there are but three things that last; faith, hope and love, and the greatest of these is love. (cf. 1 Corinthians 13:13)

We don't have to be theologians to know that patience, mercy and empathy for the poor is conditional to being authentically Christian. Jesus, within the first few days of his ministry, stood up in the synagogue and publicly declared his mission as one to the poor; not to the rich and powerful. The latter were the ones that he knew one day would crucify him. On this particular day, he read from the scroll of Isaiah and then said he was the fulfillment of its message. Jesus read, *"The Spirit of the Lord is on me, because he has anointed me to preach good news to the poor. He has sent me to proclaim freedom for the prisoners and recovery of sight for the blind, to release the oppressed, to proclaim the year of the Lord's favor."* (Luke 4: 18-19)

My mother is a wonderful person, don't get me wrong. But if she judged you as "lazy," such as a homeless guy, a poor person or a certain racial minority that she stereotyped as slothful – well you get the picture . . . Someone she pegged this way, could potentially drown and die before she would throw out a donation or a "life jacket" in the form of compassion or even a dollar bill to them.

Mom's predicament of struggling to integrate a strong prayer life along with the pure virtues of mercy and compassion is not uncommon. Her story reminds me of a couple of daily Mass-going "church ladies" who a few years ago cornered me at a local restaurant and said, *"We decided we don't want to be a part of your prayer group!"* I said, *"Oh, why is that?" "Well we heard that it is primarily going to be a way to help the homeless,"* they replied. *"And here's the point,"* they said. *"We're both immigrants. When we came to this country we hardly had clothes on our backs. We started out with nothing. We worked hard for the nice houses and cars we have today. The homeless are just lazy bums!"* What can you say to that? I was speechless and remained silent.

After my NDE, mom occasionally discussed, out of curiosity, my work with the homeless, especially those living under bridges and in remote alleyways. She was frequently perplexed by it all and had a lot of sometimes unkind and edgy questions about these poor and broken souls. Every few months, just when you think all her concerns had been addressed, she would be right back to square one and say something like, *"But aren't they lazy? Why don't they go out and get a job and work for a living like your father did?"* After the past three – four years of this, it seemed as though there was no way of making sense with her on the matter of integrating her awesome prayer life with compassion for the poor. But with God, all things are possible. Before her death, here is how God miraculously initiated that very important dialogue with her:

Tuesday, January 1, 2008 – Just as I was about to awaken, I received a profound locution from the Lord. *"I am going to give your mother wisdom,"* Jesus said. Instantly, I had an intense interior awareness that my mom is going to be blessed very soon with a strong spiritual wisdom and insight that she has never had before. Thank you Jesus!

It was now almost three years after my NDE and I had a track record of many visitations and locutions from the other side that were right on target. By now, I had a strong sense that when God speaks, something Big, with a capital "B" is going to happen. But because God is God, we can never really know how he is going to act or fulfill his words. I had to just wait and see.

I did not have to wait very long. Just a couple of weeks later, and right at the time of my mother's ninetieth birthday, two significant events happened to her to bring about the promised wisdom from on High. The first was on January 21, 2008. On this day she was supernaturally overcome by the physical presence of Christ when she received Communion one weekday Mass at her church. She described the event to me this way: *"I was walking up to receive the Host when all of a sudden I no longer saw the priest. I no longer saw anybody. A man appeared at my right side, put his arm around me and whispered, 'I love you darling.' I don't remember taking the Host and I don't remember walking back to my seat. I was at peace, in another world."* In that instant, she became an eyewitness to the risen Christ. That touching from Jesus had a profound effect on her – weeping and grieving for her sins was one of them. That's how I know it was Christ who had appeared to her at that Communion rail. She became more docile, more peaceful and thereafter, she would even send $50 or $100 to help the homeless! But there is more.

Also, around this same time period, within a few days of the above episode, she had a direct and enlightening encounter with an angel, in a Myrtle Beach, South Carolina Wal-Mart parking lot of all places. Over the past two years after it first happened, she would frequently retell the following story that I will share with you now. Often she recounted the event in tears, and yet, was filled with peace too. Here is what she told me . . .

"I was going to get a slice of pizza one evening at the place by the church. You know the one, the Italian restaurant in the Wal-Mart shopping plaza. I always check around me after parking the car to make sure there are no strangers lurking. I waited. I looked around and saw no one. As I opened the car door, immediately a young homeless man with a cute patch of hair under his lip was standing right next to my car door. I wasn't afraid, but I asked what he wanted. He said, 'My name is Billy. Ma'am, do you have a dollar?' I said to him, what do you want the dollar for? He replied, 'Ma'am, it's for the Spirit.' I said what do you mean 'it's for the spirit', you mean for spirits, like alcohol? You want to go drinking? 'No Ma'am' he replied. 'It is for the Spirit.'" With that, she gave him the dollar bill (*Billy*) and he cordially walked her to the door of the pizza shop. As he opened the door for her, he said, *"Ma'am, you're a saint."*

After having a slice of pizza, she exited the restaurant's front door and all of a sudden, what again seemed like out of nowhere, Billy came up on her right side and began to walk her to the car. She said to him jokingly, *"What's your problem? Do you want another dollar?"* He replied, *"No Ma'am."* He continued, *"Ma'am, you're a saint."* Next, at the car door, my mom said her goodbyes to Billy and asked if he came to this parking lot often. She then said, *"Will I see you again?" "No Ma'am,"* he replied, *"You will never see me again."* With that final exchange she got in the car, slammed the door shut, and turned around to back out. As she looked back, Billy, was no where to be found. He was instantly gone, and just as quickly as he had come into view. In hindsight, it's significant that this angel appeared as a homeless man isn't it? Only God could orchestrate that particular heavenly messenger to deliver that poignant message.

Directly, because of the encounter with Billy, my mother began to be more generous to the poor. Also, she was at peace. She greatly increased her donation to a new church school building fund too. And as I said before, she began to send me donations each month for the "lazy" homeless. Stunningly, in her last weeks, she even began to grieve, for no unexplainable reason, for certain suffering homeless souls that she heard about from our homeless ministry. For instance, she would frequently weep for the poor homeless guy who was living on the streets, while enduring the scourge of weekly chemotherapy. Compassion welled up inside of her and empathy poured out for this man's pain, suffering and the fact he had no place to lay his head to better endure the pain. At this juncture in time (because of her soon death), my mother was, by God's help, absorbing spiritual truths of cosmic proportions. She was genuinely feeling sympathy for the poor and broken like she never had before.

Personally, the weeping and grieving in this regard was encouraging to see. It tells a story that here is a soul that is also seeing God. Because, when we see the poor, the discarded, the ignored, the despised and the rejected, we are on track to see God. You see, God experiences the same rejection as the poor, so he is one with them, in total solidarity! Despite his rich testimony in mountain grandeur, hazy beaches, glorious heavens and fluffy clouds, he is ignored, scorned and despised by many. Likewise, when God came to earth, he was despised and rejected and received more of the same treatment. So when someone like my mother is now able to grieve while "seeing" the poor, she is seeing God and therefore was immediately on her way to heaven, no doubt.

In validation of what was happening to my mom in this regard is Jean Vanier, the founder of L'Arche, an international network of communities for the mentally disabled. He has become an "expert" in seeing God in the poor and broken. Pope John Paul II once referred to L'Arche as, *"a dynamic and providential sign of the civilization of love."* In a radio interview with Lydia Talbot, Vanier once said, *"If you are blind to the poor, you become blind to God, and there is the mystery because the Word became flesh, became little, became crucified. We know He is hidden in the poor and the weak and the fragile and whatever you do to the weak, whatever you do to the hungry, the thirsty, you do unto Jesus. Then, there are those incredible words of Jesus, 'Whoever among you who welcomes one of these little ones, welcomes me.'"*

Obviously my mother was being prepared for heaven by having all these peculiar and other-worldly experiences leading up to the time of her death. God was orchestrating for her many gifts and graces that would prepare her soul to go directly to heaven on Sunday, February 21, 2010. That is the day she passed away of breast cancer at the age of ninety-two in the early morning hours.

On Sunday, January 17, 2010, my mother met her doctor right inside the church after Sunday Mass. It was there that the doctor told her that there was not anything more that could be done. *"It will just be a matter of time"* he said. She immediately called me with the news. She was distraught and yet resigned to the fact that moving on from this life and going to God is what she has longed for and prepared for all her life. The news was bittersweet.

That same afternoon, while getting dressed to go out with friends, I received a locution from the Lord. Here is how I recorded it in my journal:

Sunday, January 17, 2010 – Lord, *"In three weeks"* is what I heard you say this afternoon shortly after speaking with mom on the phone and receiving the news that she does not have much more time to live. [Indeed, it was exactly three weeks later that I left to go to mom's house to care for her in her final weeks. Miraculously, there was at this same time period an outpouring of donations from members of various churches. Everyone was coming together, sensing urgency for me to get to my mom. It was all happening at the same time without anyone ever talking to each other.]

I arrived at my mother's house on Sunday, February 7, 2010. We had her favorite pizza together and reminisced about the encounter with "Billy." Many friends were over visiting and it seemed like a party more than an upcoming funeral. I had no way of knowing that the next four weeks were going to be a speedy decline for my mother. I also had no way of knowing the final – final preparations that God was going to ask her to make in her life. As Fr. F. said,

"Apparently you are there to be her spiritual guide." Deacon Peter from her church one day said, *"Brother, you are 'Jesus' for your mother. God is going to use you."* In all humility, yes, God did use me. But it is only because he came through with a lot of conversation to make me ready to do my job. It was miraculous what he did to help me be a better spiritual guide for my mother at this difficult time period of death and dying, when a soul is in great anguish. Here is what I wrote in my journal in this regard:

Tuesday, February 9, 2010 – In the early hours of the morning Lord, you appeared in my room and embraced me in my bed. The peace and the joy you give are amazing. Next you took me in your arms on an amazing journey into heaven. The colors Lord, the colors are spectacular. The sky was what I like to call "Mother Mary blue" and the clouds were perfectly fluffy and white. Then, you let me go and I could fly freely through the heavens. But sometimes I got carried away and I would fly too fast or felt like I was falling. It was here that you taught me to always say, *"Jesus I trust in you."*

The same morning that the temporary transportation to heaven took place; I shared with my mother the elated and amazing journey I had just taken. My spirits were high and I was at peace. I was now more than equipped to be a strong spiritual guide for the last days that we had together before she eventually slipped into a coma. I confidentially described to her the afterlife, some elements of heaven that I was personally aware of and what to expect when she gets there. She had no reason to fear, I said, but only one thing to say, *"Jesus I trust in you."* She was very comforted and agreed that she could say, *"Jesus I trust in you."* Mom was a devoted follower of these same words as they were promoted by Saint Faustina Kowlaska in her *Divine Mercy* revelation and as recorded in her diary as mentioned earlier.

Lastly, I would like to draw attention to the fact that God cares about bringing everyone into the conversation, including the unborn. My mother, for many weeks right prior to her death, had repeatedly been seeing a small, tiny baby appearing to her. I knew for a fact that she was authentically seeing the child, because, often we would be carrying on a rich and well thought out conversation verifying her sound mind, and then all of a sudden she would stop and say, *"There's that little baby again. It's right here in front of me."*

It took me some weeks of reflecting on this to receive inspiration as to who this baby was and why it was appearing to her. One day I just blurted out, *"Mom, do you know who the baby is?"* *"No!"* she said. *"That baby is the miscarriage you had way back in 1952!"* *"The baby is anxiously waiting to be with you so it can be with its mother and mature into full adulthood."* I replied. Astonished at the revelation she then replied, *"Yes, I think you're right!"*

Before I was born, my mother had a miscarriage at approximately four months' term. She aborted quite suddenly and right in the house where she was living at the time. The doctor was concerned for her welfare and so he had to examine the remains to make sure nothing was left inside that may cause her problems later. Because of this post miscarriage analysis, there was never a formal burial for the child that I'm aware of. Since that time no one has thought much more about the baby or discussed it until now. Personally, seeing the baby's love, compassion and initiative to track down its mother after all these years inspired me to pick a name for the baby, "Francis" (that was more than three years *before* Pope Francis). So, as of a few weeks ago, our family grew to include five children, not just the four that were normally known. This event makes me wonder who could ever think that voluntary abortion is a good idea. Obviously, from this encounter it's not. Choosing to kill poor unborn little ones is the wrong thing to do. Pre-born children, like the one my mother had, are real souls, and most importantly, they are very loving and devoted to their mothers, and one could only imagine, their fathers too.

Coincidentally, with no real planning in mind, I finalized this chapter about my mother on Sunday, May 9, 2010, Mother's Day.

Lastly, right before this book went to press, I spoke with my cousin Ronda, whom I had not personally been in touch with for more than thirty years. She had left a kind message of condolence for our family on my voice mail a few days after mom's death. It was now, six months later and I was finally getting a moment to return her call. Hearing my voice, elatedly, she said, *"You're going to think I'm crazy, but I heard from your mom a few weeks after she died."* Calmly, I replied, *"No I won't, I promise! Tell me what happened." "Well,"* she said. *"I spoke with your mom at length about two months before she had passed. She had called me to say that she was in the latter stages of cancer and would be gone soon. Concerned, I asked her to give me a sign after her death that she is okay* [in heaven]. *And do you know what she said?"* *"Tell me,"* I replied, inquisitively. With great enthusiasm in her voice she said, *"Your mom immediately said, 'I'll break something in your house!'"* *"And the point being?"* I replied. Excitedly, Ronda continued . . . *"About two months after your mom's death. I was home alone watching television in the living room. It was ten o'clock at night. All of a sudden I heard a crash in the basement. When I investigated, I discovered a small box filled with many glass items had mysteriously fallen off a storage shelf. Everything in the box survived the fall, except one piece. One item was busted. Just as your mom had promised, 'something' broke letting me know that she is okay!"*

Paula's very holy, peaceful and joy-filled death, bursting with lots of love, hugs, visitors, daily Eucharist, flowers and candles.

Chapter Six
Cousin, Kim

As I had mentioned in Chapter One, my cousin Kim was a favorite since childhood. She came from a military family, but in all reality she was not the "military brat" we often hear about. Her father, my uncle Ralph, was a Lieutenant Colonel in the Air Force and their family at one time was stationed in Thailand, as well as Washington, DC, among other places. She grew up with an international cosmopolitan flare. Her mother was my father's youngest sister. Kim was raised with all the charm and grace that one could expect to see in a medieval castle princess, not necessarily a modern American military household. Her long blonde hair, model physique and tasteful dresses, only enhanced her interior charm. As children, we rarely saw each other except on special occasions or an annual vacation.

Right after I had begun work on a Ph.D., in Law and Ethics at Duquesne University, in the early 80s, Kim and I had reconnected. At that time I received a call from Kim with an invitation to interview at a new company she had just joined in the New York area, PEOPLExpress Airlines. They were particularly interested in hiring managers who had no airline experience in order to groom them their way.

Within a couple months of the interviews, Kim and I were not just cousins, but also founding managers and stock owners of one of the hottest and controversial non-union airlines in the history of the aviation industry. They provided us rich business skills training, under the tutorage of *In Search of Excellence* authors and business gurus, Tom Peters and Robert Waterman.

After a few years there, PEOPLExpress (PE) was purchased by *Continental Airlines* in the late 80s. We soon left PE, merging our talents, and began a successful upstart career job fair company and business consulting group. However, by the late 1990s, Kim had reunited with a high school sweetheart and relocated, in order to marry and start a home. We stayed in touch from time-to-time by phone and after her sudden run-in with lung cancer in July of 2005, we spoke frequently. I offered her my prayers and as I shared in Chapter 2, I began to go to daily Mass for both her and my health woes and our special intentions.

On a cold winter's day in December of 2005, I attended early morning Mass at the downtown Cathedral before the hustle and bustle of the day had begun. After receiving communion, I knelt down and began to pray about what I could say or share with my cousin Kim, when I make the few thousand-mile journey to see her in a few weeks. What do you say to a person you deeply care about and who does not have much more time to live? Of course I had the details of my NDE to speak about. That was encouraging. But I was praying and asking the Lord what else could I say and how would I say it. Immediately after whispering that prayer, I heard the following locution. I did not know at the time what a locution was for, I was still ignorant and unaware of what these things were, until Fr. F. and I had spoken about it in the months to come.

Friday, December 30, 2005 – As I was kneeling and praying after Communion, I heard the following, [make known to Kim] *"I the Lord have seen the blue stone in the ring that you love to wear. I have seen its star in the middle. The blue in the ring is the sea of faithful witnesses that have followed me throughout the ages and that I have welcomed you into. The star in your ring is you shining brightly. I see your star. I see you! Do not fear, for in my mercy I have prepared a place for you. In my grace, I will keep you free from pain. Let this be a sign unto you, a shining diamond ring has been left at the foot of my altar to proclaim your brightness. This is the word of the Lord and my covenant with you is eternal."*

Within just a few seconds of this locution, I began to deny it ever happened. Up until now, whenever something like this happened, it was at nighttime. That somehow seemed to make it better or more believable for some strange reason. But this was broad daylight. In my mind I was thinking, *"There's no way I am going to tell Kim about this locution. Besides, I have not seen her in many years. Does she even have a blue ring on her hand with a star in the middle?"* Then I surmised, *"I will look like a fool if all this turns out to be a hoax, a product of my imagination!"* But overtime, I realized that part of the nature of doing God's business is the willingness to be a fool. In hindsight, now I'm okay with that. I'm a fool!

Well, it was no hoax. A few more brief seconds passed, Fr. Kevin, the celebrant of the Mass, stood at the altar with a bright shining diamond ring in his hand. Jokingly he said, *"One of you ladies is now throwing rings at me. I have up here* [holding it up] *a nice shiny diamond ring and someone just left it at the altar while receiving Communion. Please see me after Mass and I will return it to you."* At that, he abruptly went on with the closing prayer and blessing. Wow, God is amazing! His ways are so far above our ways. With the sudden appearance of the diamond ring, God confirmed the authenticity of him speaking to me right then and there.

In spite of seeing the diamond ring displayed at the altar, I still had a very oh-so-slight tinge of doubt that this was God at work. (It's amazing how cold we humans have become; our minds seem to want to deny God is having a conversation, rather than readily embrace it.) As a result, I had no plans to call Kim and discuss the event with her. However, that same day, out of the clear blue, Kim called me in the late afternoon. Because my cousin obviously had her own woes, she almost never had the time to call. But on this particular day, surprisingly, she initiated a phone call – just wanting to talk. What are the chances? Here is what I recorded in my journal in this regard on the same day as the above entry:

Friday, December 30, 2005 – Unexpectedly, Cousin Kim called me today at about three o'clock in the afternoon. I was amazed to hear her voice because she almost never has time to call. It was odd that she should call me on this particular day because of what happened this morning at Mass. Her calling was just enough push to put me over the edge and share with her this morning's locution.

"Kim," I said. *"Do you have a blue ring that you like to wear?"* She promptly replied, *"Yes! I am wearing it right now."* Intrigued by my question, Kim continued, *"It's my most favorite ring – possibly more than my wedding ring because my husband Jim bought it for me when we first got married ten years ago. I wear it all the time. I love it!"* The next detail I knew was going to be the final test as to whether this conversation actually came from God or not. So I went for it and said, *"Kim, does your blue ring have a star in the middle?" "Yes, yes it does!"* she excitedly exclaimed. *"How did you know?"* she queried. Next, I shared with her all that had transpired at this morning's Mass and the prophecy that was meant for her and her alone. I assured her that she is on God's radar; he sees her and loves her very much. And how interesting, I mused with Kim, *"God used the imagery of the blue sea to get your attention – all your life, along with your father, both of you loved boating and the sea so very much!"*

About three weeks later, I boarded a flight to go and spend a long weekend with my cousin. The night before I left, when I was preparing my luggage, I was planning to give Kim an original handwritten copy of the locution, as well as a typed printed one. While I was preparing a sheet on the home printer, I received a word from the Lord. He said, *"Frame the words for Kim. Don't just hand them to her. Make it nice! Go to the discount store near the corner of Broadway and 8th Street. There you will find a blue frame. Place my words in a blue frame." "Wow, Lord,"* I thought. *"You really know how to make a gift presentation. Yes, of course! A blue frame would be the most excellent way to present your words about the blue ring."*

But to be honest, I did not even know that dollar stores stocked picture frames, let alone a blue one. It seemed to me that these places were known for inexpensive cans of cleanser, dish detergent, dollar bags of candy bars and the like. Besides, it was seven o'clock at night. Weren't downtown stores already closed? But I was not going to question the Lord further or argue with him. I knew that he infinitely knows better and so out the door and off I went. Sure enough, upon arriving, they were open, and checking in at the front cash register, the cashier pointed me to a section that actually had picture frames in it. Low and behold, among all the many wood and chrome frames stood one and one only blue picture frame!

Kim and I had a wonderful three-day visit. She gratefully received her framed words and vowed to keep them next to a candle at a makeshift altar on her bedroom dresser. Over dinner one night, we celebrated the blessed assurance God was giving her. He was most definitely showering her with special graces. She then shared how, as a result of the cancer, she had become much more active in her church and was seeing the pastor there for spiritual direction. She even gave a reflection at a Good Friday service about a year before she passed on. Kim emailed me her manuscript and shared her thoughts with me. Recently, her husband Jim thought it would be good to pass her thoughts along to others in hopes of allowing Kim to speak to us from her vantage point in the afterlife. I am going to share parts of her Good Friday reflection now. May you find inspiration and solace in her words. Here in part is what she said . . .

"Friday, July 29, 2005 was the day my and Jim's world turned upside down, and in some ways, right-side up. We were at the doctor's office for a follow-up visit after some tests . . . The doctor came in, made small talk for a moment, and then Jim asked *'What is it, doctor?'* He said gently, *'Its lung cancer'*. To say we were shocked is an understatement . . . We left the office feeling shaken, lost, numb. During the drive home, we were silent for a while, lost in our thoughts. Then Jim said, *'Let's pray'*. My first prayers were very elementary—-a simple *'Help me Lord, show me the way'*.

"Somehow we made it through the weekend. Monday brought more bad news. The cancer specialist said, *'You have a very advanced form of lung cancer — it's not curable. At your stage, you can expect to live 6 to 9 months, without treatment . . .'* Wow. There it was, the cold, hard facts . . . [But] my nine-month anniversary is in two weeks. I'm still here. My bags are packed, but my flight has been delayed. What an opportunity, a new lease on life. In many ways I feel so much more alive than I did nine months ago. People who meet me just can't believe there's anything wrong.

"It hasn't been an easy journey. Without my faith, and the support and prayers of my husband, family and friends, I don't know how I would have coped with the many disappointments along the way. . . Through it all, I've never given up hope. Each disappointment was simply a test that we turned into an opportunity to seek new treatment options . . . After six new treatments, the latest scans indicated my cancer has stabilized, for the most part, for now. That doesn't mean I'm cured, but it does give me some extra time. What a blessing! Now, I'd like to take a moment to share with you what I have learned and the blessings that have come while on this journey. I learned a lot about myself. I learned that before cancer, I was sort of sleepwalking through life. I was caught up in the everyday hustle bustle, working hard Monday through Friday, and trying to squeeze in as much fun as possible on the weekends. We've always attended Mass on Sundays, but to be honest, I didn't do much during the week to really live my faith. Sadly, even morning and evening prayers had gone by the wayside. But what a wake-up call I received.

"I'm not sleepwalking anymore; I can tell you that! This journey with cancer has been a blessing in so many ways, a blessed tragedy as Father mentioned. I'm so much closer to my husband now, and to my mom and the rest of my family and friends. Cards, emails, Mass cards, books and phone calls have come not only from family, but even from strangers who care enough to comfort and sustain me. What a blessing to love and be loved! Most times, I can't wipe the smile from my face; I'm just so full of joy.

"Jim and I end each day as never before, in prayer. He so sweetly and fervently takes holy water from Lourdes and blesses my head, my lung, my liver, and prays for my healing. And I wake up each morning, watch the sunrise with such appreciation for his creation, and thank our Lord for another blessed day. I've learned so much about the power of prayer. After the cancer diagnosis, I felt lost and afraid. In my brokenness, I placed myself at the foot of the cross and prayed. I prayed as Jesus did; *"Father, please take this cup away from me, but your will be done."* What peace came to me from that prayer! I'm full of hope that the cup will be taken away, but I accept God's will without question.

"Early on, we called on Father Tobin for spiritual direction. At the time, I was still feeling a bit fearful of my terminal condition. I felt that I hadn't done enough good in my life, and I felt "unworthy" to meet God. Father explained that we're all "terminal", we're all going to die sooner or later, and none of us are worthy of God's mercy, but He gives it to us anyway. Father introduced us at Mass to the Ascension Community, and asked the community to pray for us. I really believe that day was a turning point for me. I felt so renewed in spirit after Mass, the fear completely disappeared. Today, I have absolutely no fear of the future, I know that God is with me, and live or die, I can't lose. Today I am healed; perhaps not physically, but definitely spiritually, and what a blessing that is. Is it any wonder that, for the first time in my life, I feel truly alive? Now, I certainly wish that I did not have this cancer, and could have received my wake-up call in some other way. But I'm so thankful that I've had the opportunity to change my life.

"None of us know what the future holds, and none of us knows the day or the hour that God will call us. Today could be the day for any one of us. I pray that if there's anyone here who feels like I did "BC", caught up in the hustle bustle, taking things for granted, sleep walking through life – that you'll wake up today and smell these beautiful roses that our Lord has given us. Give your husband or wife, mother or father and kids an extra hug today and every day. Take time to appreciate this gift of life and the glory of God that is so evident in His creation. And most of all, pray."

On Thursday, May 25, 2006, about one year before Kim passed on, the Lord spoke to me in a nighttime locution that he was going to take Kim home very soon. And in indeed he did. Cousin Kim died on Wednesday, May 30, 2007. What is most profound about this locution is that the Lord proceeded to tell me that Kim will have the ability to see and hear those who attend her funeral. He said, *"If you don't attend Kim's funeral, she will ask, 'Where's my cousin Gary at?'"*

Similarly, Maria Simma, in her vast experience with the souls in the afterlife once stated, *"A soul in Purgatory sees very clearly on the day of his funeral if we really pray for him, or if we have simply made an act of presence to show we were there. The poor souls say that tears are no good for them: only prayer! Often they complain that people go to a funeral without addressing a single prayer to God, while shedding many tears; this is useless!"* (*The Amazing Secret of the Souls in Purgatory*, Queenship Publishing Co., Goleta, California, 1997.)

Unfortunately, because of the thousands of miles' distance, and the expense of air travel, I regret that I was unable to attend Kim's funeral, even though I knew she would be looking for me. However, Kim did appear to me in my bedroom one morning not long after her death. Here is how I recorded the event in my journal:

Friday, February 20, 2009, 7:30am – After reading from 5:45 to 6:30 in the morning the book, *The Peace of St. Francis*, something in particular spoke to me. It was the fact that St. Francis *"preferred duty to pleasure."* The point was stunning and caused me to rededicate my life to the Lord. Next, he interiorly spoke to me saying, *"fall back asleep, I would like to speak to you."* I was obedient and tried to do what he asked. But after thirty minutes had passed I was still wide awake and nothing. Then, suddenly as if overcome by a supernatural sedative, I fell into a suspended state and in walked my cousin Kim with another Kim, possibly the little girl my Uncle Ralph had adored and thus named his daughter after. They both looked thirty-something and extraordinarily beautiful.

Kim and I interacted for some time, about fifteen minutes. She was glowing with pure white skin and radiant golden-blonde hair. Given her propensity for style, she was wearing a fine-looking long white gown. In addition, my cousin was filled with lots of smiles, peace, joy, compassion and tenderness. Casually, she lay down on the sofa to talk. I remarked, *"Your skin is so white and pure. It's not the dark-skin tan we Italians and Latinos like to get!"* [This is an inside joke because Kim spent many a day tanning, either poolside at her Florida condo or on her sailboat in the Upper Keys. Anything that had to do with serene blue ocean waters, sunshine and sailing, Kim loved.] Next, my cousin joked back and said, *"No more lying in the sun and getting a tan for me!" She was* alluding to her new-found lifestyle in the afterlife.

We hugged and kissed many times in that momentous encounter. At first, I must say that she was hesitant to hug. Not because of not wanting to, but because she was pure spirit and without her body. I could tell she was not quite sure how these exchanges on earth played out in the afterlife. But then she took a moment, folded her hands and prayed to the Lord to see if it was okay. He said it was okay and she was completely relaxed about interacting the way we did when she was here. Next, we hugged and kissed some more. [We're an Italian family!]

Lastly, she held me very close to her, and sincerely and lovingly said she was very sorry for any wrong she had done in running our business venture in the 90s together – for hurting me in any way. I collapsed in her arms crying and said, *"No, no! Forgive me for hurting you and for being such a jerk!"* She laughed and said, *"No, you're not a jerk. The Lord loves you very much."* Because I was aware that she had direct interior communication with the Lord (more instantaneous than we experience here on earth), I asked her to beg Christ to forgive me for being such an idiot in this life. She tenderly laughed, loved and hugged me as I knelt at her feet crying with joy to see her again.

Eternal life and heaven is all about people that know how to forgive and want to forgive. Kim taught me that lesson loud and clear when she took the time to come and visit with me from the afterlife. Doing what she did, and saying what she said, taught me a powerful lesson about how we "work out our salvation" and how we get welcomed into paradise. We all know the ability to pardon is not rocket science, but nevertheless, it is very profound to know that it is at the heart and soul of the hereafter.

The prayer that Jesus taught us backs this up. He taught us to call God our Father and to pray . . . *"Our Father who art in heaven hallowed be thy name. Thy kingdom come, Thy will be done on earth as it is in heaven. Give us this day our daily bread and forgive us our trespasses as we forgive those who trespass against us . . ."* (Matthew 6:9-13)

Immediately after introducing the prayer to his followers, Jesus drew attention to its meaning when he said, *"For if you forgive others their trespasses, your heavenly Father will also forgive you; whereas if you do not forgive others their trespasses, neither will your Father forgive your trespasses."* (Matthew 6:14-15)

As I have shared many times, heaven is only for those who know how to forgive! It's not about how much money one gives to the church. It's not about receiving a scholarly theological education and getting ordained. And for most, it's never about doing the impossible – living a "perfect" morally squeaky clean life. Because of being human, God knows that over the course of a lifetime, eventually one is going to lie, cheat, look at another lustfully, experience casual sex – straight or gay, have extra marital affairs, "worship" their homes, automobiles and other possessions and participate in other forms of idolatry. Unfortunately, for all of us, it's normal to do these things. And unfortunately, being normal along with leading a life of being judgmental of others; being unmerciful, vengeful, uncompassionate, ignoring the poor, unloving and unforgiving will, upon death, facilitate a one-way ticket to hell. And even more unfortunate, having what many believe to be a "faith" in God cannot save these types of individuals unless they repent of unloving behavior before their death.

If one is rich and therefore powerful (most people in this country are), living a life of no mercy, no compassion and no forgiveness is dangerous for the soul. So, as Dr. Phil likes to say, "Get real!" Let's get real and embrace ourselves as the sinners we truly are. Then, let us go out and be merciful to others, spread our wealth around by caring about the poor, and start to forgive other people living all around us, ones who are steeped in their own sins and particular brands of brokenness. In conclusion, recently I heard it said, *"the Church is not a courtroom filled with judges, but a hospital for the sick and broken filled with servants and care-givers."*

Our Family's Conversation
In Pictures

Mom and Dad, 1939 Engagement
Paula, in Her Wedding Dress

Christmas 1956, Family Photo

WWII, Jim was with the Army in France and Holland, 1940-1945

Mom and Dad Celebrating Second Child in a 1950s Photo Booth

Jimmy and Santa Claus, 1959 V.F.W. Christmas Party

Paula, Hosting a "Donna Reed" Dinner, Circa 1950s

Me, Mom and Jimmy 1966 at Aunt Mary's House

Me in 1961 at St. Dominic's Church
First Communion Photo Op

Mom and My Brother, 1972
Jimmy and Aunt Marie

Family 1971 Thanksgiving Dinner
in the Main Dining Room

Mom and Grandma, 1968
Cousin Kim and Mom, 1974

Cousin Kim and Husband Jim, Christmas 2005

Mom and Dad, Last Family Photo, Late 1990s

Chapter Seven

Jesus

My first encounter with Jesus was at the time of my near-death-experience. As I described in Chapter 2, he is pure love. In the NDE, when Jesus came down off of the luminous white cross, he embraced me as both Lord and lover. As I said earlier, visualize the best hugs you have ever had – possibly from a spouse, mother, father or friend. Multiply the hugs you are now imagining times millions and millions. You're touching upon a small sense of how much Jesus loves each of us. He wants to hold each of us and, like he did for my mother, say to each, *"I love you darling."*

Shortly after Christmas in December of 2005, while I slept in the nighttime and spilling over to the next morning, the Lord Jesus gifted a continuous conversation with me throughout the night. It was a lengthy dialogue where I remember saying to Him, *"You speak Lord and I will listen!"* Here is what I absorbed about who Jesus is, and what he would like us to know about himself, from that long night of conversation:

Thursday, December 29, 2005 – Lord, Jesus, all of the Christian rites and Sacraments use humble elements such as water, bread, wine and oil. These poor elements point to the profound humility and the holiness of the very character of who you are. When you came here Lord, through external signs – those now famous symbols of humility; the manger, the bread, the wine and the cross, you revealed to us your very nature – love, mercy, compassion and forgiveness. Lord, you did not show us yourself as high and mighty, but as a servant.

To this very day Lord, you continuously reveal yourself in the unassuming flowing waters of Baptism, the simple broken bread and crushed grapes of Communion and the pressed plain oils of Confirmation and the Anointing of the Sick. Your humility, Lord, and these humble elements of the Church Sacraments do not make much logic to those, who, in their arrogance, crave wealth, riches and power. The Sacraments of your Church, your body, the Body of Christ make no sense to many. The noisy excess of the world has disordered our passions and deafened our souls to what is Real.

Many of your Father's children hunger for more of everything, but they will never be satisfied until they find you. In their arrogance, many try to flee death by acquiring more things, working excessively, having shopping sprees, playing many sports and other addictions – as if these pursuits could make one eternal. However, pride, arrogance and earthly quests have kept us from the humble knowledge of you in your Sacraments. However, for the sick, the crushed, broken and the poor, their humility allows them to readily welcome you, Lord. Their emptiness and need are profoundly satisfied through the humblest elements of the

Sacraments. These modest sacramental gifts are a stumbling block for those who see it all as foolishness, but for those who are being saved, they are amazingly recognized by the humble, lost and broken souls who depend on the sacraments for eternal life.

I could never have written that on my own accord. That came by way of an intense and illuminating conversation with the Lord, continuing on and off, throughout an entire night of sleep. As a result, there is no doubt in my mind that he wishes to clear up misconceptions and underscore his true character of humility for us today. Let's face it; there are a lot of false notions going around about the nature of God. If you're like me, for decades I perceived God to be judging, condemning and ready to pounce on me when I lie, cheat or fulfill a lust, passion or desire. I had no idea that he is pure love and mercy, for those who are willing to humble themselves by believing in him and then going out and forgiving others. God is pure love and pure humility for those who are being saved. But, woe to the rich and the powerful who condemn, judge and control others – in their day-to-day sin, they fall under the judgment of God.

Also in this chapter, I believe Jesus wants us to know that he *is* unequivocally the Messiah, the Savior of the world. Why is that so important? Well, if you don't clearly know there is a guiding captain at the helm of a ship, how can you be assured that your boat, when in a storm, will arrive at its destination? Jesus *is* the Captain that we can count on to bring us all to heaven collectively and individually throughout life's tempests.

Until Jesus came on the scene, we humans were barbarians. We take for granted the order, and for the most part, the civility we have around us in the world today, 2,000 years after Christ and Christianity. Yes, a couple of World Wars and conflicts have marred the planet since his birth, but thanks be to God we're not living day-in and day-out with the meathead brutality of the early Egyptians, Greeks, Romans, Vikings, Aztecs, Mayans and American headhunters and so forth. When you or I go for a day picnic in the park, or to the beach and there are no brutal Vikings around or headhunters scalping us, we have Christ our Savior, the martyrs and the Body of Christ, both Catholic and Protestant, to thank for the civility of our world today.

Here is what the Lord conversed with me in this regard one night in January of 2006. Here is how I recorded it in my journal:

Sunday, January 1, 2006 – While I slept Lord Jesus, you came to me three times on and off throughout the night. You asked of me one thing – the same question three times. You inquired, *"Who do you say that I am?"* Each time I emphatically answered, *"You are the Christ, the Son of the living God."* After answering the question as I did, you replied back to me repeatedly, *"You could not know this unless it was revealed to you by the Holy Spirit."*

Lord, your coming on this occasion and in this way is reminiscent of the time that you arrived in the region of Caesarea Philippi with the disciples. You had just been confronted by the religious leaders. They had asked for a sign, apparently to test and see for certain whether you were the Messiah. But Lord, you are no puppet and refused to give them a sign. Instead, without giving any further signs, a little while later you asked the disciples, *"Who do people say the Son of Man is?"* They replied, *"Some say, John the Baptist; others say Elijah; and still others, Jeremiah or one of the prophets."* Lord, then you said, *"But what about you? Who do you say I am?"* Simon Peter convincingly answered, *"You are the Christ, the Son of the living God."* (Matthew 16:13-16) Lord, you told Peter that he could not have known this unless it was revealed to him by the Father in heaven.

A lot of people wish to make Jesus out to be just some sort of a nice guy or a cute bearded prophet filled with nice sayings for wall plaques. For some reason, diminishing Jesus is an important agenda for some. Possibly those who do this may be just badly informed of the verifiable historicity of Christ as the Messiah, as well as the authenticity of the ancient scrolls making up Holy Scripture. Be that as it may, what makes Jesus the Savior of the world and different from Buddha and other great spiritual leaders, is the fact that Christ rose from the dead. We must always keep in mind that there is no grave with a body in it for this very real person in history. We have ancient graves for other greats, like the Pharos of Egypt for instance, but not for Jesus. He's an enormously larger than life figure and because of that fact, if he were just dead, there would be preserved to this very day a grave with a body in it for people to go and visit.

The fact of the matter is that Jesus is not dead. Three days after his burial he resurrected from the dead. That is a fact, not fantasy. Mary, Mary Magdalene and eleven other disciples saw him many times over. For forty days he made many appearances, even ate with his disciples and appeared to five-hundred others who knew him. No one else has ever done this. Why? Because no one else has ever risen from the dead, but Jesus did. Here is what I wrote in my journal in this regard:

Friday March 31, 2006 – In a late morning vision, right before awakening, I heard the voice of an angel speaking to me . . . "Consider this Jesus, is he God and born a man? You may say *'no, that's unbelievable!'* Was he humble? You may say *'no, that's unbelievable!'* But was he wise? You may say *'possibly.'* Did he suffer and die? You may say *'no, that's unbelievable!'* But did he rise from the dead? Yes! Truly this man is God!"

On Tuesday, December 19, 2006, the Lord Jesus came to me in morning hours, right before I awoke. He spoke to me about God the Father, the Son and the Holy Spirit and their very nature in this way, saying, *"God is great – to the enormous measure of his greatness, so too is his responsibility to his greatness."* That's powerful! Of course it is potent, that is God having a conversation with us – his words are Spirit and life.

That locution is one that I have shared with many over the years. It is significant and that is why I am sharing it again now. Think about it for a moment. Go to the countryside and gaze into the enormity of the night sky away from the urban lights. Focus in on the endless stars, galaxies, black void, planets and moon. Next, take a moment to reflect on the delicate intricacies of the human body; the mind, the heart, the veins, the toes, the eyes, seeing colors and how you walk or even swim and dance.

Here is what I believe the Lord is illuminating with the words, *"God is great – to the enormous measure of his greatness, so too is his responsibility to his greatness."* It is the fact that from the endless reaches of the heavens and the complexities of the human body to the unfathomable depths of the ocean – that all this greatness we see around us also tells an enormous "Love Story." To the same degree we see the vast grandeur around us, so too, that is exactly how magnificent and infinite God's loving responsibility is to the creation he has made.

What does that mean to you and me? It means God loves each and every one of us deeply. Don't let anyone say otherwise. *"For God so loved the world that he gave his only begotten son, that whosoever believes in him might not perish but have eternal life."* (John 3:16) God not only infinitely creates; he also infinitely loves and is responsible for his creation. The fact of the matter is that he, who created all things, was also willing to come to his creation and love it to death – even death on a cross. He is so amazingly responsible for what he has created that he was willing to suffer, die and forgive his persecutors – the very people he created. How awesome is that? If he is willing to do all that for you and me, should we not listen and join in the conversation, instead of acting as though he does not exist? Worse yet, not only denying him, some also use his name as some sort of derogatory expression or swear word.

If we are in awe of what we can see, just imagine how breathtaking everything is that is unseen. The Apostle Paul concurs when he writes, *"No eye has seen, no ear has heard, and no mind has imagined the things that God has prepared for those who love him."* (1 Corinthians 2:9) One night, in January of 2007, I was up praying at about three o'clock in the morning and briefly had an opportunity to share with the Lord, through his own initiative of course, some glimpses into what heaven might be like. Here is how I recorded the events of that night:

Tuesday, January 9, 2007 – Lord, thank you for what Fr. J. [another Spiritual Director] refers to as "cooperative grace!" Lord, your grace is enough and amazingly you showered it upon me throughout this past night. I awoke at around three in the morning and was reading parts of the book *"My Life"* by St. Teresa of Avila. Then you inspired me to pray the rosary in a unique way. Using the *"Five Sorrowful Mysteries,"* I recounted the way of the cross and the death of Christ. Remorsefully, I also linked five personal failures that I wanted to confess to you and get off my chest. After each decade of the rosary, I sensed a growing lightness in both my body and spirit. As I sat up in bed praying and while I was still not quite finished – Lord, you walked into the room and gently asked, *"Can I take you?"* And of course I said, *"Yes!"*

Next, your great loving arms wrapped around me and you took me upwards through the top of the building. Lord, you are a great gentleman in the way that you came and gently asked to take me, lifting me high into the heavens.

The peace and joy of being with you in the heavens is indescribable. It was my joy to yield completely to your will as I gave you great praise the entire time we were away. Lastly, you returned me to my bed. You placed me gently down and under the covers in the same tender way my mother or father did when I was a small child. It is my delight to be your little child, Lord! You left me to sleep for a while and then you visited again and took me a second time into the heavens. How enormous is the peace of your caress, the love of your embrace and the joy of soaring into the heights with you! Truly, eye has not seen and ear has not heard what you have prepared for us.

But Jesus, as he matured from childhood, was not on the "mountain tops" soaring into the heights with one foot in heaven, as one may think. He had work right here on earth to do. Although Jesus was God, keep in mind that he was also fully human. He lived, ate, drank, laughed, celebrated, had temptations, cried and suffered in the same way we do. Just because he was God, he was not exempt from being fully human too. He was like us in every way. From the moment he was born, he matured and grew in wisdom in the same fashion as any child today. His mother, Mary, and his guardian father, Joseph, had to raise him, show him how to tie on his sandals, the way to school in the morning and then help him with his Hebrew homework at night.

Jesus grew in the knowledge that he was also divine and that he would have to do his Father's will, suffer and die. This insight was not acquired the moment he was born. Over time, he grew in the knowledge that he, like Isaac, the son of Abraham was going to be sacrificed, killed for the sins of the people. However, he would not be treated the same way Isaac was, who was released at the very last moment from being sacrificed. Jesus had to go all the way.

On the surface, it seems farfetched that flesh needs to be sacrificed in order for life to be gained. It is not so mind-boggling if we think about the reality that sacrificing flesh is an every-day-of-the-week occurrence because most people consume meat at mealtimes. If it were not for the sacrifice of animals, life would not continue on the earth the way we know it now. So too, Jesus sacrificed himself, his flesh not as food for a day, but food for an eternity, feeding us forever within the realm of the spirit. In February of 2007, the Lord firsthand revealed further insights into this aspect of his life. This is what I recorded in my journal about the event:

Tuesday, February 20, 2007 – Lord, thank you for this morning's vision, where in it I was crying because you revealed to me a moving insight into your early adolescent years. In your twelfth year, while you were still yet a boy, it was at the Jewish feast of the Passover holidays that you began to realize that you were "different." You were just twelve years old when you grew in the understanding that you would be killed for your great love for us, your compassion and beliefs. You discovered, while reading the scrolls in the temple with the rabbis, that you would be sacrificed and killed just as the perfect young lamb was lead to slaughter at Passover time. You were so consumed by these inspirations that you forgot to board the caravan with your mother and father, Mary and Joseph, for the ride home.

And because you are fully human, you came to these realizations gradually, through the power of reason and direct illumination from your Heavenly Father. It was here at this holiday Passover that you began to unite the symbols of bread and the wine and the festal lamb with your own passion and death that would come in about twenty years. A significant part of your suffering here on earth was connected to this twenty-year period where you had to internally wrestle with the knowledge that the inevitable was going to happen to you in your thirties. You knew that your death was going to be horrendous and humiliating.

Because of Jesus' death on the cross, we have an advocate, actually a "lawyer" who empathizes with us in every way. Jesus lived the life we live and thus he is adequately informed about our condition and he reliably pleads our case for mercy before God the Father. He is like the Old Testament high priest who had to intercede for the sins of Israel and offer temple sacrifices to God. However, Jesus offered himself as one final sacrifice once and for all. He can now plead each of our cases in heaven before God.

If this all sounds too farfetched, pick up a copy of the movie, *Defending Your Life* starring Albert Brooks and Meryl Streep. After seeing this romantic comedy about the afterlife, the idea of having an advocate in heaven will make somewhat more sense. In April of 2007, the Lord communicated the following to me about his heavenly "law firm" that has freely paid the price for you and me. That's good news. His services are free. Everyone can afford Jesus as their lawyer, especially the poor!

Saturday April 28, 2007 – Lord, thank you for the locution and gift of your communication in the night. In it you said, *"We have a high priest who is constantly pleading our case before the Father."* When we sin, Jesus, you are always speaking up for us before the Father. You are our advocate. Lord, you also said to me, *"We talk about you!"* meaning you, the Father and the Holy Spirit. Of course I was curious as to what you meant when you said that.

I suspect that as long as we are in the habit of extending mercy to others, even though we sin, you plead our case for leniency because you said, *'blessed are the merciful, they shall receive mercy.'* Lord, you showed me that when we do sin, you immediately have a conversation with the Father about extending mercy to us. It is reminiscent of Paul's letter to the Hebrews. *"Consequently he is able for all time to save those who draw near to God through him, since he always lives to make intercession for them."* (Hebrews 7:25)

So in the locution I asked you Jesus, what you and the Father talk about. You said, *"We don't talk about what you are doing wrong. We talk about what you are doing right! Mainly, how you show mercy and compassion to others, as the Father is showing mercy and compassion to you. That is the pleading I make for you on your behalf – what you are doing right."*

That sure is amazing! The words of the Lord here go against everything many have ever assumed about him. Contrary to popular belief, God does not look at what we are doing wrong. He's looking at what we are doing right! How profound is that? However, when I don't do much right, there's a problem. That is why it is important to weave into our lives time to help the poor, the homeless, elderly, sick, dying, broken and lost. The more that we are doing things right, the more we are giving God the Father, Son and Holy Spirit something to talk about. Conversely, the more self-centered that we are, and as a result, do very little good for others, more-than-likely, it is then that we fall off God's radar. That's not a good situation to be in.

When I was growing up, the Smothers Brothers had a funny routine that they did quite frequently on their television comedy-hour. Inevitably, there was almost a weekly dig from Tommy Smothers to his brother Dick. Rubbing it in, Tommy would say, *"Yeah, well mom always did like you best!"* I think that sometimes Catholics and Protestants each like to think that they are liked best. Not to mention, among the Protestants, some Lutherans or Baptists may like to think they are liked best, over say, Presbyterians or Methodists. Catholic groups are funny too. Some like to think that God favors Dominicans over say, Franciscans. One day I was visiting a diocese-run church, when I happened to mention to the pastor that I was visiting from a Paulist parish. He joked, *"Oh the Paulists! Are they still Catholics?"* With that said, I was surprised to receive the following locution from Jesus in November of 2007. Here is what I heard him say:

Sunday November 11, 2007 – Lord, thank you for the locution in the early morning hours where you said, *"I see Catholics and Protestants as one people, one Church."*

It's nice to know that God's love and mercy is so great that he does not see division. He only sees unity. He is "color blind." His all-encompassing love is reminiscent of those heroic moms and dads that have regular active children, then they go out and adopt disabled children and everyone gets treated the same. These are parents with huge hearts of love. After what I heard in the locution on November 11th, I can only now imagine that God has a huge heart of love for all his people here on earth. We're the ones with the problem of how to get along. For God, loving us equally has never apparently been a problem.

Whether Catholic or Protestant, one of the many things everyone agrees on is that Jesus will come again. Catholics in unison profess, at the time of the Eucharist, *"Christ has died, Christ is risen, Christ will come again"* All mainline Protestant denominations believe in the Second Coming as well. Jesus spoke of his return when he said, *"At that time, the sign of the Son of Man will appear in the sky, and all the nations of the earth will mourn. They will see the Son of Man coming on the clouds of the sky, with power and great glory."* (Matthew 24:30) In conclusion of this chapter about Jesus, here is a clip from my journal in regard to His coming:

Tuesday, June 24, 2009 – Lord, thank you for the locution in the night where you spoke, *"The sign of the Son of Man will be seen all over the earth."* Then you gave me a strong interior awareness that your "sign", the sign of the cross, will appear in the sky for many days so that everyone on the earth will see it and have an opportunity to turn to you. Yet, some hearts will be so hard and cold that they will deny the cross and its sign in the sky. Apparently, the sun and moon will be darkened for a time and the cross will illuminate the sky. Lord, you have said in the scriptures: *"And I, if I am lifted up from the earth, I will draw all men to Myself."* John 12:32

I suspect that when the sign of the cross appears in the sky, it will be one more example of God being merciful to us all. He'll be exhausting every last means to get our attention. When this event takes place, it will be like a *"Repentance for Dummies"* book. It will be a blaring sign, to non-believers and marginal Christians, to wake up and change. Here is how the Gospel of Matthew further describes this coming event. *"Immediately after the distress of those days, 'the sun will be darkened, and the moon will not give its light; the stars will fall from the sky, and the heavenly bodies will be shaken.' At that time the sign of the Son of Man will appear in the sky, and all the nations of the earth will mourn. They will see the Son of Man coming on the clouds of the sky, with power and great glory. And he will send his angels with a loud trumpet call, and they will gather his elect from the four winds, from one end of the heavens to the other."* Matthew 24:29-31

There have been other revelations about the person of Jesus Christ. Following, are more entries about him from my journal. They are insights that were granted in the months right prior to this book's publication.

Sunday, May 9, 2010 – Lord, thank you for speaking this morning, saying, "[I] *bore in the crucifixion all of your diseases."* And so, Lord, interiorly, you have shown me that there is not a disease in any hospital room or doctor's office that you did not experience in your own brutal passion, suffering and death. When we think about the ravages and weakness of cancer, you experienced the same on Good Friday. You carried your cross in pure exhaustion, and then Simon had to help you. In the scourging at the pillar, you bore the pain of leprosy, cancer and all extreme skin disorders. At the crowing with thrones, you lived through debilitating migraines and brain disorders. All diseases, Lord, you experienced, and you have sympathy for all those who suffer today. All who are sick can turn to you because you understand. By your cross Lord, we are healed!

This was to fulfill what was spoken through the prophet Isaiah: "He took up our infirmities and carried our diseases." Matthew 8:17

Surely our grief's He Himself bore, and our sorrows He carried; yet we ourselves esteemed Him stricken, smitten of God, and afflicted. Isaiah 53:4

The next revelation speaks to the age-old debate: Does Jesus save us by faith, by works or by both? It was at the heart of the Protestant Reformation controversy. Theologians, both Catholic and Protestant, often find it difficult to reconcile Paul's teaching of "faith only" and James, the brother of Jesus' teaching of "works."

Saturday, Jul 10, 2010 – Lord, thank you for the vision this morning, where in it I saw a large circle. At the top of the circle [twelve o'clock], was printed the words, *"Salvation by Faith."* Then I heard you speak, saying: *"Walk around the circle, which are your works of mercy, compassion and kindness. Where does it bring you back to?"* Then, Lord, you swiftly responded, *"It brings you back to 'Salvation by Faith.'"*

Lord, in this revelation, you showed that the circle is a life lived filled with mercy, compassion and forgiveness and it's your *complete* plan for our sanctification, but always leading us back to salvation by faith. It's a reminder and confirmation of similar lessons learned from the letter of James, *"You see that a person is justified by what he does and not by faith alone."* James 2:24

Chapter Eight
God the Father

It is impossible for me to write this book without taking time to share about the person of God the Father. One reason, is because it is he, whom I first met in my NDE experience. For those who were not raised with any catechism training, it is important to note here in this chapter that God is three Persons in one; God the Father, God the Son and God the Holy Spirit. Just remember this, one God – three persons!

But how is that possible? Nobody really has the answer to that because God is God. If God were other than God, then we would have the possibility of understanding this mystery. But because God is God, he is therefore infinite. Humans are not built to understand the infinite. We have a hard enough time understanding how to program a DVD player, let alone the infinite heights and depths of the nature of God.

With all that said, and having been momentarily on the other side, I think I can shed a small spec of light and some very limited insight into what is ultimately an unexplainable mystery of God in three Persons. Because the Bible tells us that we are made in the image and likeness of God, let's first look at our own humanity for clues of the trinity in all of us. As we do this, remember, from the earliest of ancient days, in the book of Genesis, God referred to himself as a plurality when he proclaimed, "Then God said, *'Let us make man in our own image and likeness.'"* (Genesis 1:26) If he was only one person he would have said, *"Let me make man in my own image and likeness."* But he did not. He said, *"Let us make man in our own image and likeness."*

We who are similar to God in our composition, are also made up of three parts; body, soul and spirit. There are three yous! That is why we have heard stories of certain saints who have experienced bilocation – being in two places at one time. Namely, in recent years, Padre Pio (+1968) had this gift.

Look at it this way. When you get into a car and drive down a highway, your body is physically in the automobile and it's operating the car skillfully – that is one part of you, your body at work. However, did you ever notice that while you are driving you can simultaneously speak with a passenger or take a phone call, safely we hope? That is your spirit at work, talking and recalling various memories and thoughts. Now, while you are having a conversation and driving, you also have the ability to experience emotions, regrets, joys and frustrations. That is your soul at work. The body and spirit sit inside of definition (words), while the soul sits outside of definition.

Words are completely unable to describe the very core, "soul" part of you. That is why we call some music, "soul music." That term means to say that although the music itself sits inside definition such as its notes and instrumentation (body and spirit), other wonderfully rich aspects of the music can not be explained or put down on paper. That unwritten feature refers to "soul music," and it is the musician's soul expressing itself outside of definition.

Did you ever notice the three parts of you can talk to each other? We call that, "wrestling with an idea," so-to-speak. When we wrestle with a decision or plans to be made, we use up all three parts to have a conversation about a particular concern. This internal chatter is a conversation going on inside of us every moment of our waking and even sleeping hours. Our dreams are a product of this triune conversation as well.

You see, if we were only one person, then we would be more like a computer than a human being. Computers deal with data in singularities, processing bits in orderly split moments of time. They do not have a soul or a spirit. They function and act in a single way and no matter how much data they hold, they are finite. Humans are much more advanced than this. We function in complete integrated conversations with ourselves to not only process data, but to also simultaneously consider many other complex factors such as good, evil, hate, concern, compassion, mercy, anger, frustration and love.

Humans, in a somewhat similar way are like God who is also three Persons. When Jesus was on this earth, he had a body like ours and he was fully human. He also had a Spirit, the Holy Spirit. Lastly, he had a soul – just as we do, but his soul was very God himself. When he was alive, like us, he was able to converse interiorly between his Body, Soul and Spirit. To this very day, this is how God communicates within himself. He is a community of three persons that talk creation out among the three of them. If God was a singularity, he would do things like a computer, cut and dry. But he is a community of three. He has the ability to balance the law, duty and the offense of evil with compassion, forgiveness, justice and kindness. Thanks be to God that God is a community of three Persons. If he were not, all of us would be in a lot of trouble because in that case, he would decide matters cut and dry like a computer – essentially throwing the book at us with no consideration for the good we do in this life. Thankfully, God can dialogue within himself and, as a result of that conversation, offer each one of us simultaneously perfect justice and mercy in a completely fair and balanced way.

A discussion about "God in Three Persons" is incomplete without drawing attention to Saint Augustine (+430) and his book, *On the Trinity* (De Trinitate). This original treatise turns out to be one of his most important accomplishments. According to Augustine, human beings are created in the image of God and therefore the mystery of the Trinity is imprinted in each one of us. Augustine started with God the Father as being Love. Saint John in his first letter tells us, *"God is love."* (1 John 4:8) But there is no such thing as love without a beloved which is why the Son is necessary. Ultimately, love cannot just stay locked between two individuals or else it becomes sort of a dual egotism. The love between the Father and Son wants to be shared, which is where the Holy Spirit comes in. Therefore, God (Love), the Son (Beloved) and the Holy Spirit (Shared Love) proceed forth from them, being one God in three Persons. It is within this same triune model that humans are created, in order that we love and are not self-centered or egotistical creatures.

The previous chapter addressed who Jesus is in the mix of these three Persons. But in this chapter I would like to focus more on the person of God the Father. (The layout of the book does not include a further discussion about the Holy Spirit. We will save that for another time.)

One of the most comprehensive insights we have into the character of God the Father is Jesus' story of the "Prodigal Son." In the story, Jesus intends to give us an authoritative glimpse into the very nature of the Father. That's a good thing because many people are confused about him. They think God is a mean ogre just waiting for us to do something wrong so he can cast us all into hell fire. Jesus is going to clear up the misperception. Here is the story Jesus tells. It's worth knowing about if you have never read it. If you have, it's always good to read it again and again. It's that good.

Jesus said, "There was a man who had two sons. The younger one said to his father, *'Father, give me my share of the estate.'* So he divided his property between them. Not long after that, the younger son got together all he had, set off for a distant country and there squandered his wealth in wild living. After he had spent everything, there was a severe famine in that whole country, and he began to be in need. So he went and hired himself out to a citizen of that country, who sent him to his fields to feed pigs. He longed to fill his stomach with the pods that the pigs were eating, but no one gave him anything.

"When he came to his senses, he said, *'How many of my father's hired men have food to spare, and here I am starving to death! I will set out and go back to my father and say to him: Father, I have sinned against heaven and against you. I am no longer worthy to be called your son; make me like one of your hired men.'* So he got up and went to his father.

"But while he was still a long way off, his father saw him and was filled with compassion for him; he ran to his son, threw his arms around him and kissed him. The son said to him, *'Father, I have sinned against heaven and against you. I am no longer worthy to be called your son.*

"But the father said to his servants, *'Quick! Bring the best robe and put it on him. Put a ring on his finger and sandals on his feet. Bring the fattened calf and kill it. Let's have a feast and celebrate. For this son of mine was dead and is alive again; he was lost and is found.'* So they began to celebrate.

"Meanwhile, the older son was in the field. When he came near the house, he heard music and dancing. So he called one of the servants and asked him what was going on. 'Your brother has come,' he replied, *'and your father has killed the fattened calf because he has him back safe and sound.'*

"The older brother became angry and refused to go in. So his father went out and pleaded with him. But he answered his father, *'Look! All these years I've been slaving for you and never disobeyed your orders. Yet you never gave me even a young goat so I could celebrate with my friends. But when this son of yours who has squandered your property with prostitutes comes home, you kill the fattened calf for him!'*

"'My son,' the father said, *"you are always with me, and everything I have is yours. But we had to celebrate and be glad, because this brother of yours was dead and is alive again; he was lost and is found.'"* Luke 15:11-32

Henri Nouwen in his book, *The Return of the Prodigal Son,*

flip-flops the "central character" of the story, giving that vital title to the Father. At times he refers to Jesus' story as the *Prodigal's Father,* instead of calling it by the name which it is known, the *Prodigal Son.* I agree. Yes, it is true that the son musters up a lot of humility and good sense to come back to his father and apologize. That is difficult for most of us to do – to admit when we are wrong. So, in that regard, the son is quite central to the story. However, the merciful character of the father in this parable is truly heroic. Instead of reading his lazy-bum-of-a-son the riot act when he returns home, he compassionately welcomes him as some kind of war hero, not the loser that he actually is.

Perhaps many fathers that read this classic New Testament story would have a difficult time being merciful in this way, because many are all about duty and expectation and prone to little compassion. However, the father in the parable of the Prodigal Son shows us a completely different scenario. He is one of unconditional love and humble support.

In March of 2006, I was gifted a tremendous insight into the Father of Jesus' story. Indeed, the following revelation about God the Father may have been given, in part, because of the contradictions and difficulties with my earthly father that I described in Chapter 4. Here is what I recorded in my journal about this event:

Tuesday, March 14, 2006 – In the early morning hours I awoke in tears of joy from a stirring and emotional vision. In it, I am standing on a dimly lit backstage waiting to go out and perform on a theater's main stage. The red velvet curtain is closed, hiding us from the audience. I and two other brothers are standing off-stage behind a black drape scrim and are receiving a pep talk from our director. He wants us to go out and give a stellar performance before a live audience. He admonishes, *"Go out there and cry, and make it good!"* In the show, we boys play the characters of three teenage brothers who terribly and suddenly lose their parents. As a result, we are each in desperate need of adoption or we will individually and collectively become homeless. We are about fourteen years old. While still offstage, the director huddles us together. He barks, *"Make this next scene powerful and convincing for the audience."* He's very demanding and continues saying, *"I want to hear heavy crying and sobbing. Got it?"* Although the pressure was on, we agreed and shook our heads saying, *"yes."*

Next, he pushes us even more. *"But please don't go out there and cry and let the audience believe that you are crying because you are all sad that your parents are dead. No!"* he said. *"These must be tears of joy. You must show tears of joy!"* the director continued. And one last thing he said, *"Show the audience that quite unexpectedly, out of nowhere, a father stepped up to the plate, came forward and adopted all of you at one time. He rescued you from homelessness and kept your entire family together. Those are the tears of joy I want to see communicated."*

We came out of the huddle and he patted us on the shoulders. Immediately, we went out and positioned ourselves at front, center-stage to do the scene. The curtain opened, revealing a full-house. The theater lights went down and a spot came up on us three brothers clustered together. Barely holding each other up in emotional support, we wept heavily and convincingly many tears of joy. I remember feeling exhausted by the time the scene was over.

Next, wiping tears from my eyes, I left my brothers, walked down the riser steps at center stage and then sat upon one of them facing the audience. A spotlight followed me, the house lights came up and I could see the bewildered faces of the individual audience members. They looked stunned by our powerful performance. I began to speak to them, pointing out to the audience with my right hand and saying, *"Why did you come here tonight? Was it, to see a play? To see us brothers perform an imaginary story? No, my friends, this was not a play. What you saw here tonight was real life. We could have been angry and sad at the sudden loss of both of our parents. But our sadness has been turned to tears of joy, when just at the right time, out of nowhere, a father decided to adopt all of us. Did you come to see fiction? No, what you have seen here tonight is reality."*

Immediately I awoke wiping lots of wet tears from my eyes and face. I was still emotionally drained from the intensity of the adoption scene. In a daze, as I contemplated the meaning of all this, I asked the Lord to help me receive its interpretation. And of course he did. Without delay I was lead to the Bible passages that instruct us about our adoptions as sons and daughters of God the Father. He confirmed the vision with the Scriptures.

The first Scripture that came to mind underscoring our adoption by our merciful God the Father, is one that is frequently said as part of *Liturgy of the Hours* evening prayers:

"Praised be God and Father of our Lord Jesus Christ, who

has bestowed on us in Christ every spiritual blessing in the heavens. God chose us in him before the world began to be holy and blameless in his sight. He predestined us to be his adopted sons through Jesus Christ; such was his will and pleasure, that all might praise the glorious favor he has bestowed on us in his beloved." (Ephesians 1:3-7)

This next scripture not only underscores our adoption as sons and daughters of God the Father but also the emotion of us crying because this is magnanimously so:

"But when the time had fully come, God sent forth his son, born of a woman, born under the law, to redeem those who were under the law, so that we might receive adoption as sons. And because you are sons, God has sent the Spirit of his son into our hearts, crying *'Abba Father.'* So, through God you are no longer a slave, but a son and if a son, then an heir." (Galatians 4:4-7) And lastly, one more Biblical confirmation of the vision's message:

"For all who are led by the Spirit of God are sons of God. You did not receive the spirit of slavery to fall back into fear, but you have received the Spirit of sonship. When we cry *'Abba Father'*, it is the Spirit himself bearing witness with our spirit that we are children of God; and if children, then heirs, heirs of God and fellow heirs with Christ, provided we suffer with him in order that we may be glorified with him." (Romans 8:12-17)

The theater stage story and its Biblical lesson taken in companionship with the story of the *Prodigal's Father* in the Gospel of Luke, speaks volumes to us about the very nature of God the Father. No matter how much of a sinner you are, no matter how much of a loser you are and no matter how badly your father treated you here on earth – you can have confidence that there is one Father in heaven that is all merciful and loving. He will take you back. He will forgive you. He will throw a party for you when you return to him, even right now as you are reading this book. You can confidently know that God the Father wants to adopt you and make you his very own son or daughter for an eternity. That's a long time! Like the prodigal son, all you have to do is fess up, return home, apologize to God for the wrongs you have done, acknowledge his fatherhood and he will take you back no matter what. What's the caveat? When you kneel at your heavenly Father's feet and receive his mercy, he will then wish you to go out and be merciful and forgiving of all those around you. Mercy has to be a flow. It can't be a dam.

Sony artist, Cecil Kim, a founding member of the *Servants of the Father of Mercy* conceived and created a representation of God, the Father. He is also the creator of *Sony's, "God of War."*

Chapter Nine
Mary & Joseph

As I mentioned earlier, in the chapter about Jesus, there are always those who wish to discredit him from his rightful title, "Savior of the World." Likewise, there are some, who for whatever reasons, wish to discredit Mary, the "Mother of God." Since about the time of the Reformation, there have been outspoken ones who want to deny her of our devotion and prayers of thanksgiving and adoration. Personally, I think there is something inherently wrong when anyone takes the time to put motherhood and a woman down, especially the Mother of God. If it were not for the motherhood of women, the whole cycle of life would be nonexistent. So too, without Mary the Mother of God, the whole cycle of Eternal Life would be nonexistent. Possibly, that is why Mary has many female devotees. Most women are mothers or have innate motherly abilities, and so therefore they get it. If more Catholic and Protestant men spent time connecting with Mary, more-than-likely there would be a plethora of more compassionate and merciful husbands, fathers and leaders in the world today.

What many fail to contemplate, or fully appreciate, is the fact that only after thousands of years of civilization and millions of women later, only *one* woman had a life worthy of being chosen as the Mother of God. Only *one* woman in all of history would ever have the resume and qualifications to do the job, to be the mother of God. What are the chances? Now if you or I went all our lives playing the lottery, then suddenly we won the jackpot, wouldn't you be excited about those phenomenal chances? Of course, and its doubtful anyone would play it down.

What did Mary actually do for us, if anything, that deserves our acclamations and adoration? A lot! When the entire world celebrates Christmas every year, we get the fairy tale version of her story. We see beautiful manger scenes for sale in the Christmas aisle at places like Kmart, twinkling stars atop city skyscrapers, halos on angels, glittering comet tales on Christmas cards and more. Combine it with sappy holiday tunes and it sounds like Mary really did not do much for us. She lived a fairytale! Mary appears more like a privileged queen in a romance novel, rather than the extraordinarily humble, longsuffering and obedient woman of God that she actually is.

Let's be real and put it all into a genuine perspective. Here is a woman that said *"yes"* to God. We should all take a lesson from Mary. Do not say *"yes"* to God or even like Isaiah, who once said, *"Here I am Lord, send me,"* unless you are ready for hardship, suffering and pain. Picture this, right after Mary said *"yes,"* her fiancé, unaware of her miracle pregnancy, thinks possibly she is a cheater more than a saint. How would you or I live with a horrible misunderstanding such as this and its corresponding interior suffering? Eight months into her pregnancy, Mary has the "privilege" to travel by donkey over hot, dirty, dusty roads and all of it so she can wind up in a barn lying on a stack of hay to have her baby. Not to mention the chickens and smelly barn animals prancing around. How many married women today, would say *"yes"* to that?

And the list of her heroic deeds for us goes on and on. Ultimately, she receives the "wonderful" opportunity to flee King Herod for Egypt, becomes an exile in a foreign country, has to learn a new language, and then barely escapes a blood bath of Roman soldiers killing hundreds of Innocents. Ultimately, Mary, wholeheartedly supports all her life what she thought was going to be a "winner son," but ultimately, is a loser by Roman standards, and witnesses his brutal crucifixion. And all those decades she lived day-to-day by Faith.

For more than thirty years, in fact, she lived within a very dark "cloud of unknowing," and she did it all for you and me! In all reasonability, shouldn't this woman deserve some on-going love and devotion from all of us? If she had not freely chosen to say *"yes"* to God and choose to suffer these hardships, who then would have brought the world its Savior? No one! You and I would have been up the proverbial "creek without a paddle," perpetually drowning and forever lost. She was our only chance, and thanks be to God, she did it. She never thought of herself, she only thought about you and me, and that is why Mary toughed it out.

With that said, let me share an insight from my journal about Mary and Joseph. It confirms a little bit more about Mary being the Mother of God and also tells us some about the unique role that Joseph played in our salvation story:

Monday, February 13, 2006, 5:00am – I had a vision in the night. In it, the statues high above the altar of St. Peter's Church came alive. There were three statues over the altar and from left to right were Saint Joseph, Christ and Saint Peter. Suddenly, the statues morphed into the actual persons of Saint Joseph, the Lord and Saint Peter. The two saints turned left and right and entered into a conversation with Christ. Next, a voice, like that of an angel, came out of nowhere and spoke to me saying, *"Do you know how Mary is referred to as 'the Mother of God?'"* I responded, *"Yes."* The angel continued, *"In much the same way, from now on, I want you to refer to St. Joseph as 'the Hands of Christ.'"* I replied back, *"But why?" "Because,"* the angel said, *"When Jesus was a child he could not do things for himself. Joseph did everything for him. And so he is to be called 'the Hands of Christ.'"*

This vision sealed up in my mind that giving our love and thanksgiving to Mary for being the Mother of God, is the right thing to do. After all, the confirmation came directly from an angel. I figure we can trust angels because they, if anyone, should know what they are talking about. Also, the vision revealed the unique role Saint Joseph played in our salvation story and stimulated in me a great devotion to him. Particularly because working with the homeless, I was inspired to see Joseph now as *"the Hands of Christ."*

Joseph is a guy that serves the poor! How so? Well, Jesus was rich but he left his riches in heaven and became poor and "homeless." So now, there is this wonderful man Joseph, who has a willing heart to help Jesus in his poverty and his "homelessness." Jesus, in this life suffered both, separations from his Heavenly Father and loss of his home in paradise. But Joseph adopts him and cares for him in his enormous poverty. How heroic is that? Joseph does for Jesus what God the Father does for all of us. He adopts us and Joseph adopted Jesus!

So, it was right after that vision I wrote this prayer to Saint Joseph. I will share it with you in hopes that you will pray it and ask for his help with all the poor and homeless in your community.

"Dear Saint Joseph, you took the poor Christ child into your home. For many years he could not do things for himself. As a carpenter and as a true laborer, you became the very hands of Christ. Help us to become the hands of Christ for those who are helpless, those who are homeless; for they can not do things for themselves as well. We build ourselves into a home to serve those who labor to exist through your intercession and in your son's Name, Jesus Christ the Lord. Saint Joseph, patron saint of the homeless, hear our prayer. Amen."

Another image of Mary that we all have is one of her standing tall, crushing the head of a serpent with her feet. This picture is for good reason. It is inspired by an ancient Biblical passage from the book of Genesis, as well as by a vision that the Apostle John had in the book of Revelation, which is recorded in chapter twelve. In January of 2008, I received a vision from the Lord backing up the same image and revelation. Here is what I recorded in my journal:

Saturday, January 5, 2008 – Lord, thank you for the vision this morning where in it, first I heard the words, *"Mary has shut the mouth of the serpent."* In the vision, I saw a serpent standing tall around a tree at the entrance of a garden gate. He could watch me and others enter, but we were not afraid of him or his "puffed up" terrifying presence there. He tried to look scary, but had no ability to sting with venom. He was disarmed and docile.

Obviously, the serpent is the devil himself. Genesis 3:15 says, *"I will put enmities between the serpent and the woman, and your seed and her seed: She shall crush your head, and you shall lie in wait at her heel."* This is one of the most famous passages in Scripture because it is one of the first ancient mysterious prophecies in the Bible about a coming Savior. The Scripture speaks of future conflict between a Woman, her Seed, (Jesus) and the Serpent that deceived man in the Garden.

This same conflict is spoken of in other places as well—even outside of the Bible. There are many stories across multiple ancient cultures about a conflict between a woman, the child she gives birth to, and a snake or dragon. For instance, the story is even reflected in the constellations our ancestors projected onto the stars of the sky. The constellation Hercules is using its foot to crush the head of the constellation Draco, the Dragon. In mythology, Hercules had a divine father (Jupiter) and a human mother (Alcmene), making Hercules half mortal and half divine—a distorted presentation of the Incarnation. In some ancient accounts, the constellation Draco guards the golden apples (forbidden fruit) from Hercules. These apples had the unusual property that any mortal who picked them would die.

This is one example among many. Apparently, the original ancient story of the Hebrew Scriptures, initially written thousands of years ago, may have been passed around from culture to culture over hundreds of generations.

What does it all add up to? That just as by one woman (Eve) did sin and disobedience enter the world, so too, by one woman (Mary), righteousness and obedience entered the world. A woman not only initiated the first problems of the human race in collaboration with a consenting man (Adam), but a woman also initiated the salvation of the human race in collaboration with her Son, a fully consenting man (Jesus), who was bent on obediently following his Father's will.

The Blessed Mother has other kudos and images too. On my mother's birthday, Thursday, January 25, 2007, I received a locution right before waking. In it, I heard the words, *"Holy Mary, Mother of God, 'Consultant of Grace.'"* (As mentioned earlier, most locutions are rarely long or wordy.) In this very short revelation, the word "Consultant" appears to be central to unraveling the sentence's meaning and lead us to an important spiritual message. According to the dictionary, to "consult" is a word that means to ask the advice or opinion of an expert, colleague or a friend perhaps. Professionally speaking, we all "consult" doctors.

The other key word here is "Grace." What is grace? There are two types of grace, "sanctifying" and "actual."

Sanctifying grace lives in the soul beginning at Baptism and makes our soul holy. It is an unmerited act of God that gives us eternal life. Actual grace is transient and it does not live in the soul. It is a free gift from God, working on our soul from the outside to bring about some special good in our lives, for instance, when God gifts events or inspirations that help to solve a problem with a particular sin or resolve non-forgiveness of a certain person in our life.

In the locution, *"Holy Mary, Mother of God, 'Consultant of Grace,'"* I take this to mean that Mary is *the* person for each of us to go to, who like a doctor, to ask for her advice about how to prepare ourselves to live holy lives and to receive special graces from God to make that happen. We can talk to Mary as we would any consultant and ask her for aid. Also, consultants are specialists with an expertise. Mary is an expert when it comes to grace. The Bible says that she was filled with grace (cf. Luke 1:28). When we go to her as our *"Consultant of Grace,"* she can accurately tell us what to do and can assist us too. In the words of the "Hail Mary" we pray, *"Hail Mary full of Grace."* Now, she has apparently also earned the title, *"Mary, Consultant of Grace."*

Sometimes visions have a spiritual meaning, but they are not readily known or seen. As it was with the Apostle John's vision in the book of Revelation, in instances like this, one may never completely know its interpretation. One such vision occurred in February of 2007. I will do my best to try to explain its practical interpretation out of the peculiar imagery that it contains. Here is what I wrote in my journal:

Monday, February 5, 2007 – In a vision this morning, I

and a few others waited in a small house on an insignificant side street eagerly awaiting the birth of Christ. Everyone gathered was anxious for his coming. Finally, the word came by a courier that he was born. They sent me out of the house to go and find him. I walked up a side street and I saw Mary, Jesus' mother, in a beautiful neighborhood tree. Next, I saw Jesus. But instead of him being a baby, he was a full-grown man and covered in blood. I took him by the hand to go with me so that the others back at the house could meet him. However, as one could imagine, being just born he could not walk or talk very well. I helped him along. Once at the house he spoke, but surprisingly his words were childlike.

When I awoke, I prayed for the interpretation. Here is a possible explanation of the vision . . . Mary, who is the *"Consultant of Grace"* is the one who delivers Christ to each of one us to this very day. Her delivery of Christ into the world did not end at his birth. How do we know this? Well the Apostle Paul said, *"The gifts and the call of God are irrevocable."* (Romans 11:29) When God gave Mary the gift to be the bearer of the Christ, delivering him to the world, that was a forever gift.

Her role as womb and temple of the Incarnation has never changed. Through her, we find Jesus born anew in each one of us. And, although we are adults, we have trouble walking and talking since we are still babies in the Lord. Therefore, we are not to be surprised when many adults are infant-like in their walks in Christ. We should be patient with them. Mary is the mother of all those who continue to be the incarnation of Christ in the world today. Mary, through grace, gives birth to each one of us who are called by his name.

As I was writing this part of the chapter, I received a locution from the Lord where I heard, *"Bathed in a sweat of blood."* Apparently it is alluding to the fact that Jesus, the central character of this vision described above, was covered in blood. But it was not any blood; it was the blood of the Passion of Christ. The Bible tells us this about his passion . . . *"And being in anguish, he prayed more earnestly, and his sweat was like drops of blood falling to the ground."* (Luke 22:44) We can be assured that all those Christians today who are the Incarnation of Christ, they being delivered to the earth through Mary will also suffer Jesus' Passion as well as the triumph of his Resurrection.

Before carrying the discussion about Mary further, I would like to share here a short clip from my journal taken from January of 2007 that substantiates this talk about Mary, her perpetual gifts, her permanent calling and the fact that the *"Call of God is irrevocable."* Here is what I wrote:

Sunday, January 28, 2007 – Lord, thank you for the locution and then a vision in the night. First, I heard the words, *"The call of God is irrevocable."* Next I saw the vision of an older professional who was seated and looking very contemplative. He was reflecting on once being called to religious life, got side-tracked in his career and is now being called again after a long occupation in business. He comes to the realization, once called, always called. *"The call of God is irrevocable!"* [God has been referred to as the *"Hound of Heaven."* Once called by him, one is forever called. He will track you down like he did Jonah.]

Through the most recent mystical appearances and revelations of the Blessed Mother at Lourdes, France – Fatima, Portugal – Medjugorje, Yugoslavia and Garabandal, Spain, it is evident that Mary is forever involved in the evolution of our modern world to this very day, right now in this digital age. Although, the latter two appearances of Mary are not yet officially recognized by the Church, they have a large following throughout the world. At Garabandal, Spain, in the 1960s, the Blessed Mother spoke of a soon coming Warning, a Great Miracle and a Great Chastisement. At four o'clock in the morning, one Saturday in 2006, a mystical occurrence took place that highly backs Mary's various messages for our world today. Here is what I wrote:

Saturday, December 16, 2006, 4:00am – In a vision, an angel appeared to me and said, *"I must tell you two very important pieces of information."* I politely replied, *"Please do not share private information from the Lord with me."* But he insisted and sternly said; *"No!"* Then again he said, *"I must share it with you."* Courteous but persistent I responded, *"Please do not share this with me because then I will have to become personally responsible for whatever you tell me."* *"No!"* he replied. *"I must share it with you."*

What he said next caught me off guard. He said, *"Look, you're considered to be one of the Lord's 'saints' and for that reason I need to tell you the message. You need to know what's going on!"* Well, when I heard the "saint" word I became extremely uncomfortable with that inference and got a little edgy with him. *"I'm no saint believe-you-me. You have the wrong person. I am not a saint but a sinner and a loser!"* I retorted.

Angels can be pushy when they are on a mission. He ignored my resistance and had an agenda that he clearly was not going to compromise. Then he spoke these two pieces of information to me. He said, *"First, there are angels on the earth, at this very moment in time, that are agents of God's government and his eternal Kingdom. These angels appear dressed as men and women and can intervene looking like "real" human beings at any time. Particularly, they are moving about at high levels in world governments to influence global affairs."* He continued, *"The angels can transform from spirit to human form, blending, still retaining their supernatural powers."*

He said he had one additional piece of information that I must know about. He spoke authoritatively, *"Secondly, the Blessed Mother will also be appearing to people around the globe to influence the Lord's will in the world today."*

"Miracle of the Mother", Sunday, November 13, 2016 at 3:00pm, unknown spotlight shines on the BVM in the darkness of our homeless warehouse altar and a rainbow appears at her waist.

Chapter Ten
Relatives and Friends

When I was a small child, usually on Sunday afternoons our family had a fairly regular ritual of visiting various relatives that lived in surrounding cities not too far from our home. Between my mother and father, the relatives were divided up into "two camps." There was one set of relatives on my father's side who were more middleclass and slightly affluent having nice houses and cars. They all lived near each other in nicely groomed suburbs. My father's family was a kindhearted people, very welcoming too and every time we visited we shared awesome mealtimes together. Then, on my mother's side, there was our poor Aunt Sarah, a humble woman that lived next door to my grandmother with her husband Peter in a small, very ordinary house on the railroad tracks of a tiny steel town. Freight trains blew their whistles while passing at full speed rattling the entire house at all hours of the night and day. The meals were plain and simple too. It was always spaghetti and *"ball-a'-meat"* as she called it in her English-Italian accent. The menu almost never changed.

It's hard to put into words as a child why, but it was Aunt Sarah's house that I mostly preferred to visit, not necessarily the other families with big nice houses, awesome dining and wealthy accoutrements. To me, there was something unexplainable about Aunt Sarah that was simple and *Real,* with a capital "R." Although poor, she was always smiling, joyful, compassionate and quiet, giving lots of hugs and kisses. We always got our cheeks pinched too! Standing only about four feet tall, Aunt Sarah was affectionately dubbed, "Aunt Shorty," and that always made her chuckle every time we said it. Because of the special bond I had with this humble soul, even as I got older, I always made it a point to visit her and Uncle Pete. She never judged anyone and always loved us just the way we are. I never recall her gossiping or saying a bad word about anyone, ever! She just didn't do that sort of thing, although that is a common practice in most families today as it was in ours. Surviving my uncle by about twenty years, in her latter days I visited Aunt Sarah in a nursing home. She died at the age of ninety-three in 2007.

About nine months after her death, one evening Aunt Sarah suddenly appeared to me radiant with love, affection, smiles and joy. She was seated in a rocking chair gently moving back-and-forth and chuckling, as if I had just called her "Aunt Shorty" again. She was not ninety-something anymore. She was very youthful, looking about twenty-eight years old. When I described the appearance to Fr. F., he said her smiles and joy was a good thing, a solid inference that she is in heaven. Reflecting on this vision brought me to a well-known Scripture adding further affirmation and consolation about Aunt Sarah's whereabouts. [Jesus said] *"Blessed are the poor, theirs is the kingdom of heaven . . . Blessed are the pure in heart, for they will see God."* (Matthew 5:8)

All the while I was growing up, my mother had a wonderful best girlfriend by the name of Ida. My brother Jimmy liked her a lot too. At one time, I understand she had a husband and through that marriage had a brilliant son who eventually became a church pastor. But all the years that I knew her, she lived alone. She was one of those self-made 60s women, *"hear-me-roar"* types that had her very own and quite successful *John Hancock Insurance* business. She had the sharp ability to get right in there and talk with the men and could sell ice to Eskimos. Ida was a huge contrast to the naïve homemaker that mother was. Possibly because they were opposites, that was the attraction in the relationship. According to my mother's recollection, Ida passed away in 2000. I had not thought of Ida nor had seen her in decades. That was all about to change.

Early one day in September of 2009, overwhelmed by what I had seen and heard in an appearance of Ida in my room, I called up my mom at six in the morning alerting her to the fact that her friend needed our prayers. Here is what I wrote in my journal regarding that event:

Monday, September 28, 2009 – This morning, a poor soul from the dead came, a friend of my mom's. Her name is Ida. She had passed away about nine years ago. Today, she was a wandering soul, still drifting without an eternal home. How sad. The best way to describe her would be "homeless." When she appeared, Ida was quite elderly and resembled how one might look right after death, very pale and sickly. I immediately recognized who she was, however.

My brother Jimmy was there too; peaceful and silently looking on as I grabbed Ida's hand to speak with her. *"Tell me how you've been since you died."* I said. *"They don't want me in heaven!"* she whispered; looking sad, worried and rejected. She continued, *"The angels said I am not welcome there unless I give my life to Jesus." "But, He is God!"* I emphatically replied. *"He is God; you must listen to Him!"* forcefully repeating myself. I then embraced her lovingly and said, *"Ida, promise me that you will do whatever they tell you to do when you return. You must promise me that you will do that."* As I continued admonishing Ida, I held her close and insisted she choose to follow the Lord. Thankfully, she agreed and then departed.

It seems as though, now that I am telling my story, more and more friends are willing to tell me theirs as well. A close friend by the name of Filomena, who is the chef in an area church parsonage, recently shared details with me from two unique encounters she had with the other side that are quite significant. After immigrating to the United States from Italy with her fiancé in the late 1950s, upon arrival they set out to get married and start a family in their new homeland. Within two years of the marriage, her husband was tragically killed in an automobile accident that also left Filomena in a coma for weeks. Their two little girls survived in the backseat, sustaining only scratches and other minor injuries. What happens next is remarkable.

After some weeks, Filomena came out of the coma and made progressively small steps in recovering her health. It was at this time that family and medical staff broke the news to her that her husband had died in the car crash. The information was overwhelming and as one could imagine, devastated the new bride and mom. As she tells the story in her English-Italian accent she said, *"I cried alone in my room every day for months-and-months-on-end, frequently calling out my husband's name."*

After months of uncontrollable sobbing, something phenomenal happened to help end the terrible sadness that filled her heart. Filomena continued, *"One night while I was asleep, my husband appeared to me and spoke in his broken English-Italian accent.* He said, *'Filomena! What are you weeping about? Please stop your crying!" Every time you start to cry, I have to leave what I'm doing in heaven to come here and visit you. I'm happy where I am at. So please don't cry any more.'"* With that he disappeared and as Filomena tells the end of the story, *"It was all so real, he comforted me and I never cried again after that!"*

After a couple of years of gaining strength and taking physical therapy, Filomena had to go get a job and become the bread winner for the family, which she continues to do now, some four decades later. After a few years of being a hard working mom, she was comforted in her toils by a unique appearance of the Lord that changed her life. This is what she witnessed:

"One night while I was fast asleep, I was taken up in a dream or a vision to an old-fashioned Sears store near my house. It was a place that I frequently shopped for the children. When I got on the escalator, I looked up and I saw Jesus standing at the top waiting for me. As I got closer I said, *'I know who you are. You are Jesus!'* At the top, I stood in front of him and excitedly said, *'What would you like Jesus? I will buy you anything you want in the whole store. Anything! You just name it and I will buy it for you.'* Next, Jesus put his hands on each of my shoulders and said, *'Filomena, there is nothing that I want. Everything here is mine. What I want from you are your prayers.'* With that, he left me and I woke up immediately and in my bed thinking *'What happened to me? I just met Jesus!'"*

Another family's amazing encounter with the afterlife was recently shared with me by Catalina, who has been the organist and choir director for the same church in small-town America since the 1950s. Even at her senior age now, and after having given birth to more than a dozen children, she continues to serve and to play at services, sometimes five nights a week. Here is Catalina's family story:

"When my oldest son Marty was still a boy, my father was not doing well and was not expected to live much longer. My father loved his grandson Marty in a special way. Marty would hand him tools while they worked on special projects and car repairs. They always loved being together. One day around five o'clock in the morning, Marty heard some noises in the kitchen. Without waking the rest of the house, he went out to see what was going on. That is when he saw his grandfather in the kitchen and began to speak with him for some minutes, thinking he had come over to the house for a visit. Soon, my husband got up and went to the kitchen because he heard Marty talking. Just as he arrived, my father left by the back door of the house and walked out into the garden. Marty was standing at the back door waving goodbye to him. Marty told his dad, *'Grandpa was just here visiting us!'"* It was just about then that a knock came at the front window; Catalina received word from her sister that her father had passed away around five o'clock in the morning.

But sometimes, God kick-starts conversations among us souls that are living on earth right here and now, mainly so that we will help one another by extending healing hands of mercy, love and compassion. Recently, Mary Lou, shared a remarkable story about a time in her life, some years ago, when she was in the hospital and was scheduled for dangerous surgery. While still in her room, she remarked to her husband that it would be great to find a priest in order to receive the Sacrament of Reconciliation (Confession) one last time. Unfortunately, the staff did not know of a clergy member in the hospital and was unable to help. At the very same moment, Monsignor Biedermann, from Sacred Heart Parish, had just entered his car in the hospital's parking lot planning to return home. Upon opening the car door, he heard an auditory locution, *"Someone needs to go to confession on the second floor."* Filled with charity and compassion for the sick and obedient to the voice of the Lord, he visited every room on the second floor asking if the person had called for a priest. Having no luck, he walked in the last room on the floor and saw Mary Lou. He inquired, *"Did you call for a priest? Would you like to go to confession?"* *"Yes!"* she replied. *"How did you know?"*

In many respects, the impetuous of charity seems to be at the heart of the dialogue God is having with us. He is moving everyone to greater selfless acts of kindness and love, modeling us after his son, Jesus Christ. One night, a visitor by the name of Alvaro had been staying at our house for a couple of weeks and was preparing to leave the next day to fly back to his hometown with his teenage daughter. I had only spoken to Alvaro once; the first day he had arrived. Mainly, we spoke at length about his faith and interest in the things of God. He had a lot of wonderful insights and a lot of great questions too. Because this particular visit was the first time I had ever met him, I really did not know him or even what he may need while being this far away from home to make his stay more comfortable. The entire two weeks he and his daughter were very busy, mostly traveling the area visiting family and friends. We were out of touch, but that was about to change.

On this particular night, his last before having to depart for home, I walked into the house at nine o'clock at night and stopped in the bathroom on the way to my bedroom to wash up and call it a night. I heard Alvaro's voice in a far room talking and did not want to interrupt. While standing at the bathroom sink, the Lord approached and engaged me in the conversation of the night. Here is how I recorded that event in my journal:

Saturday, November 29, 2008 – On this night, I went into the bathroom, and while washing up, I heard an interior locution from the Lord while standing at the sink saying, *"Offer to take Alvaro the hour and a half trip to the airport tomorrow." "Be prepared,"* he continued, *"When you go, it will be a very early flight, so be ready to wake up at three in the morning!"* Then he said, *"Are you willing to sacrifice a little sleep to help him out?"* With an oh-so-slight hesitation, I said, *"Yes, Lord."* I walked out of the bathroom, found Alvaro and as prompted said: *"Hey Alvaro, do you need a ride to the airport?"*

He was stunned, as if I had been reading his mind. *"Did my sister call you?"* he said. *"No,"* I replied. *"How did you know?"* he inquired. Filled with frustration in his voice, he had just been on the phone for over an hour trying to find a ride. Gratefully he accepted my offer, but with a word of caution, *"Our flight is at six. We have to get up around three in the morning, are you up for it?"* Without hesitation I said, *"Yes!"*

At that moment, he was completely unaware of what prompted a strong positive response to such an early flight and ungodly hour of the morning. Not only were friends and family unable to help this poor guy out, the Airport Shuttle did not even want to take him either! The company did not resume operations until five, much too late for him to arrive in time for a six o'clock flight. To make matters worse, the ride that he had counted upon cancelled at the twelfth hour, leaving no opportunity to make alternate plans. He was at that very moment out of options and out of luck. But God had mercy upon Alvaro and used a poor loser like me to extend help to someone in need.

Well, there is not enough room here in this book to tell all the many stories that I am now aware of since I have begun to tell mine. But to me, it is evident that the conversation is going on all around us, both here and in the afterlife. Specifically, in this chapter it was important to share a few stories from others and including others because it illustrates that God is working in all of our lives continuing his dialogue with us. We only have to believe in him, trust him, pray and follow him in a life of sharing mercy, compassion and forgiveness.

Chapter Eleven

The Poor, Homeless, Lost And Broken

Unbelievably, God daily suffers rejection by the many who see his handiwork in nature, yet all the while ignores him and pretends as though he doesn't exist. When God physically came to the earth, he was also despised and rejected, primarily by the rich and powerful. This is one reason why, to this very day, God is mystically present in the poor, broken, despised and rejected living among us. God is no stranger to the rejection and suffering of the poor, and therefore he lives in solidarity with them.

Dorothy Day (+1980), the founder of the Catholic Worker movement and advocate for the poor once said, *"Christ remains with us not only through the Mass but in the 'distressing disguise' of the poor. To live with the poor is a contemplative vocation, for it is to live in the constant presence of Jesus."* St. Mother Teresa of Calcutta once said, *"At the end of life we will not be judged by how many diplomas we have received, how much money we have made,* [or] *how many great things we have done.* [Because Jesus said,] *We will be judged by – 'I was hungry and you gave me to eat. I was naked and you clothed me. I was homeless and you took me in.'"*

Saint Faustina Kowolska in the mid-1900s concurred with this notion when she recorded an amazing encounter with God himself in her journal. One day, St. Faustina encountered a poor beggar of a young man at the front gate of the convent. She had been placed in charge of serving the homeless that occasionally would show up pleading for help. In her own words, she tells the story this way . . .

"There was this young man, emaciated, barefoot and bareheaded, and with clothes in tatters, was frozen because the day was cold and rainy. He asked for something hot to eat. So I went to the kitchen and found nothing there for the poor man. But, after searching around for some time, I succeeded in finding some soup, which I reheated, and into which I crumbled some bread, and I gave it to the poor young man, who ate it. As I took the bowl away from him, he [suddenly] gave me to know that he was the Lord of heaven and earth. When I saw Him as He was, He vanished from my sight. When I went back in and reflected on what had happened at the gate, I heard these words in my soul: *'My daughter, the blessings of the poor who bless Me as they leave the gate have reached My ears. And your compassion, within the bounds of obedience, has pleased Me, and this is why I came down from My throne – to taste the fruits of your mercy.'" Diary of Maria Faustina Kowalska,* Notebook IV, #1312.

In the Bible, Jesus also tells us a story about the "Rich Man and Lazarus" which is significant in this same regard. As you read the story below, keep in mind that the real sin of the rich man is not prostitution, it is not for being adulterous-straight or promiscuous-gay and it is not for lying, cheating or stealing either. The real sin of the rich man that winds him up in hell is what he actually had complete control over; he was arrogant and unmerciful to the poor and presumably others. He was so haughty; he could not even see the utter poverty of Lazarus. Further, because of his uncompassionate behavior here on earth, when he asks for mercy in the afterlife, mercy is denied him. Anyone that has hopes of going to heaven, there is an important lesson to be acknowledged here. This is only one of many significant things Jesus says and does that backs up his claim that God desires "mercy, not sacrifice." If you have never read the story, please enjoy its intricacies. If you know the story, read it slowly again and pray for the Holy Spirit to enlighten you as you entertain its various levels of meaning.

[Jesus said,] "There was a rich man who was dressed in purple and fine linen and lived in luxury every day. At his gate was laid a beggar named Lazarus, covered with sores and longing to eat what fell from the rich man's table. Even the dogs came and licked his sores.

"The time came when the beggar died and the angels carried him to Abraham's side. The rich man also died and was buried. In hell, where he was in torment, he looked up and saw Abraham far away, with Lazarus by his side. So he called to him, *'Father Abraham, have pity on me and send Lazarus to dip the tip of his finger in water and cool my tongue, because I am in agony in this fire.*

"But Abraham replied, *'Son, remember that in your lifetime you received your good things, while Lazarus received bad things, but now he is comforted here and you are in agony. And besides all this, between us and you a great chasm has been fixed, so that those who want to go from here to you cannot, nor can anyone cross over from there to us.'*

"He answered, *'Then I beg you, father, send Lazarus to my father's house, for I have five brothers. Let him warn them, so that they will not also come to this place of torment.'* Abraham replied, *'They have Moses and the Prophets; let them listen to them.' 'No, father Abraham,'* he said, *'but if someone from the dead goes to them, they will repent.'* He said to him, *'If they do not listen to Moses and the Prophets, they will not be convinced even if someone rises from the dead.'"* Luke 16:19-31

Jean Vanier, the founder of l'Arche communities for the disabled, whom I spoke of earlier in this book, expands upon the lessons to be learned from "Lazarus and the Rich Man." While speaking on radio with Lydia Talbot, he once said, *"I think there is a whole mystery which we find in Luke. Lazarus was an excluded outcast, a leper, and he is the one that enters into the kingdom. The rich man, who wasn't able to see him, rejected him. He goes into the place of torment. You see, the danger for rich people is that they become frightened and they build up barriers around their hearts, defense mechanisms, because they have to preserve their riches, preserve their image, preserve their power. So they become people with lots of fear, whereas Lazarus has nothing to defend. He's just himself."*

In September of 2009, a poor homeless soul from Purgatory appeared to me, quite possibly someone who knew me from the streets or whom I may have served under the bridges. Now having read the story of the "Rich Man and Lazarus," one can't but help to feel for the poor soul described here, especially because of the wretched condition he was in. Here is what I recorded about the encounter in my journal:

Monday, September 28, 2009 – One recent morning, a young man about thirty-something appeared to me. At first I thought he might be a demon because he was in such bad shape and even scary-looking condition. So I poured Holy Water on him, just to be sure he wasn't the enemy! He responded humorously to the drenching and said, *"Yuk! "Why did you do that to me?"* I then realized he was a poor soul from the afterlife, but he was inept and confused. That prompted me to ask, *"When did you die?"* *"A half hour ago"* he replied. He was definitely a newbie to the afterlife. Apparently, from his tattered looks, he was a homeless person – one in jeans, basic t-shirt and his teeth were in bad need of repair. At the time of his taking leave from my room, I reassured him that my Mass intentions would be offered for him the next day, praying that the Lord would grant him eternal rest.

Some people believe that Jesus said, *"The poor you will always have with you,"* because he was encouraging us to realize this will always be an unmanageable plight and because it is so large, so-as-if-to-say, *"Ignore the problem as you wish."* Wrong answer! Jesus said, *"The poor you will always have with you,"* in part, because without the poor the middle-class and the wealthy do not have the ability to *"lay up treasures in heaven."* We need the poor, they will always be with us, because by seeing them, they help us middle-class-rich people to go to heaven. They give us the chance to practice the virtues of charity that make heaven possible. If we did not have the poor, the middle-class-rich and the ultra-wealthy folks too, would remain self-centered and thereby doomed to the fate of the rich man in Jesus' story.

In the summer of 2008, I was, for one week, visiting a homeless ministry when the director got in my car while hitching a ride back to his home a few miles away. Candidly he said, *"I disagree with guys like you coming here and handing out rosaries to homeless people. I wish you wouldn't have done that today,"* I remained silent. He continued, *"Now I have to deal with the Rescue Mission across the street seeing our homeless people over there with rosaries hanging around their necks. They're Protestants and they don't want to see Catholic rosaries paraded around and irreverently draped over peoples' heads."* He escalated the discourse further by holding the rosary hanging in my car and said, *"And furthermore, I don't like it when people hang rosaries around their necks or from the rearview mirror of a car, its disrespectful!"* Of course, I strove to understand this odd point of view and continued to remain silent, never discussing his sore subject again.

Not long before this man's angry encounter, the Blessed Mother had granted me an auditory locution of her voice on Saturday, April 26, 2008. I had awoken in the middle of the night, after a horrific attack of the devil in a vision. To counter the assault, I sat up in bed and prayed the rosary at four o'clock in the morning. While praying, a beautiful woman's voice, made of pure crystal and total charm, spoke out of nowhere, saturating the entire room with sweetness, *"I will help you!"* she said. The amazing audio of her voice was better than anything that can be heard in an ultramodern movie theater's surround sound system. Drenching every fabric of the space with her charismatic presence, peace and consolation, I overwhelmingly knew the Blessed Mother had just spoken to me. Wow! From that night forward, after hearing Mother Mary say, *"I will help you!"* I was encouraged to never worry about any type of difficulties again. That was good enough for me. Since Mary is going to help me, there is really nothing ever to be concerned about, even if someone might get angry because I was passing out Mary's rosaries to the homeless and cheering on devotion and prayers to her! But I digress and I am actually sharing this story for another reason.

In July of 2008, not long after the encouraging words from the Blessed Mother, the conversation about the rosaries was ready to escalate and heat up even more. Here is what I recorded:

Thursday, July 17, 2008, 7:00am – In the early hours of the morning, I received a vision that our newly formed congregation to serve the homeless, *Servants of the Father of Mercy,* had received its first piece of mail at a new post office box established just about a week ago. In the early morning revelation, I saw my hand enter the box and surprisingly, I pulled out our first-ever piece of mail. [At this juncture in time, we were brand-spanking-new, no one had even heard of our name or address, but a few very close friends.] While in the neighborhood of the post office, I stopped in to check the mail and to see if the vision had any validity to it. Miraculously, there was one piece of mail laying there inside the box, just as I saw it in the revelation. I thought to myself,

"Who knows our address and that we even exist? This is really strange!" The post card was actually a notice to pick up a small package at the counter. Upon opening it, the box was filled with handmade rosaries intended for us to give out to the homeless and donated by someone whom I had never heard of, or met before, according to the return address. There was no note inside. So, it was not a donation of money that first arrived for our newly formed nonprofit, it was a gift directly from the Blessed Mother!

A couple of weeks after this, I had the inspiration to investigate the return address and find the person behind the miracle rosaries. The donor was an elderly woman in her eighties, who spends most of her time at home, whiling away the hours making them for missionaries. She told me on the phone, *"When I read in an old newspaper, or magazine recently, that you gave rosaries to the homeless, I made them extra-long so they can be placed over their heads."* I responded, *"Maam, it would have been impossible for you to have read about us or our address in any publication, we're brand new, no one has ever heard of us!"* She never did find the journal that she thought she saw the organization listed in.

The first miracle taking place here was the early morning vision that later that same day brought me to the post office and "got the ball going." The second is the fact that the donor apparently saw a vision too; one containing our ministry's name and address inside of a journal article that does not really exist. The third miracle is that rosary maker, by the power of the Holy Spirit, was inspired to make the rosaries long enough to fit over the head of a homeless person, countering what had happened a few weeks earlier by the man in my car. Lastly, the name of the woman is a miracle too – Claire Donner. Her name, when translated from the French, Claire meaning *"clear"* and Donner meaning *"to give."* Her name loosely translated means *"Clear Giver."* Only God could orchestrate a miracle with this many intricacies and layers to it.

Since the time of Claire Donner, hundreds of others ladies and men have supported making rosaries for the 80,000 + homeless we serve in Southern California. Namely, *"Our Lady of the Rosary Makers"* society of the United States and Canada and the extraordinary work they do in their parishes by hosting fundraisers, buying beads and handmaking more than 10,000 rosaries for the poor over the years: Janet Fanucchi at *St. Raphael Church* in Santa Barbara, CA – Irene Haines at *Assumption Church* in San Leandro, CA – Rosemary Stiles at *St. Monica's Church* in Mercer Island, WA – Fr. Andrew Pyon, Margaret Mary Marks and Frances McGlaughlin at *St. Mary's Church* in Cochrane, Alberta, Canada and Pauline DiMarco at *Our Lady Star of the Sea* in North Myrtle Beach, SC.

The miracle of the Blessed Mother and the other extraordinary events in this chapter shored up for me the fact that God is first and foremost reaching out to the poor, the homeless, orphan, widow, sick and dying. Since he is so concerned, we should be too and go and do the same.

Students of *St. Luke's Church*, Pasadena, CA Team up with *Servants of the Father of Mercy,* Delivering Food, Water, Clothing, Sneakers, Socks, Blankets and Rosaries to 80,000 + People Living Homeless in Southern California

Chapter Twelve
Lessons Learned

Chapter one began with the telling of my near death experience. In particular, there is a lesson to be learned in the account of passing through the total blackness. The experience of going through the darkness is frequently sited and shared by others who have had a NDE experience. Apparently, the "black tunnel" is a sign and a symbol of our earthly need for faith in dark times. When I was in the blackness of death, it was my faith in God, fostered here on earth in dark times, which facilitated my rescue and brought me into the light.

However, a person does not need to have a NDE to pass through the darkness and experience a test of faith. In this lifetime, all the dark moments we experience are tests of the ultimate blackout each will have at the time of death. Cultivating faith right here and now, while we are still on earth, gets us ready for the big-one, so-to-speak. Intuitively, we all know that we should have faith in dark times, such as when we have lost a job, experienced a terrible accident, a divorce, loss of a child, etc. But do we realize how important it really is to have faith in all the dark times of our lives?

Right after my near death experience, a good friend, Scott

who is of the Jewish faith, shared his own experience of passing through the darkness and meeting God on the other side. Here is how I recorded his story in my journal right after hearing it.

Wednesday, October 26, 2005 – I met with my friend Scott today at Literati Café. He also had a God-encounter in 2000, while on a bicycling trip in the Desert Southwest with a friend. He had biked into a tunnel, alone. Once in the middle, unexpectedly, he was plunged into total blackness and could not see either end. The fear was tremendous as he groped the walls, passing slowly, step-by-step, and struggling with every fabric of his being, as he trusted God and had Faith that he would make it to the other side. That evening at the campsite, suddenly God descended from heaven, overshadowing Scott with his presence, shortly after midnight, while he was sitting on a hilltop high above the camp ground looking at the peaceful starlight of the pitch black sky. God chose to console Scott and reveal himself to him right after he had passed the test of the enormous faith-encounter in the black tunnel. Although not having a NDE, Scott experienced the black tunnel that many speak of, literally!

Scott and I also spoke about how when God reveals himself to us in the darkness, by our own free will, the response must be to choose God, more than ever going forward. If we should turn our backs on God after such a revelation, we would not do so in innocence as we did at other times in our lives when God seemed elusive. If we turn our backs now and do not choose to follow him, it would be out of gross error and eternal damage to the soul. *"To whom much is given much is required."* (cf. Luke 12:48)

As in the "Rich Man and Lazarus," Jesus' parable shared earlier; similarly, this book also contains lessons learned from my family's own story in the hereafter. In part, like Jesus' parable, it is a story about a man speaking back to us from the afterlife, namely my father. I sense that he and my mother are encouraging me, since their passing, to share our family's lessons learned. There's no doubt that my father is proud of what I am doing in this book. Particularly because it proclaims the message of God's mercy and forgiveness that he is a beneficiary of, from his unique vantage point in the afterlife. In part, my dad is accomplishing in this book what the rich man had hoped to do through Abraham, but was not done because he did not deserve mercy or any special consideration.

Putting it all into perspective, my father suffered greatly in Purgatory; however, by speaking from the afterlife here, he does not wish anyone reading this to have to undergo much of the same. It is better to learn one's lessons of mercy, compassion, kindness and forgiveness in this life, than to have those issues purged out in the hereafter. At least on earth, if one needs a break from the pressure of thinking through love and charity – there is always the possibility of a cleansing walk, inspiration at the movies, or having a comforting piece of chocolate cake. In Purgatory, there are no consolations. For many it can be isolation, desolation and suffering and with no breaks. One should always remember, heaven is a place only for those who know how to forgive, and it's better to work that out sooner than later.

This book speaks a lot about being merciful to others, since our going to heaven basically hinges on Faith in God *and* heroic acts of compassion to those around us. But what is mercy? Jesus said, *"Blessed are the merciful, they shall obtain mercy."* (Matthew 5:7) Succinctly, mercy is *not* giving to others what they deserve, but giving them the opposite. That is hard to do, isn't it? It can be illustrated this way . . .

A few months ago I stopped in at a breakfast diner and sat at a fairly empty counter on one of the barstools. There was no initial conversation with the server but, *"Coffee please. Give me a minute to read the menu,"* – you know, the usual restaurant ordering chit chats. After dropping off the coffee, the young lady occasionally passed by, but twenty-five minutes later still had not stopped by with refills or had taken the order. Once I realized, that for whatever reason, I was not going to be served; I paid the coffee at the front register and left the server a five-dollar tip.

Once in the car, I thought about what had just happened. The usual way to respond to this sort of unkindness is to call it to the attention of the server, possibly have a few words or report the incident to the manager or owner. All of which probably is what the person may have "deserved." But mercy is about giving the person the opposite of what they deserve. In this instance, I thought to myself, *"What is the opposite here? I know! The opposite would be to give an awesome tip as if I had just experienced winning customer service."* So, that is exactly what I did. That was mercy in action. In hindsight, I suspect that the person learned more from receiving mercy than could have been learned by the usual reprimanding methods. She will forget ninety-nine percent of her customer encounters; this particular encounter will never be forgotten. It will always speak to her heart, calling her to conversion. That's what mercy does; it calls each one of us to change.

Adults and children both need mercy in order to grow in the knowledge of a loving God, but children need huge amounts of it in special ways. How does our definition of mercy play out with little ones? Similarly, as it did in the story about the server. Fathers and mothers are God's loving representatives here on earth. Little ones learn about the characteristics and qualities of God through their parents' merciful or unmerciful behavior. As we all know, sometimes children mess up really bad and they may deserve a severe scolding, but "the law of mercy" tells us to make it lighter or completely opposite of what is expected. For instance, the next time a child gets a "D" or "C" in say, math or science on their end-of-year report card (all the while dreading to come home), try surprising the little one with, *"Don't worry, we'll work on that harder next year. Let's go out and have a nice big dish of ice cream and celebrate the beginning of summer break!"* Over time, children will succeed and grow more from mercy than the traditional and confrontational ways of handling these sorts of things. Facilitating change in children, as it is in adults, is always a delicate balance of the law, discipline, repentance and more than anything else, lots of genuine mercy.

Frequently, many recognize that they want to be understanding and forgiving, but don't know if they have completely achieved the goal. In this regard, we've heard it said, or have even said it ourselves; *"I forgive, I just haven't forgotten."* That dilemma raises the question, *"How do I know that I have sincerely forgiven someone?"* There are two ways that I am aware of, that one can be certain.

First, the measure you are merciful and forgiving of yourself, that is itself a strong indicator of how merciful you are toward others. That's powerful to think about! Only you and I know best the same sins, failures and errors that are being committed time after time throughout the span of our own lives. Interiorly, the more that one can have a compassionate internal conversation about these errors saying something like, *"That's okay, with God's help, I'll do better next time."* Or, *"Jesus, I trust in you to change this in my life."* The more that one's interior dialogue toward self is patient and kind, it is also a strong indication that others will be treated with the same love and understanding. However, the more that the interior self-dialogue is condemning and unkind with phrases like, *"You idiot, you did it again!"* Or becoming despondent saying, *"You can keep working harder at this but you will never conquer it."* Obviously, one clearly has the same ability to be judgmental, impatient and condemning of others. Therefore, the best place to begin living a life of mercy and forgiveness is right within one's self.

Presumably, it is unlikely that God will ever perfect a soul here on earth from habits or patterns of sin, if the person entertains even the slightest judgmental or unkind attitudes in his or her heart and mind toward others. God allows each of us to remain in repetitive sins because it is his way of keeping us humble, dependent on receiving his mercy and thus we are obligated to be merciful toward others.

Look at it this way; when one harbors even the slightest judgmental attitude toward others (almost all of us do); it's not in God's best interest to provide perfection to anyone living with that mindset. Why? You and I both know that the more perfect one becomes, more often than not, a bad attitude comes along with it; being impatient, unkind and unforgiving. We say phrases to ourselves and others like, *"Why doesn't he get it?"* or *"She's so stupid!"* and worse yet, *"I would never do what he just did. How rude is that?"* In our "perfectness" and our self-righteousness, we angrily walk away from another's brokenness, judging them and condemning them. In love with our own perfection, we go out and belittle others by spreading hate, discord, lies, exaggerations and disharmony. Why would God want to grant perfection to anyone that he knows is going to go out and beat up the little guy in his brokenness? He won't. Here lies the reason why any person with hopes of obtaining heavenly help to become truly perfect, by God's standards, must also pray for and pursue the complete virtues of charity, patience, kindness, meekness, gentleness, empathy and sympathy for others. It is within the context of a hundred-percent-of-the-time nonjudgmental attitude, that God grants complete, personal sanctity to each of his children. How many people do you know that are willing to live that way?

Bede Jarrett, a pastor from England, before the time of his death in 1934, gave a similar explanation as to why we are not perfected here on earth and the reason most will remain with continuous imperfections of sin until they are buried six-feet-under. He said, *"If we were truly humble, we should never be astonished to find ourselves giving way to sin. We should indeed be horrified but not surprised . . . Once we have really begun to try to see what we are like, we recognize ourselves to be the evilest of creatures. This is no mock humility, for there is no room for anything mock in the spiritual life. This is true humility. . . God wishes me out of my past sin to come nearer to him, find somewhere in that unhappy past a motive too for love."*

While basking in God's kindness and forgiveness of my own sin, that self-sinful realization should indeed propel me to genuinely love others who are broken and sinful as well – not condemn them. Yet, some will read this and be completely oblivious to their sins. If one feels perfect, better than others or has a sense of being right (self-righteous) all the time – that is in itself a false notion and a deception of the largest kind.

Jesus tells a parable about a similar lesson. The story is titled, "The Unmerciful Servant" Here it is, check it out:

"Then Peter came to Jesus and asked, *'Lord, how many times shall I forgive my brother when he sins against me?* Up to seven times?' Jesus answered, *'I tell you, not seven times, but seventy-seven times.'* Therefore, the kingdom of heaven is like a king who wanted to settle accounts with his servants. As he began the settlement, a man who owed him ten thousand talents was brought to him. Since he was not able to pay, the master ordered that he and his wife and his children, and all that he had, be sold to repay the debt. The servant fell on his knees before him. *'Be patient with me,'* he begged, *'and I will pay back everything.'* The servant's master took pity on him, canceled the debt and let him go.

"But when that servant went out, he found one of his fellow servants who owed him a hundred denarii. He grabbed him and began to choke him. *'Pay back what you owe me!'* he demanded. His fellow servant fell to his knees and begged him, *'Be patient with me, and I will pay you back.'* But he refused. Instead, he went off and had the man thrown into prison until he could pay the debt. When the other servants saw what had happened, they were greatly distressed and went and told their master everything that had happened.

"Then the master called the servant in. *'You wicked servant,'* he said, *'I canceled all that debt of yours because you begged me to. Shouldn't you have had mercy on your fellow servant just as I had on you?'* In anger his master turned him over to the jailers to be tortured, until he should pay back all he owed." [Jesus then said] *'This is how my heavenly Father will treat each of you unless you forgive your brother from your heart.'"* Matthew 18:21-35

Secondly, there is another way to know if one is sincerely forgiving someone or not. Jesus said, *"Love your enemies and pray for those who persecute you."* When one has the ability to pray for those who have been acting unkindly, that caring behavior speaks volumes about the merciful goodness going on within. Yes, you may still feel hurt by the wrongdoing, but that is not the judge of the fact that you are being compassionate by praying for your "enemy".

Along with the theme of mercy, the absolute main subject matter of this book obviously has been proof of the afterlife, which I have laid down in a somewhat methodical and coherent way so that you may also come to believe and trust in God's promise of eternal life. And with that said, there will always be some people, with sharp tongues and thinking, who will try to explain away any clear proof of life after death. That's normal! We've all known a naysayer, they exist. For instance, if you see *"black"* they will see *"white."* Usually when people are this adamant about denying obvious evidence, they have a hidden agenda. I suspect one possible hidden agenda of an afterlife naysayer is *"to dodge accountability and responsibility."* If a cynic ever admitted that there is proof of the hereafter, they would therefore also have to believe in God. Many do not want to do that. Why? One reason being is that it would also be to admit we are no longer an end unto ourselves. In acknowledging the hereafter, one accepts the reality there is Someone we must ultimately be accountable to and who expects us to live our lives with a sense of duty and responsibility, kindness, compassion and humility. Many teens and adults do not want to do this.

Frequently, another question comes up, *"What is our age in the afterlife?"* That depends. Similar to my Aunt Sarah and Cousin Kim, it appears as though when a person is welcomed into heaven because of having acquired purity of heart in this life or having been purged in the afterlife, the person immediately becomes regenerated to a youthful twenty – thirty-something. Essentially, the two non-corporal components of our "trinity," the soul and spirit, they immediately take on the image of one's young-looking resurrected body, although it has not been yet received. The regenerated soul and spirit will eventually be reunited to a very youthful body on the day of the resurrection of the dead.

However, apparently individuals that go to Purgatory retain the age and condition that the soul and spirit was in at the time of death. That is why in the story of the homeless man who appeared to me, he was still wearing a tattered t-shirt, looked worn and his teeth were in bad condition. The more a person descends to lower levels of Purgatory (depending on the amount of suffering and purgation that is applied to cleanse the soul of selfishness, a hard heart and self-centeredness), the original age at the time of death is retained as well as a charring and blackening of their image, denoting great suffering, as it was in my father's life.

Lastly, in this same regard, some souls, for whatever reasons, are permitted by God to wander for a time after death, as it was in the case of Ida. That is why we always pray for eternal rest for our departed loved ones. It is also, most probably the reason we frequently see the cliché, R.I.P. (Rest in Peace) on gravestones. The souls that wander tend to take on the appearance of their dead body, pale and emaciated. Possibly, this wandering may be a state of "limbo" that is spoken of in Catholic spirituality.

Sadly, some souls drop off the "radar" at the time of death. These are individuals who never cultivated a Faith in God while they were alive and they were self-seeking, unkind, unrepentant and unmerciful to others. Persons in this situation retain their age at death; they do not have regeneration and immediately experience the eternal pains of hell in soul and spirit. At the time of the Resurrection, those individuals in hell will also be reunited with their bodies and together with their soul and spirit will experience the pains and sufferings of hell for an eternity.

It is safe to say that it's highly unlikely that these souls could ever appear here on earth or have discussion with us. It would be more realistic that the devil could counterfeit such an appearance in order to deceive. He has been known to appear even as the crucified Christ and the Blessed Mother for reasons of deception. So, we should never put anything past him. The way we know such afterlife appearances are authentic is the fact they always lead one to greater peace, forgiveness, charity and love. If these qualities do not grow and flourish after such an encounter, guess what? Someone has just been duped by the devil himself! Also, one's mind can play tricks too, but even these types of perceived encounters can never replicate the charity and peace of God when afterlife appearances are authentic.

Putting it all into perspective, because of the immeasurable mercy of God, most people go to Purgatory, or they wander until they figure things out (as in the case of Ida) or they go directly to heaven. One has to work very hard in this life at power, control, evil, hatred and self-centeredness in order to actually wind up in hell for an eternity. As it was in my brother's case, despite a self-centered "party lifestyle", his belief in God, the just consideration by God of his childhood abuse, my and my mother's prayers for him, along with his one genuine act of mercy, won him a wonderful place in Purgatory and a clear shot at going to heaven by God's mercy.

It is important to acknowledge that the real sins that get one into hell, and we should be most fearful of, are the diabolical sins of power, control, pride, arrogance and hatred. The sins connected with our animal nature such as lust and addiction, although bad, they do not necessarily determine eternal perdition. C. S. Lewis, in his bestselling book, *Mere Christianity* agrees. He once wrote, "Finally, though I have had to speak at some length about sex, I want to make it as clear as I possibly can that the center of Christian morality is not here. If anyone thinks that Christians regard unchastity as the supreme vice, he is quite wrong. The sins of the flesh are bad, but they are the least bad of all sins. All the worst pleasures are purely spiritual: the pleasure of putting other people in the wrong, of bossing and patronizing and spoiling sport, and back-biting; the pleasures of power, of hatred. For there are two things inside me, competing with the human self which I must try to become. They are the Animal self, and the Diabolical self. The Diabolical self is the worse of the two. That is why a cold, self-righteous prig who goes regularly to church may be far nearer to hell than a prostitute. But, of course, it is better to be neither." (*Mere Christianity*, Chapter 15)

And now a word of caution; with all this discussion about the hereafter, please be aware that the counterfeit practice of "spiritism" is never a good idea. For example, calling up the spirits of the departed, Ouija-boards and incantations should never be practiced or participated in. We are not supposed to summon up souls from the other side. Their visitation strictly comes as a gift from God for the purpose of furthering charity, love, forgiveness and for the cultivation of peace and inspiration. People who practice Spiritism, such as moving tables, ghost hunting and calling up souls, are collaborating with the devil himself. Those who do this sort of thing, such as diviners, seers and witches, are in danger of eternally harming themselves and those who go to them for advice. Whoever appears should always come as a gift from God and we should never pray for and request, or seek, after this gift.

It is also important to make perfectly clear that this book is neither about being a Conservative nor about being a Liberal. One should be neither! But everyone should be Merciful, with a capital "M!" For instance, when a Conservative is unkind, spiteful, insulting, hateful and judgmental toward a Liberal, God is no longer on the side of the Conservative. God is always on the side of the downtrodden, the despised and the rejected and in this case, the Liberal. Conversely, when a Liberal is aggressive, malicious, arrogant and judgmental toward a Conservative, God is no longer on the side of the Liberal. He supports the Conservative.

Why is this so? Jesus himself knew very well what it was like to be unjustly judged. The self-righteous priests of his day thought they could read the motives of the heart (*only* God can do that) and so they thought they had Jesus "all figured out." Jesus gets killed because of this horrible, judgmental, assuming behavior of the church leaders. Thus, whenever a person is being judged and maligned, God immediately is in solidarity with the persecuted one. That is why we should welcome persecution. It is the only way to know for certain that God is solidly on one's side. He empathizes with those who are being judged, because God first-hand knows what it is like to be treated in such an ill and assuming manner.

Along these same lines, the following post was recently published at our blog, www.HomelessInAmerica.BlogSpot.com

"When Jesus said, *'The poor you always have with you,'* (Mark 14:7), he was pointing out that we are sinful in permitting poverty. For his allusion is to, *'There will be no poor among you if only you will obey the voice of the Lord.'* (Deuteronomy 15:4-5)

> *"Therefore . . .*
>
> *"There should be no liberals in America, just the merciful.*
>
> *No conservatives, just the compassionate.*
>
> *No liberals, just the forgiving.*
>
> *No conservatives, just kindness.*
>
> *No liberals, just the patient.*
>
> *No conservatives, just love."*
>
> (*Liberals and Conservatives* www.HomelessInAmerica.BlogSpot.com, Sunday, June 6, 2010)

It is for this reason that we are never to criticize or condemn others. Jesus said, *"Do not judge others, and you will not be judged. For you will be treated as you treat others. The standard you use in judging is the standard by which you will be judged. And why worry about a speck in your friend's eye when you have a log in your own? How can you think of saying to your friend, 'Let me help you get rid of that speck in your eye,' when you can't see past the log in your own eye? Hypocrite! First get rid of the log in your own eye; then you will see well enough to deal with the speck in your friend's eye."* Matthew 7:1-5

On Monday, January 7, 2008, I was engaged in a vision, one that has implications about generously and lovingly extending out the proclamation of the Gospel just as Peter's vision had asked him to do in book of Acts, Chapter 10. If you are not familiar with his revelation, which allowed the "Good News" to be spread to non-Jews, (most of us today benefiting from Peter's vision), here is the text, just as it appears in Acts:

"About noon the following day as they were on their journey and approaching the city, Peter went up on the roof to pray. He became hungry and wanted something to eat, and while the meal was being prepared, he fell into a trance. He saw heaven opened and something like a large sheet being let down to earth by its four corners. It contained all kinds of four-footed animals, as well as reptiles of the earth and birds of the air. Then a voice told him, *'Get up, Peter. Kill and eat.' 'Surely not, Lord!'* Peter replied. *'I have never eaten anything impure or unclean.'* The voice spoke to him a second time, *'Do not call anything impure that God has made clean.'* This happened three times, and immediately the sheet was taken back to heaven." Acts 10:9-16

And so it was. Peter wakes up, comes downstairs and immediately there is a knock at the door. Three men meet Peter and lead him a day's journey to Caesarea, to a man by the name of Cornelius, and by God's inspiration; Peter, open-mindedly, gave this Italian a shot at heaven too. Prior to this, they all thought heaven was only for the Jews. Some people today think heaven is only for those individuals that live in nice houses, have the "white picket fence" lifestyle and are deemed morally "religious" by society. It's a similar confusion the early church had about who goes to heaven, until God corrected the mistake with visions and inspirations from the Holy Spirit. The next vision uprights a modern misunderstanding of who gets invited to paradise.

In the early morning hours of one winter's day in January of 2008, I saw throngs of people all gathered together in one huge ballroom. Shockingly, not one person attending a great "ungala" was even close to "normal" by society's standards. I was touched by their endurance of overwhelming rejection, pain and anguish. Many were grossly overweight, uneducated, retarded, gay, marginalized, physically unattractive, migrants, immigrants and oppressed. As I looked around the room at each one and witnessed their anguish, I thought to myself, *"These poor people, they suffer so from the rejection, judging, and the persecution that they receive from others."* Pitifully, they looked up desperately calling out, *"Please help us!"* Next, what they said is truly significant. *"We are abused. Could you please speak up for us by proclaiming Christ's command, 'This is my commandment that you love one another as I have loved you.'"* [John 15:12]

Evidently, these poor souls have a message; calling out for mercy from the Church today – both Catholic and Protestant. Are we listening?

Ultimately, the poor, the broken, the persecuted and the marginalized have already suffered much more than the powerful and wealthy in this life, who usually can buy comfort, and more-often-than-not, they do. It is unlikely that the discomforted here will have to do much more suffering in Purgatory in the afterlife. However, the middle-class, rich and powerful who may never have experienced this sort of rejection and despisement, and who may never have hit rock bottom as the poor and some with addictions do, they will have to do something now to "bring the bottom up."

What is meant by that? Well, there are a variety of ways to "bring the bottom up." For instance, a comfortable wealthy or middle-class person could volunteer a few hours a week at a Rescue Mission. Another possible way would be to "live without" certain comforts. Recently, I read about an Atlanta family of four, that convinced each other to sell their $1.5 million home, give half to the poor and give half of their belongings as well. They chronicle their journey in a new book, *The Power of Half*, by Kevin and Hannah Selwan. Thus, by cultivating a Faith in God and finding ways to "bring the bottom up," by those who have never received the gift of "hitting rock bottom," is how the wealthy and powerful can make it directly into heaven.

Conclusion

And so, in closing, James, the brother of the Lord was right after all, *"Faith without works is dead!"* (James 2:26) Appropriately, now a James or "Jim" will have the last word in this book:

"Listen, my dear brothers: Has not God chosen those who are poor in the eyes of the world to be rich in faith and to inherit the kingdom he promised those who love him? But you have insulted the poor. Is it not the rich who are exploiting you? Are they not the ones who are dragging you into court? Are they not the ones who are slandering the noble name of him to whom you belong?

"If you really keep the royal law found in Scripture, *'Love your neighbor as yourself,'* you are doing right. But if you show favoritism, you sin and are convicted by the law as lawbreakers. For whoever keeps the whole law, and yet stumbles at just one point, is guilty of breaking all of it. For he who said, *'Do not commit adultery,'* also said, *'Do not murder.'* If you do not commit adultery but do commit murder, you have become a lawbreaker.

"Speak and act as those who are going to be judged by the law that gives freedom, because judgment without mercy will be shown to anyone who has not been merciful. Mercy triumphs over judgment!

"What good is it, my brothers, if a man claims to have faith but has no deeds? Can such faith save him? Suppose a brother or sister is without clothes and daily food. If one of you says to him, *'Go, I wish you well; keep warm and well fed,'* but does nothing about his physical needs, what good is it? In the same way, faith by itself, if it is not accompanied by action, is dead.

"But someone will say, *'You have faith; I have deeds.'* Show me your faith without deeds, and I will show you my faith by what I do. You believe that there is one God. Good! Even the demons believe that—and shudder." (James 12:5-19)

Delivering a Christmas blanket to Greg
(living homeless 15-years behind a gas station).
At one time, he was a New York attorney.

Postlogue

An Invitation

Millions of homeless Americans are waiting for someone just like you to extend mercy to them – the conversation of this book. The *Servants of the Father of Mercy* is Catholic community and we also welcome people of Faith to join our team as lay volunteers, brothers and sisters helping just five hours a month homeless men, women and children in Southern California or in your very own community, anywhere in the world. Please contact us today and consider "bringing the bottom up" by spiraling down, joining up and helping the homeless. Email us at Contact@ServantsoftheFather.org.

Also, our vowed religious vocations for Catholic

Brothers, Sisters, Priests and Deacons are open to those individuals of all ages, eighteen and older, who are in touch with their own brokenness and poverty. We look for former fishermen, prostitutes, the uneducated, despised and rejected to come and share our mission. Get the discussion going by emailing us at: Vocations@ServantsoftheFather.org.

Above, children in Newtown, CT receive comfort and joy at a recent Christmastime gathering with gifted copies of *This Bible Talks!* The first-ever talking Bible for children created by *Servants of the Father of Mercy* lay sister, Pam Fischer.

Annually at Christmastime, the *Servants of the Father of Mercy* look to donate our children's "press and play" talking Bible, *This Bible Talks!* to poor and homeless children living in America and on the global mission field. We believe there is a great need, in these growing tumultuous times, to urgently form toddlers and pre-readers early on in their developmental years with the Word of God. You can discover more about the Bible mission to little ones and how to support it at www.ServantsoftheFather.org and www.ThisBibleTalks.com.

Have an on-going conversation about the message of mercy by subscribing to our blog – HomelessinAmerica.BlogSpot.com. Since 2007, it's America's only weekly journal for triumphal insights into everyone's poverty, illusions and brokenness.

You are invited to donate alms of mercy and compassion to the homeless, providing them with snacks, fresh fruits and vegetables, beverages, clothing and spiritual supplies. However large or small, your monthly donation provides for regular deliveries of bottled water, food, blankets, shoes and more – preventing dehydration, hypothermia, malnutrition and the untimely death of a homeless person. Give online at ServantsoftheFather.org or send a check to: *Servants of the Father of Mercy, Inc.*, P.O. Box 42001, Los Angeles, CA 90042.

Servants of the Father of Mercy, Inc. is a private association of the Roman Catholic Archdiocese of Los Angeles and is listed in the *Official Catholic Directory*. The organization is a nonprofit, tax-exempt IRS 501 (c) 3 California corporation. All donations are tax deductible. Like us on Facebook!

Addendum

Help the Homeless in Purgatory

Some estimates approximate billions of souls could still remain homeless in Purgatory at this present time, and for the moment, they are unable to access their eternal home. St. John Vianey once said, *"Yet how quickly we could empty Purgatory if we but really wished to."* Possibly he is referring to a special prayer that can bring these poor souls home, as told to St. Gertrude the Great (+ November 17, 1301) by the Lord himself. He indicated the following prayer would release 1,000 souls from Purgatory each time it is said:

> Eternal Father,
> I offer You the Most Precious
> Blood of Your Divine Son, Jesus, in union with
> the Masses said throughout the world today,
> for all the Holy Souls in Purgatory, for sinners
> everywhere, for sinners in the Universal Church,
> those in my own home and within my family.
> Amen.

Upon one's own death, why risk the possibility of personal poverty and hardships in purgatory? The next set of prayers listed below prevent afterlife "homelessness" and honor the seven times Jesus spilled His Precious Blood for us, as revealed by Our Lady to St. Bridget and approved by the popes Clement XII and Innocent X.

7 Prayers of St. Bridget Said Daily for 12 Years

Our Lord Made 5 Promises To Saint Bridget

If the soul praying these seven prayers dies before the entire twelve years have been completed, the Lord will accept them as having been prayed in their entirety, because the intention of the soul was to complete them as directed. If a day or a few days are missed due to a valid reason, they can be made up for later, at the soul's earliest opportunity. Our Lord made these five Promises to anyone who recited/prayed these prayers daily for twelve entire years:

1 The soul who prays them will suffer no Purgatory.

2 The soul who prays them will be accepted among the Martyrs as though he had spilled his blood for his faith.

3 The soul who prays them can choose three others whom Jesus will then keep in a state of grace sufficient to become holy.

4 No one in the four successive generations of the soul

who prays them will be lost.

5 The soul who prays them will be made conscious of his death one month in advance.

The 7 Prayers of Saint Bridget

Opening Prayer - O Jesus, now I wish to pray the Lord's Prayer seven times in unity with the love with which You sanctified this prayer in Your Heart. Take it from my lips into Your Divine Heart. Improve and complete it so much that it brings as much honor and joy to the Trinity as You granted it on earth with this prayer. May these pour upon Your Holy Humanity in Glorification to Your Painful Wounds and the Precious Blood that You spilled from them.

1st Prayer - The Circumcision: Pray 1 Our Father: Our Father who art in heaven, hallowed be thy name; thy kingdom come; thy will be done on earth as it is in heaven. Give us this day our daily bread; and forgive us our trespasses as we forgive those who trespass against us; and lead us not into temptation, but deliver us from evil. Amen

Pray 1 Hail Mary: Hail Mary full of grace. The Lord is with thee. Blessed art thou among women, and blessed is the fruit of thy womb, Jesus. Holy Mary, Mother of God, pray for us sinners, now and at the hour of our death. Amen.

Eternal Father, through Mary's unblemished hands and the Divine Heart of Jesus, I offer You the first wounds, the first pains, and the first Bloodshed as atonement for my and all of humanity's sins of youth, as protection against the first mortal sin, especially among my relatives.

2nd Prayer - The Suffering on the Mount of Olives: Pray 1 Our Father, 1 Hail Mary

Eternal Father, through Mary's unblemished hands and the Divine Heart of Jesus, I offer You the terrifying suffering of Jesus' Heart on the Mount of Olives and every drop of His Bloody Sweat as atonement for my and all of humanity's sins of the heart, as protection against such sins and for the spreading of Divine and brotherly Love.

3rd Prayer - The Flogging: Pray 1 Our Father, 1 Hail Mary

Eternal Father, through Mary's unblemished hands and the Divine Heart of Jesus, I offer You the many thousands of Wounds, the gruesome Pains, and the Precious Blood of the Flogging as atonement for my and all of humanity's sins of the Flesh, as protection against such sins and the preservation of innocence, especially among my relatives.

4th Prayer - The Crowning of Thorns: Pray 1 Our Father, 1 Hail Mary

Eternal Father, through Mary's unblemished hands and the Divine Heart of Jesus, I offer You the Wounds, the Pains, and the Precious Blood of Jesus' Holy Head from the Crowning with Thorns as atonement for my and all of humanity's sins of the Spirit, as protection against such sins and the spreading of Christ's kingdom here on earth.

5th Prayer - The Carrying of the Cross: Pray 1 Our Father, 1 Hail Mary

Eternal Father, through Mary's unblemished hands and the Divine Heart of Jesus, I offer You the Sufferings on the way of the Cross, especially His Holy Wound on His Shoulder and its Precious Blood as atonement for my and all of humanity's rebellion against the Cross, every grumbling against Your Holy Arrangements and all other sins of the tongue, as protection against such sins and for true love of the Cross.

6th Prayer - The Crucifixion: Pray 1 Our Father, 1 Hail Mary

Eternal Father, through Mary's unblemished hands and the Divine Heart of Jesus, I offer You Your Son on the Cross, His Nailing and Raising, His Wounds on the Hands and Feet and the three streams of His Precious Blood that poured forth from these for us, His extreme tortures of the Body and Soul, His precious Death and its non-bleeding Renewal in all Holy Masses on earth as atonement for all wounds against vows and regulations within the Orders, as reparation for my and all of the world's sins, for the sick and the dying, for all holy priests and laymen, for the Holy Father's intentions toward the restoration of Christian families, for the strengthening of Faith, for our country and unity among all nations in Christ and His Church, as well as for the Diaspora.

7th Prayer - The Piercing of Jesus' Side: Pray 1 Our Father, 1 Hail Mary

Eternal Father, accept as worthy, for the needs of the Holy Church and as atonement for the sins of all Mankind, the Precious Blood and Water which poured forth from the Wound of Jesus' Divine Heart. Be gracious and merciful toward us. Blood of Christ, the last precious content of His Holy Heart, wash me of all my and others' guilt of sin! Water from the Side of Christ, wash me clean of all punishments for sin and extinguish the flames of Purgatory for me and for all the Poor Souls. Amen.

Durable, laminated copies are available of Saint Bridget's 7 Prayers, by donation for the homeless. Each is 8.5 x 11 and perfect to take along in a brief case or backpack, as well as laying it on a night stand or coffee table, wearing well for twelve years with normal daily use. Specify English or Spanish.

For more information, email Info@ServantsoftheFather.org, or write: SFM, P.O. Box 42001, Los Angeles, CA 90042. Order online with a credit card, secure PayPal - www.servantsofthefather.org.

Recommended Reading

C. S. Lewis, ***Mere Christianity***, New York, MacMillan Publishing Company, 1978.

Henri Nouwen, ***The Return of the Prodigal Son***, New York, Doubleday, 1994.

Jean Vanier, ***A Door of Hope***, London, Hodder & Stoughton, 1999.

John of the Cross, ***Selected Writings - Classics of Western Spirituality***, trans. Kieran Kavanaugh, New York, Paulist Press, 1987.

Mike Yankoski, ***Under the Overpass***, Colorado Springs, Multnomah Books, 2005.

Nicky Eltz, ***Get Us Out of Here - Maria Simma Speaks with Nicky Eltz***, Dekalb, Illinois, The Medjugorje Web, 2005.

Saint Augustine, ***City of God***, trans. Marcus D. D. Dods, New York, Modern Library, 1950.

Saint Augustine, ***Confessions***, trans. Henry Chadwick, New York, Oxford University Press, 2009.

Saint Maria Faustina Kowalska, ***Divine Mercy in My Soul - The Diary of Sister Faustina Kowalska***, Stockbridge, MA, Marian Press, 1987.

Simon Tugwell, ***The Beatitudes: Soundings in Christian Tradition,*** Darton, Longman & Todd Ltd., Great Britain, Templegate Publishers, 1980.

The Little Flowers of St. Francis, trans. Raphael Brown, Garden City, NY: Hanover House, 1958.

Teresa of Avila, ***The Collected Works of Teresa of Avila,*** 3 vol., trans. Kieran Kavanaugh, Washington, D.C., ICS Publications, 2001.

How to Order this Book for Your Church, Prayer Group, Family and Friends

On the Internet, you may conveniently order additional copies of *Proof of the Afterlife* 2 – *The Conversation Continues,* at

www.ServantsoftheFather.org
www.ProofoftheAfterlife.com
www.Amazon.com.

Quantity discounts are available for churches, prayer groups and hospitals, as well as discussion and support groups. Send your email request to Info@ServantsoftheFather.org, with the number of books, your name, phone number and "ship to" address information, or post the same in a letter to:

PROOF OF THE AFTERLIFE 2
Servants of the Father of Mercy
P. O. Box 42001, Los Angeles, CA 90042

Easily get in touch with the author to schedule a church event, group presentation or speaking engagement by sending an email request to Contact@ServantsoftheFather.org.

Lastly, my first encounter in the afterlife was with God the Father. He said, *"No, you cannot see me or you will be dead."* The Father was veiled behind a large gray screen. Next, after momentary blackness, I saw Christ descending from a brilliant cross. Here you can see the gray screen and cross are the identifying elements of the community's logo.

Book 2

Table of Contents

FOREWORD

Grow and Go!

In April of 2010, as I wrote the first book, *Proof of the Afterlife – The Conversation Continues,* you may remember I was holed up for many days in a mountain cabin that a friend so generously provided. Located in the high desert of the San Gabriel Mountains, I elaborated on how the usually dry desert fields nearby were ablaze with a lavish carpet of springtime flowers, lush green vegetation and a rainbow of blooming cactus. Now, today as I write *Proof of the Afterlife 2* it's March 2016, six years later and springtime has come again to mid-coastal California where I am composing this new and expanded edition in the picturesque wine country of Solvang and the nearby rocky beaches and cliffs of the region.

In hindsight, the not-so-coincidental thread of springtime surrounding this book then and now speaks vociferously about all that was born out of my 2005 near-death-experience (NDE) and life-changing encounter with God the Father and the Lord Jesus Christ. Eleven years have passed. But as you can see from the chapter photo, it is no longer just me. Many have joined with me. Together, helping to tell a unique afterlife story in what seems to be a plethora of near-death-experience stories booming in the book publishing industry.

Over the past eleven years a team of nearly two-hundred men, women and children have risen up and joined with me delivering to 80,000 + homeless living under bridges, in alleyways and on the city streets of Southern California and beyond. Through deliveries of food, water, clothing, blankets, jackets, hygiene supplies, rosaries and more we help to prevent dehydration, hypothermia, infections, ER visits, and death among the homeless.

As you may remember from the first book, we're on a mission to the poor that was commissioned directly from the afterlife a few days following the NDE. Then, after attending *Saint John's Seminary*, we formalized the mission and named the team, *"Servants of the Father of Mercy."* Officially, the community was welcomed into the Church as an association of the *Archdiocese of Los Angeles* by Cardinal Emeritus, Archbishop, Roger Mahony in 2008. At the same time, we had incorporated as a California, IRS nonprofit, 501 (c) 3 tax-exempt organization.

But in all reality, our blossoming springtime was graciously prophesied by the Lord on July 7, 2009, in a nighttime dream recorded in the journal that I had been keeping since my NDE on September 26, 2005. Here is what I wrote just one year after our launch.

On Tuesday, July 7, 2009, in the early morning hours, I saw a newly planted field of seeds. But nothing had sprouted because the farmer had just planted the crop. Then I heard a loud voice saying, *"Grow and go!"*

Upon awakening that morning, I interiorly knew the Lord intended this dream to refer to the *Servants of the Father of Mercy* one-year anniversary. The group had celebrated its opening Mass, July 26, 2008. Now in July of 2009 at the time of this dream, all the seeds had been planted, all the groundwork had been laid, and we were ready to *"Grow and go!"* infused with a mission to serve the homeless in America. Our winter of starting up was over, and thanks be to God springtime had arrived!

So maybe that is one way we know when someone has had a genuine God-encounter, they *"Grow and go!"* The person is not stagnating so-to-speak. That is why I am writing *Proof of the Afterlife 2.* My story is ongoing and continuously emerging. It's alive, vibrant and flourishing. Eleven years after my NDE, time around me is still in a constant state of buds, blossoms and almost always generating new life. I liken it to an earthquake, there is the big one and then a series of aftershocks rocking my world daily.

Another strong motivation in writing this book coincides with the fact that dozens of readers have called or sent emails over the years requesting a second book containing more journal notes, insights and revelations from the hereafter. Students of the last book frequently and favorably remarked at the fact that a hundred percent of book sales benefit the homeless mission of the Church and the *Servants of the Father of Mercy*. Having taken the vow of poverty, I never have and never will personally gain financially from my NDE testimony. Clearly, book one has touched thousands of readers in many and diverse ways. Peruse the reviews on the back cover of this book and inside the last chapter. They all tell a story of people moved by the Holy Spirit, nourished with inspiration and truth.

So, I feel like I owe it to the Lord and readers alike to share book two's on-going God-encounters recorded in my journal. It's a way to plant seeds, fertilize and grow others who want to immerge out of the winter of their lives and welcomed into springtime. This new book, like the last, will infuse the joy of sprouting if you let the truth be told and let it take root. Jesus promised us, *"You will know the truth and the truth will set you free."* John 8:32 But for that to happen, on each of our parts there is the grit and grime – the dirty work of cultivating humility, embracing brokenness and rooting out our pride.

"Grow and go!" The saying also reminds one of the words of Jesus when he said, *"Go into all the world and preach the Gospel to the whole creation."* Mark 16:15 It was here that Jesus ordered that no barriers shall stop the preaching of the gospel. When God is involved and infused, you can count on growth and expansion. Wherever there is a child, woman or man; there God is to be proclaimed. To every sinner he

offers life, and when he says *"Go!"* all the world is included in His message of mercy.

Lastly, in this Foreword a little bit more about the good, the bad and ugly! As I said earlier, the first edition of *Proof of the Afterlife* received wide acclaim over the past six years from pastors, church leaders and readers, both Catholic and Protestant alike. It reached the top in its categories at Amazon.com and has maintained a nearly solid 5-star ranking after all these years; in spite of a few grouches, naysayers and curmudgeons!

And so there is a lesson learned here; haters are a gift from God and make an important contribution to all our lives. Jesus, in fact, told us, *"If the world hates you, keep in mind that it hated me first. If you belonged to the world, it would love you as its own. As it is, you do not belong to the world, but I have chosen you out of the world. That is why the world hates you. Remember what I told you: 'A servant is not greater than his master.' If they persecuted me, they will persecute you also."* John 18:18-20

It is because of them that the Good News is spread. They energize it, our message and us. That is what the book of Acts is all about. It's all good! In fact, it is the only surefire way to know that we have had an encounter with God and doing His work, isn't it? Having everyone love you is a danger sign. Jesus warned, *"Woe to you, when all people speak well of you, for so their fathers did to the false prophets."* (Luke 6:26)

Following Christ with his message of mercy and works of charity will at times lead you to being ridiculed and even persecuted. But if the happens, Jesus has something to say about it. *"Blessed are you when men hate you, and ostracize you, and insult you, and scorn your name as evil, for the sake of the Son of Man. Be glad in that day and leap for joy, for behold, your reward is great in heaven. For in the same way their fathers used to treat the prophets."* (Luke 6:22-23)

As it turns out, only a minuscule group did not like the first book. If you are inclined to dislike this new edition, please circle one of the following issues and send it back for a refund. The book is truly meant for those who want and need it. Makes sense? So what was the brouhaha all about the first time? Here it is in a nutshell

1 After the book had documented dozens of real-life NDE-driven supernatural encounters with angels, afterlife meetings with God the Father and Jesus along with mystical dreams, visions and apparitions, one critic writes, *"The book has nothing to do with the reason I bought it: to learn what the person experienced on the other side."*

2 And, of course, as you may know, some churchgoers, whether Catholic or Protestant already have life and the afterlife totally figured out being avid Bible readers. A person with a robust attitude of *"I am right, and you are wrong"* (pride) and a strong *"let's disagree with Catholics"* attitude is not going to accept my testimony that documents the real existence of Purgatory, especially in the section about my father (Chapter Four). One critic writes on behalf of the many with the same beliefs, *"As a Bible believing Christian...I was particularly disturbed by the part where the author's father, apparently a very negative and*

unloving man, wound up in a purgatory-like place after he died. This is preposterous beyond words... I do not discount that he is writing about what he experienced, but I seriously question where this experience originated. I don't think it was God." Well, may God bless her dear heart! But in all seriousness, I think I met this person on a book speaking tour while traveling on the east coast in the spring of 2011. One morning I was getting ready to leave a small east-coast town after an appearance on Greenville, SC, *Nite Line,* a regional Christian television show airing live the night before. While standing in line at a neighborhood coffee shop, a lady with her teenage son in front of me began to speak after seeing my shirt, and its silk screened cross, shield, and words, *"Servants of the Father of Mercy." "Are you a Catholic?"* she snapped, loudly alerting all the customers around to the fact, *"We have a Catholic out-of-towner among us!" "Yes!"* I replied, *"I am a Catholic."* She continued rather aggressively, *"I was a Catholic too at one time. But as soon as I get my coffee, I can show you in a few minutes how the devil himself deceives Catholics."* I just pleasantly smiled and did not say a word while the teenage son, embarrassed, sheepishly hid behind the other customers in line. Over at the cream and sugar bar, she continued the outburst. But the son pulling on her arm spoke up, *"Mom, let's go."* Quickly I responded as if something or Someone had come over me and said, "M*a'am, apparently you are going to heaven, and I'm not. Would you do me one favor?" "Yes,"* she replied hesitantly. *"Please pray for me that I do not wind up in hell. I need* *your prayers the rest of your life. Would you always pray for me?"* With that, I walked out the door, sped off to the airport for a flight back to Los Angeles and thanked God that I had just found a new Christian friend who will pray for me the rest of her life!

3 Then there are the critics that cannot write, spell, construct full sentences correctly and seem to lack critical thinking skills. It's always a challenge to understand their actual concerns. Here is one such criticism. *"I've read quite bit on Near Death Experiences. This one is written by a Catholic. I understand that being a practising Catholic. I could not read all of it, it was poorly written. Did not like it all. If this man works with the honeless, God bless him, and the people he works with/for. Like I said at beginning, having read a lot on Near Death Experience - this is just not of the calibre of 'experience' I am used reading about."* Well, apparently what we have here is a case of *"the pot calling the kettle black!"*

4 Lastly, one guy goes out of the realm of critic and hater into outright attacks, perjury and evil actions to try to stop the book sales that are directly impacting the gifting of life-giving food and water to the homeless; also seeking to terminate its message of mercy. Surprising when it's a book so in line with the worldwide "Church of Mercy" mandated by Pope Francis who came on the scene three years after it was published. Mother Antonia, the *Prison Angel,* and a friend of St. Mother Teresa of Calcutta; one of the last things she said to me a few days before she died on October 17, 2013, while living in and serving the

incarcerated in a Tijuana, Mexico prison since 1980 was this…*"Brother Joseph, the real evil in this world is not people who have done something wrong; it's people all around us who engage in perjury, lies, and gossip."* King David knew about these people all too well, and that is why in the book of Psalms he wrote, *"How long will you assault me? Would all of you throw me down—this leaning wall, this tottering fence? Surely they intend to topple me from my lofty place; they take delight in lies. With their mouths they bless, but in their hearts they curse."* Well, there's always one in every crowd isn't there? So back to our mystery man – from the bottom of our hearts, all the *Servants of the Father of Mercy* thank, love and pray for his many blessings. The apostle Peter encourages us to this end while reminiscing upon the life of Christ, *"To this, you were called, because Christ suffered for you, leaving you an example, that you should follow in his footsteps. 'He committed no sin, and no deceit was found in his mouth.' When they hurled their insults at him, he did not retaliate; when he suffered, he made no threats. Instead, he entrusted himself to Him who judges justly."* 1 Peter 2:21-23

In summary, I'd like to share an insight from the other side that was gifted to me recently in the spring of 2016, recorded in my journal and sharing with readers now.

On Wednesday, March 16, 2016, a friend, a mom and a grandmother whom I have known since 1968 posted on *Facebook, "Being gay is not a choice, but being a bigot is."* Immediately, I was stirred by an interior locution and posted a response to her thoughts . . . *"Judging and hating others is a perfect match made in hell, but feels like heaven when you're doing it."*

Chapter Thirteen

God Bless America

American Persecution

While traveling to foreign countries on and off over the past thirty-five years for business, leisure and church work, it is apparent that many citizens overseas just love Americans! I found this to be especially true in France and Holland. Countries in which our extended Dutch and French families, Harry and Ria Verstraten and Michele and Jean-Claude Jérôme, their spouses, children, and grandchildren have often and appreciatively reminisced how my father and troops heroically took part in the Normandy invasion, physically clearing the region and even their homes of Hitler's torturous assault. Conversely, I've met ordinary folks in bars, pubs, and cafes who are most aggressively critical of the U.S. and "love to hate Americans." Since the 1970s, their voices, actions, and disgust are louder throughout the world.

Saturday, October 29, 2005, it's been just about a month now since my NDE; in the early hours of the morning, I suddenly awoke because of a very loud locution. It audibly startled me out of a sound sleep. A man's voice from the other side had urgently and convincingly shouted a prophetic warning of a coming, *"American persecution!"* he exclaimed.

Okay, so I wrestled with the event all day long and did not notate it in my journal right away, all the while contemplating its meaning. In fact, I have to keep reminding myself it had been only a month since the NDE. All that has been happening supernaturally is so very new and startling. Next, I prayed about what I heard and asked for assurance that this was from God. I also looked forward to sharing it with Fr. F. my spiritual advisor who had just begun to meet with me every few weeks.

On one level, it seemed as though the message *"American persecution!"* pointed to a coming oppression of American Christians, increased sufferings and even possible martyrdoms. The next day, after prayer time, I was inspired to randomly open up the Bible as a way to possibly receive a confirmation as to its message. The scripture that "accidentally" turned up said, *"The hour is coming when whoever kills you will think he is offering service to God."* John 16:2

Monday, October 31, 2005, Halloween (All Saints Eve), I've been pondering Saturday's locution, *"American Persecution."* Today, with no business appointments scheduled, I asked the Lord to lead and guide me what to do on my self-prescribed day off. I ended up spending the day in the Los Angeles central library and for the first time browsed the history section. The first book I glanced at and pulled off the shelf was titled, *"The Bushes: Portrait of a Dynasty"* by Peter and Rochelle Schweizer. According to one national review, *"In fact, for all its detail on the Bush family, this volume is really a chronicle of how the old-boy network works in this country."* Next, I visited the religion section. The book catching my eye is *"The Gospel According to America"* by David Dark. The author asks the questions we ought to ask of all the varying authorities and their faith that shapes the cultural, social and political landscape of America. How does faith and politics mix, or do they?

After my day retreat in the library, an inner awakening began to reveal insights into the *"American Persecution."* Was it somehow connected to those here and abroad who disdain the American groups and politicians that in the 80s and 90s used Christianity to energize their selfish gains and to further their "prosperity gospel?" Will their hatred be targeting all Christians for lack of better discernment, compassion, and understanding?

In combination, it also occurred to me that the *"American persecution"* may also refer to and target the unknown members of the authentic merciful American church regardless of the denomination, by certain ones of a false group that is deeply rooted in both the mainstream Catholic and Protestant political structures. The true *"Church of Mercy"* as Pope Francis identifies it will be persecuted by the politically-connected wealthy, the powerful, "religious," controlling and the bourgeois who call themselves Christian. They are unkind, unhelpful and even unmerciful toward homeless, migrants, immigrants, the poor and the broken in our society, country, and the world.

As I contemplated its meaning in the weeks and months following, it also seemed entirely possible that the *"American persecution"* coming may be just as it was in the days of Nero, the emperor of Rome, Christianity will be blamed for America's woes, especially by secularists and atheists. In the summer of A.D. 64, Rome suffered a terrible fire that burned for six days and seven nights consuming almost three-quarters of the city. The people accused the Roman Emperor Nero of the devastation claiming he set the fire for his own amusement. To deflect these accusations and placate the people, Nero laid the blame for the fire on the Christians. The emperor ordered the arrest of a few members until the entire Christian populace was implicated and became fair game for retribution. As many Christians as could be found, were rounded up and put to death in the most horrific manner for the amusement of Romans.

So too today, many will blame Christians, their faith, and religion for many of our tragedies and terrorist attacks on America here and abroad. Hate groups, lawmakers, judges, atheists, agnostics and so forth are progressively seeing religion, especially Christianity as the root of all evil. And so the previous shaky and volatile mix of God and politics has come back to bite us. Now, by attacking Christians, the ones who do it will think that they are doing God and America a favor.

"Whenever Christ calls us, his call leads us to death . . . When Christ calls a man, he calls him to come and die." Dietrich Bonhoeffer, *Discipleship*. Dietrich Bonhoeffer (+ April 9, 1945)

was a German Lutheran pastor, theologian, a participant in the German resistance movement against Nazism.

This Land Was Made for You and Me

Thursday, October 4, 2007, in route on JetBlue from Los Angeles International to Washington DC, Dulles, I heard an audible warning while half asleep on the flight rang out in my ears, *"Fifteen days of woes!"* It was followed up a little later with, *"You are not mistaken."*

Upon arriving back to the west coast, I shared this with my spiritual director. We both considered what type of situation could last fifteen days. We did not know. Then, two weeks later in the month of October, it was fulfilled. Southern California was drenched in exactly fifteen days of forest fires popping up like wildflowers from Malibu to San Diego, leaving about one million people homeless. Wealthy and middle-class Americans discovered that homelessness could happen to anyone. It's not a problem isolated to the poor, but homelessness is a terrible condition that should cause concern for everyone. Jesus warned us to be merciful so that in our own time of need God would come to our aid and strengthen us. He said, *"Blessed are the merciful, they shall obtain mercy."* Matthew 5:7

After the NDE I did not always travel by plane, but sometimes chose lengthy road trips in a 2008 Kia, Rondo to get back and forth to the west and east coast for family, business, and leisure. The trips also doubled as a "meet, greet and feed" the homeless along the way. One such trip was in the summer of 2009.

July 26, 2009, it's the first day of a nine-thousand-mile journey crisscrossing America. After leaving Los Angeles, I arrived at the south end of Las Vegas at 10 pm. Unbelievably, there was a large billboard for automatic weapon gun sales posted on the highway. An ad for automatic weapons? Shocking! I immediately began to pray the *Divine Mercy* for this town from one end of Las Vegas to the other; altogether about twenty minutes. On the north end, as the lights of the city began to fade in the rearview mirror, I made the sign of the cross to conclude the *Divine Mercy*. At that exact moment, a dazzling meteor fell from the sky just overhead the highway, streaking in brilliant colors of white, green, yellow and blue. Confirmation that God hears our prayers!

Here is a little background on the *Divine Mercy* before I share another true story from my journal in this regard. From the diary of a young Polish nun, Faustina Kowalska, a special devotion began spreading throughout the world in the 1930s.

The message is nothing new but is a reminder of what the Church has always taught through scripture and tradition: that God is merciful and forgiving and that we, too, must show mercy and forgiveness. But in the *Divine Mercy* devotion, the message takes on a powerful new focus, calling people to a deeper understanding that God's love is unlimited and available to everyone — especially the greatest sinners.

The message and devotion to Jesus of *Divine Mercy* are based on the writings of Saint Faustina Kowalska, an uneducated Polish nun who, in obedience to her spiritual director, wrote a diary of about 600 pages recording the revelations she received about God's mercy. Even before her death in 1938, the devotion to The *Divine Mercy* had begun to spread.

In 1931, our Lord appeared to St. Faustina. She saw Jesus clothed in a white garment with His right hand raised in blessing. His left hand was touching His garment in the area of the Heart, here, two large rays came forth, one red and the other pale blue.

For those that may be interested, here is how to pray the *Divine Mercy* prayers with one, two or more people.

BEGIN (using an ordinary Rosary) with the *Sign of the Cross* and say the *Apostles Creed*: (Leader) *I believe in God the Father the Almighty, Creator of heaven and earth, and in Jesus Christ His Only Son who was conceived by the Holy Spirit, born of the Virgin Mary and became man. For our sake, he was crucified under Pontius Pilate, was crucified, died and was buried. He descended into hell. On the third day, he rose again according to the scriptures and he ascended into heaven. He is seated at the right hand of God, the Father the Almighty. From thence He shall come to judge the living and the dead. (All) I believe in the Holy Spirit, the holy Catholic Church, the communion of saints, the forgiveness of sins, the resurrection of the body and the life everlasting. Amen.*

OFFER the *Divine Mercy* for a person(s). Jesus said to St. Faustina: *"At the hour of their death, I defend as My own glory every soul that will say this chaplet; or when others say it for a dying person, the indulgence is the same. When this chaplet is said by the bedside of a dying person, God's anger is placated, unfathomable mercy envelops the soul, and the very depths of My tender mercy are moved for the sake of the sorrowful Passion of My Son."* (*St. Faustina's Diary,* 811) Also, you may wish to offer the *Divine Mercy* for a group of persons such as the homeless, a town, the youth, unrepentant sinners or those lukewarm in their faith.

PRAY *The Lord's Prayer*: (Leader) *Our Father, who art in Heaven, hallowed be Thy name. Thy Kingdom come, Thy will be done, on Earth as it is in Heaven.* (All) *Give us this day our daily bread, and forgive us our trespasses, as we forgive those who trespass against us. And lead us not into temptation, but deliver us from evil. Amen.*

Ave Maria: (Leader) Hail Mary, full of grace, the Lord is with thee. Blessed art thou among women, and Blessed is the Fruit of thy womb, Jesus. (All) *Holy Mary, mother of God, pray for us sinners now and at the hour of our death. Amen.*

PRAY (Leader) *Eternal Father, I offer You the Body, Blood, Soul and Divinity of your dearly beloved Son, Our Lord and Savior Jesus Christ,* (All) *In atonement for our sins and the sins of the whole world.* (1x)

PRAY (Leader) *For the sake of His sorrowful passion,* (All) *Have mercy on us and on the whole world.* (10 x)

PRAY (Leader) *Eternal Father, I offer You the Body, Blood, Soul and Divinity of your dearly beloved Son, Our Lord and Savior*

Jesus Christ, (All) *In atonement for our sins and the sins of the whole world.* (1x)

PRAY (Leader) *For the sake of His sorrowful passion,* (All) *Have mercy on us and on the whole world.* (10 x) Etc.

CONCLUDE (All) *Holy God, Holy Mighty One, Holy Immortal One, have mercy on us and on the whole world.* (3x) END with the *Sign of the Cross.*

On August 7, 2009, I started out in Myrtle Beach, South Carolina to return to the west coast. Four hours into the trip, I began to pray the *Divine Mercy* for my thirty-something nephew who at the time, to my knowledge had not received the sacrament of baptism. His last name is very uncommon, "DeMarco" (not real name). I was on highway I-40 just east of Ashville, NC. After making the sign of the cross to begin the *Divine Mercy* for him, I looked up and miraculously saw his exact name written in 6-foot letters on a billboard. It was an advertisement for an attorney with the same name, *"DeMarco."* While praying, my mind drifted away from the miraculous billboard sign and some minutes later finished. Just as I made the sign of the cross to conclude, another billboard for the same attorney amazingly appeared! It read, *"Demand DeMarco;"* God's reassurance of his *Divine Mercy* at work!

Well, back to the road trip. While on I-40 in Tennessee, I reminisced meeting a Christian by the name of Marion at a friend's house in Ohio a few weeks earlier. She suggested that on the drive back west I stop in Kansas City and share my NDE testimony with their *International House of Prayer* (IHOP) prayer group. So, while heading west, I randomly pulled off an exit to pray, read the map and researched if a detour to Kansas City was possible. I needed confirmation that a diversion somewhat north and west while adding many hours driving was likely.

August 7, 2009, There is no reason to go to Kansas City today, but I keep thinking about the invitation from Marion to speak at their IHOP prayer group. Should I go? Should I not go? I'm not sure, but then again when I looked up a village sign right in front of the car, it said: *"Welcome to Marion."* I had never heard of Marion, Tennessee! There was only an exit number when I pulled off the highway. But there, just four feet away is a *"Marion"* sign! Because of this obvious "green light," I made it a point to drive the long hours to Kansas City meeting Marion and the group around 9:30 pm.

On Monday, August 10, 2009, it was inspirational seeing the outpouring of American patriotism while visiting Mount Rushmore, South Dakota. I was moved to pray the *Divine Mercy* for this great land we call America. May God have mercy on us in these uncertain times of the twenty-first century, now filled with terrorism, threats and the potential of mass destruction. Just as I concluded and was making the *Sign of the Cross* a large street-side sign in Keystone Village announced, *"Holy Terror Days."* May God have mercy upon us all!

Through these experiences, there is no doubt in my mind that God cares about America. In fact, the summer of 2009 was the first crossing of the United States that the *Servants of the Father of Mercy* name and our logo were brilliantly affixed with magnets on each side of the vehicle. People coast-to-coast from gas stations to state fairs commented both good and bad about the advertisement. While visiting one huge end-of-summer Midwest fair, I was parking in the corn fields at about nine o'clock in the morning. A young man and his girlfriend ten feet away shouted obscenities, hatefully despising the Christian insignia. It's always nice to receive such a cold welcome. It helps confirm that we are doing God's work!

Servants of the Father of Mercy Cross and Shield

Just returned back to the west coast after nearly four weeks on the road. It is Friday, August 22, 2009, and giving thanks to the Lord for sharing a vision last night. In it, a giant roadside billboard appeared with big letters written across it that said, *"Thank You Gary!"* Interiorly, I was given to know that the Lord appreciated the door magnets, cross and shield display resulting in nationwide "advertising" the past few weeks.

At the time of this next entry, I did not have a TV and had not seen network news or any other television programming for more than five years. As a result, for the most part, I was completely unaware of political celebrities, their thoughts, and agendas. So that is what makes this date, day and vision even more profound.

On Saturday, August 7, 2010, Lord, in a vision before waking this morning, you presented a throng of migrant and immigrant people in Arizona who were celebrating because they had been delivered by the efforts of Washington, DC politicians from an unjust law that had increased hate and biases against them. In the vision, the American people as a whole even celebrated their victory. They would now be treated with more dignity and assistance from immigration services.

Next, a woman appeared on a platform speaking to the media. She was leading a massive group that together vowed to overturn the federal government's new laws protecting the dignity of migrants and immigrants. The lady was robed in a nicely tailored pink dress, a very proper white hat, a small pink purse and white gloves. However beautiful and elegant, her words were offensive and did not blend well with her beauty and charm. She was ever so delicately sugar-coating words of hate and discrimination with a well-crafted and glib public address. Increasingly, many filled an arena and wished to follow her. They morphed into an army of men and women dressed similarly; professional, clean-cut, beautifully tailored attire and yet their words were filled with hate.

Then I found myself speaking in a stadium to a large gathering of Catholics and Protestants. I had been invited by two pastors who had organized an interfaith Christian assembly. From the apron of a very large stage, I spoke into a very powerful microphone and sound system saying . . . *"Rallies that back hate for migrants, immigrants, gays and others we don't agree with are not Christian. Remember sisters and brothers, hate is wrong. People coming together in large groups to expound hate is also wrong."* The pastors clapped, hugged and supported me. They asked if they could pray for me. But before they did, I prayed the following prayer. *"Lord Jesus, teach the American people your message of love, love, love. Help the media to get the story straight. It is not hate, hate, hate. It is love, love, love."* The pastors said, *"Amen!"* And all the people said *"Amen!"*

Chapter Fourteen

International Affairs

Visions of Cuba

Cuba first came into my life in 1980 while sponsoring a refugee resettlement for two elderly men from that island country who were sent to my home by *Lutheran Immigration Services*. As you may remember, the Mariel boatlift was a mass emigration of Cuban refugees who traveled from Cuba's Mariel Harbor to the United States between April 15 and October 31, 1980. At this time the Cuban government announced that anyone who wanted to leave (escaping communism and poverty) could do so. Primarily Miami-based Cuban-Americans organized the ensuing mass migration with the blessing of Cuban President Fidel Castro. The refugees created political problems for America's president Jimmy Carter after it was discovered that Fidel Castro had taken advantage of the exodus by simultaneously clearing out Cuban jails and mental health facilities, then placing the individuals on U.S. bound ships. The Mariel boatlift was ended by mutual agreement between the two governments in late October 1980, after as many as 125,000 Cubans had reached Florida. Coincidentally, by 1986 I was transferred to Miami, Florida along with my cousin Kim

(Chapter Six) as our home base, by the airline industry, what was then, PEOPLExpress Airlines. Cuba and Cubans had become a part of our life.

On Friday, November 24, 2006, just over a year since my near-death-experience, I was immersed in an early morning vision. In it, I can see Fidel Castro leaving power. He will resign soon. However, Cuba will be run again by a communist government. It will not end with Fidel Castro. In the vision, the other side is asking us to pray in the coming weeks and months for the conversion of Cuba. Pray that the people may be free to choose Christianity and also pray for the restoration of the Church on the island.

After immediately sharing the vision with my spiritual director, I began to do exactly that, pray for Cuba. On February 24, 2008, about two years after the vision, Raúl Castro (Fidel Castro's brother) immerged seemingly out of nowhere, officially being elected as President by the *Cuban National Assembly* after Fidel Castro, who was physically ailing, announced his intention not to stand for President. In fulfillment of the November 2006 vision, Raúl Castro kept the country on a Communist path.

Then the real shock came in 2015 when the *Associated Press* (AP) reported another aspect of the 2006 vision would be fulfilled, the restoration of the Church in Cuba. Here, in its entirety (it's that good) is how the AP reported the news . . .

VATICAN CITY (AP), May 10, 2015 — Cuban President Raul Castro paid a call Sunday on Pope Francis at the Vatican to thank him for working for Cuban-U.S. detente - and said he was so impressed by the pontiff he is considering a return to the Catholic church's fold.

"*Bienvenido* (Welcome)!" Francis said in his native Spanish, welcoming Castro to his studio near the Vatican public audience hall. The Cuban president, bowing his head, gripped Francis' hand with both of his, and the two men began private talks. The meeting lasted nearly an hour, as the Argentine-born Francis and Castro spoke in Spanish.

Francis will visit Cuba in September in route to the United States.

After leaving the Vatican, Castro, the brother of Fidel, the revolutionary leader who brought the Communists to power in Cuba, gushed with praise for Francis.

The pontiff *"is a Jesuit, and I, in some way, am too,"* Castro said at a news conference. *"I always studied at Jesuit schools."*

'When the Pope goes to Cuba in September, I promise to go to all his Masses, and with satisfaction," Castro said at a news conference at the office of Italian Premier Matteo Renzi, whom he met with after the Vatican talks.

"I read all the speeches of the Pope, his commentaries, and if the pope continues this way, I will go back to praying and go back to the church, and I'm not joking," he said.

It was a startling assertion for the leader of a Communist country, whose crackdown on dissidents in the past had drawn sharp Vatican criticism.

'I am from the Cuban Communist Party, that doesn't allow (religious) *believers, but now we are allowing it, it's an important step,"* Castro said.

Speaking about Francis, Castro said he has been *'very impressed by his wisdom, his modesty, and all his virtues that we know he has."*

Castro had already publicly thanked Francis for helping to bring Havana and Washington closer together after decades of U.S. government policy of strict isolation of the Communist-ruled Caribbean island. On Sunday, he stepped up his praise on Francis' push for the two nations to put enmity aside and work for reconciliation for the benefit of Americans and Cubans.

As he took his leave from the Vatican, Castro told journalists, *"I thanked the pope for what he did."*

Vatican spokesman, the Rev. Federico Lombardi, said the president also *"laid out to the pope the sentiments of the Cuban people in the wait and preparation for his upcoming visit to the island in September."*

After his meeting with Renzi, Castro expressed hope that his country would quickly see more fruits of the thaw between Cuba and the United States. *'Maybe the* (U.S.) *Senate will take us off the list of terrorist nations"* soon, Castro told reporters.

Francis gave Castro a medal depicting St. Martin of Tours, known for caring for the destitute. *"With his mantle, he covers the poor,"* Francis told Castro, saying do more for the poor.

Fidel Castro met with Pope John Paul II at the Vatican in 1996. That encounter helped pave the way for John Paul's 1998 pilgrimage to Cuba, the first visit by a pontiff to the island. John Paul was also eager for Cuba to grant more visas for foreign priests to bolster the dwindling corps of clergy on the island.

The Vatican's general policy of opposing economic sanctions as a foreign policy tool carries appeal for Cuban leaders and people, after decades under a U.S. economic embargo. With the Vatican keen on protecting the interests of its Catholic followers

Pope Benedict XVI also visited the island.

Castro told reporters that *'we are trying to carry forward improvements of our political, social and cultural system. But it's very difficult to do it without causing shocks, without leaving some in the street."*

He came to Rome on his way back from celebrations in Moscow of the 70th anniversary of the surrender of Nazi Germany in World War II.

In hindsight, we can see how God was at work in Cuba. But that's not all, the miracles continued! On Sunday, September 20, 2015, Pope Francis celebrated Mass in Havana's main square, the *Plaza of the Revolution.* He celebrated Mass again on Monday in the central-eastern city of Holguin and another Mass on Tuesday at the sanctuary of the *Virgin of Charity of Cobre* outside Santiago in far-eastern Cuba. After that Mass, he departed for his historic visit to the United States.

Ultimately, Cuba and the United States restored

diplomatic relations on July 20, 2015, which had been severed since 1961 during the Cold War. American President, Barack Obama called for ending the longstanding trade and travel embargo as well. Lastly, in July 2015 *JetBlue* became the first major U.S. airline to initiate a direct flight from New York, *JFK International Airport* to Havana's *Jose Marti International Airport,* indicating a final fulfillment of God's vital plan for a complete thaw in Cuban travel, people and trade relations.

Tokyo Electric Power Company

Traveling frequently for more than forty years has taken me to many lands; however, the Orient and countries like Japan I have never had the occasion to visit. That is why I was more surprised than anyone while attending St. John's Seminary, there came in March of 2007 a prophetic word, a vision of future catastrophic events that would literally shake up and potentially destroy major parts of Japan.

It's 6:00 am, Tuesday, March 20, 2007. In a vision that took place right before waking, I saw a nuclear disaster, (but not because of a weapon) coming soon and will have a terrible impact on Tokyo and another region (a name I heard over and over but too difficult to grasp). For now, while I had the vision, I called it town "K." Upon awakening, although I do not know how to spell it, phonetically, my research on the Internet confirmed it is a dual metropolis, similar to Minneapolis-St. Paul in the U.S.; its name is Kashiwazaki-Kariwa.

Immediately, I shared the content of the vision with Fr. Jim. His recommendation was that I actively begin to pray for the two areas, Tokyo and Kashiwazaki-Kariwa. He believes it may be possible that this is a "word of knowledge," a gift granted by the Holy Spirit. Because of his guidance, I began to pray daily for the people of Japan.

There was no further research done on my part after the vision of March 20, 2007. For instance, in hindsight, I could have looked up the details of the Kashiwazaki-Kariwa metro area, its economy, industries and major employers. If I had, an investigation would have uncovered the fact the area had become home to the site of the *Kashiwazaki-Kariwa Nuclear Power Plant,* June 5, 1980. The facility is a large, modern nuclear power plant on a 4.2-square-kilometer site including land in the towns of Kashiwazaki and Kariwa run by *Tokyo Electric Power Company* (TEPCO).

On July 16, 2007, a 6.8 magnitude earthquake struck the region, setting off a chain of events that fulfilled the prophetic vision. It all came to pass just four months after the initial revelation. On July 19, 2007, Michael Mariotte, a writer for the U.S.-based *"Nuclear Information and Resource Service"* (NIRS) in Takoma Park, Maryland, issued a report detailing a growing nuclear catastrophe in Kashiwazaki-Kariwa. His update was much different than what was being told in the Japanese news media. I believe through many people's prayers, and God's grace; Japan, and the world averted what could have been a bigger and more extensive disaster. To that end, here is Michael Mariotte's report.

TACOMA PARK, MARYLAND, (NIRS), July 19, 2007 – *Report on Earthquake Damage to Japan's Kashiwazaki-Kariwa Nuclear Power Facility:* In the early hours following the July 16 earthquake, *Tokyo Electric Power Company* (TEPCO) reported only a transformer fire and spill of 1.5 liters of radioactive water.

It is now clear that the damage to the world's largest nuclear power facility was far greater than initially reported and that radiation releases were also far greater than reported. Indeed, it appears that radiation releases are continuing to this very day (July 19, 2007).

According to the Associated Press (AP), on July 17, damage to the reactors was extensive. The AP found and listed the following problems the day after the earthquake:

1 Fire at an electrical transformer facility.

2 1,200 liters of water containing radioactive material leaked into the sea.

3 About 100 barrels of radioactive waste knocked over.

4 Duct knocked out of place in a major vent; possible leak of radioactive cobalt-60 and chromium-51 from five of the plant's reactors.

5 Water leak inside buildings housing all seven reactors.

6 Malfunctioning of water intake pumps at two reactors.

7 Blowout panel knocked out turbine building two reactors.

8 Oil leak from low-activation transformer waste oil pipes at two reactors.

9 Loss in the water-tight seal at reactor core cooling system.

10 Water leaks at the diesel generator facility, burst extinguisher pipe, burst condenser valve and filtration tank.

11 Broken connections and broken bolt at the electric transformer.

12 Loss of power at the control center for the liquid waste disposal facility.

13 Oil leaks from the damaged transformer and a magnetic transformer facility.

14 Oil leak at reactor water supply pump facility.

15 Disrupted electrical connection at magnetic transformer facility.

16 Cracks in the embankment of water intake facility.

17 Air and oil leaks at switching stations.

18 Land under parts of plant turned to mud in a quake-caused process known as liquefaction.

As of July 19, 2007, we now know that some 400, (not 100, barrels) of radioactive waste were knocked over, and about 40 lost their lids. Some of the waste was liquid and leaked into the building. It is not known whether radiation from these spills has leaked outside the building. The 1200 liters (about 317 gallons) of radioactive water spilled into the Sea of Japan. According to Japanese TEPCO officials, the newest reactor at the site that came online in July 1997, has been venting radioactive steam into the air since the earthquake began and continues to do so as of today (July 19).

The earthquake exceeded the basic design for the reactors, and the facility did not meet new Japanese earthquake standards put in place in September 2006. Moreover, the fault that caused the quake is apparently directly underneath the facility site and was not discovered prior to construction. It is not yet known whether this fault is capable of an even larger earthquake than the 6.8 measured on July 16.

For the United States, the lesson is unmistakable: the earthquake reminds us of the fragility and danger of nuclear power and its ability to withstand the acts of Mother Nature. Nuclear reactors and earthquake faults simply don't mix. An immediate need is to permanently end any further discussion of installation of dry cask radioactive waste storage units at the Diablo Canyon site on California's earthquake-prone Pacific coast.

In hindsight, one important lesson learned from the generous "heads up" vision the Lord granted before the TEPCO earthquake and nuclear catastrophe is that prayer is important. Prayer works! Without prayer, things in our world can get a lot worse, causing, even more, devastation and loss of life. God wants us to pray for each other individually as well as for the global community. Many thanks to Fr. Jim for making us aware of the importance of prayer through his guidance after receiving the "word of knowledge."

Secondly, another important lesson in all this speaks to the enormity of God's love for each of us. He does not care if we are Japanese, American, German, Italian or Indonesian – black, white, transgender, straight or gay – Buddhist, Catholic or Protestant – He loves us all equally, just the same. Lastly, this revelation draws attention to the fact that God is always mediating disasters, many of which we bring upon ourselves. He silently goes uncredited for all the aid, grace and mercy he supplies behind the scenes that keep the world in check and functioning; even protecting us from destroying ourselves.

Egypt

In February of 2010, the same month I was caring for my mother who was in her final days battling breast cancer (Chapter Five) I also had an out-of-body experience visiting persecuted Coptic Christians in Egypt. But first, a little background. Copts, also known as Ekhristianos, literally meaning "Egyptian Christian" are native Egyptian Christians, usually Orthodox and who currently make up around 10 to 20 percent of the population of Egypt — the largest religious minority in that country. While Copts have cited instances of persecution throughout their history, *Human Rights Watch* has noted: "growing religious intolerance" and sectarian violence against Coptic Christians in recent years, and a failure by the Egyptian government to effectively investigate properly and prosecute those who were responsible. Also, the abduction and disappearance of Coptic Christian women and girls remain a serious ongoing problem according to Reuters and many civil rights groups.

Saint Mark the Evangelist is said to have been the first to have established the Christian Church in Alexandria in the decades following Christ's ascension. By A.D. 284 the Roman emperor Diocletian initiated the first of many edicts that put to death great numbers of Christian Egyptians over the first few hundred years of Christianity. The Muslim conquest of Egypt took place in AD 639. Despite the political upheaval, Egypt remained a mainly Christian land, although the influx of Arab immigrants and gradual conversions to Islam over the centuries changed Egypt from a mainly Christian to a mainly Muslim country by the end of the 14th century.

Now in the modern era, the Egyptian government does not officially recognize conversions from Islam to Christianity. Certain interfaith marriages are not allowed either which prevents marriages between converts to Christianity and those born in Christian communities. Children of Christian converts are being classified as Muslims and must receive a Muslim education. The Egyptian government also requires permits for repairing Christian churches or building new ones, which are often withheld.

Egypt's discriminatory and increasingly hostile environment toward Christians is the climate in which this next entry in my journal is initiated.

On Tuesday, February 9, 2010, in the early morning hours, Lord, thank you, my God, for taking me on an out-of-body flight, a journey through the heavens filled with a light blue sky and beautiful white clouds. Although I could effortlessly fly unaided by an aircraft, I sometimes sensed I was losing altitude or flying too fast. But with you by my side, you equipped me with the faith to always say, *"Jesus I trust in you."*

Eventually, my feet landed on the solid ground outside a Coptic Church in Egypt. The name is *Saints Church,* (Alexandria, Egypt). I was standing in the entrance area courtyard to the right side of the front of the building. As I arrived, I could hear young people singing and playing their guitars inside. I entered the front doors of the church; hesitant at first, wondering if they could see me in the same way that I could see them. I bumped shoulders with some of the youth in the center aisle, but they did not seem to know I was there. That is until a perceptive young woman standing in the pews on the right side said to the others while pointing my way, *"Someone has just walked in. A spirit is here. I can see him!"* I quickly maneuvered through the youth gathering stepping over guitar cases, avoiding collisions with small groups chatting and walked to the other side of the church where it was more open and less congested. Then suddenly Lord, you took me back home, thousands of miles in an instant and uniting me back with my body while it lies sleeping in my mom's house in South Carolina.

In hindsight, after discussing this unique mid-east travel experience with my spiritual director; it was through his guidance that I reflected on how this most definitely was a call to prayer for Coptic Christians and the Church in Egypt. Fr. Frank alerted me to the fact there has been incident after incident of extremists attacking and killing Christians in Alexandria, Egypt and beyond. Through my visit to the mid-east, the Lord was giving us all another "heads up;" asking us to unite in prayer for our dear and persecuted brothers and sisters.

Twelve months after visiting *Saints Church,* almost to the day, on Saturday, January 1, 2011, twenty-three people died as a result of a terrorist bombing attack in the same courtyard in which I had arrived on February 9, 2010. The blast occurred as Christian worshipers were leaving a New Year's service.

The *Egyptian News Agency* reported at the time of the blast, several thousand Coptic Christians were attending midnight prayer service at the church on the occasion of New Year's Eve. The explosion resulted in scattered body parts, destroyed cars and smashed windows. Many Coptic Christians were killed immediately following the explosion, or soon after, and about 97 people – most of them Christians – were injured. The remains were covered with newspapers until they were brought inside the church. Two more Copts died in the hospital over the few days following the attack, raising the total number dead to 23, all of whom were Coptic Christians. According to one eyewitness report, the first victim was a Muslim salesperson who sells *Quran* books across the street from the *Saints Church.*

Research conducted by forensic detectives confirmed that the explosive device used was homemade and contained nails and ball-bearings. The *Egyptian News Agency* reported that the *Interior Ministry* stated the bomb was filled with small pieces of metal to serve as shrapnel, and that a foreign-backed suicide bomber was more than likely responsible for the devastation left in the wake of the barbaric attack.

Coincidentally, 2011 is also the year that Christian Egyptian youth formalized themselves into a group that was formed soon after more than 20 Christians were killed by army troops cracking down on Christian youth protests in 2011 outside Cairo's landmark state television building, known as Maspero. The youth group is now known as the *Maspero Youth Association.*

The *Associated Press* on Monday, October 21, 2013, reported that the Coptic youth group, known as the *Maspero Youth Association,* called for the dismissal of Interior Minister Mohammed Ibrahim, who heads the police. *"If the Egyptian government does not care about the security and rights of Christians, then we must ask why are we paying taxes and why we are not arming ourselves,"* said the group.

Lastly, in summary of our persecuted Christian Coptic Egyptian sisters and brothers, it is strategic that my visit there on February 9, 2010, was specifically orchestrated by the Lord to be among the youth of *Saints Church.* I began the time with them when He planted my feet in the very courtyard where many would lose their lives in an awful bloodshed about a year later.

But why has the Lord placed all this attention on Egypt? Why not North Korea or another country of the world widely-known for controversy or injustice? It's not an easy question to answer, but rather historical and complex.

Let us keep in mind that the country of Egypt itself dates back three thousand years before Christ and has always had deep roots in the earliest of our Judeo-Christian history. The first reference to Egypt in Scripture is under its ancient name of Mizraim, one of the sons of Ham mentioned in Genesis 10:6. However, the first actual mention of Egypt by name in the Old Testament occurs in Genesis 12 where it is recorded that Abraham, because of famine in the land of Canaan, went to Egypt (Genesis 12:10). There he attempted to hide the fact that Sarah was his wife and called her his sister—a partial truth. Only by intervention of God who plagued Pharaoh was Sarah rescued from the possibility of being taken as a wife of Pharaoh, and Abraham and his wife were sent out of Egypt.

Further, a prophetic message from the Lord was given to Abraham in Genesis 15:13–14 that most scholars believe refers to Egypt although it's not specifically named: *"God said to Abram, "Know for certain that your descendants will be strangers in a land that is not theirs, where they will be enslaved and oppressed four hundred years. But I will also judge the nation whom they will serve, and afterward, they will come out with many possessions."* Again, although Egypt is not named, it is inescapable that this is the reference intended by the term *"land that is not theirs."* Thus long before the children of Israel went down into Egypt, it was predicted that they would sojourn there and be afflicted for 400 years.

So Abraham has a son Isaac, Isaac and his wife Rebecca have a son, Jacob. Jacob has twelve sons, but he especially loves Joseph, the youngest and favors him because *"he is a child of his old age"* (Genesis 37:3). Jacob also knows that Joseph is exceptional and unique with God-given dreams, visions and other supernatural gifts. Eventually, the brothers can't take it anymore. Out of jealousy, pride and anger they act on their emotions. Seeing the "dreamer" approach on a back-country shepherding trip, they ambush Joseph and throw him into a pit; the first of many great depths to which Joseph will sink. The brothers soon sell him to Midianites traders who in turn sell him to an Ishmaelite caravan headed down to Egypt.

This begins a long saga of a love-hate relationship with Egypt and the people of God whom He chooses to pour out His gifts upon and call His own. As the story goes, Joseph works his way up from ball and chain gang-style slavery to a very well-groomed palace servant and administrator. But after a series of false allegations of infidelity with the captain of the palace guard's wife, Potiphar, he swiftly sinks back into the dungeons of torture and slavery. But over time with God's help, he is vindicated from a crime he did not commit and is resurrected after literally descending into "hell" on earth. He is crowned commander-in-chief over all of Egypt, second only to Pharaoh, the king and supreme leader of the land.

The stage is now set for Egypt to be front and center in fulfillment of the earlier prophecy described above. Joseph's brothers and his father Jacob seek refuge in Egypt because of an unrelenting famine throughout the land, only to discover that Joseph whom the brothers despised, now holds the keys to the life and death of this small, but growing band of what one day will become the nation of Israel. Because of Joseph's mercy and forgiveness, the brothers, Jacob and the entire family are welcomed and prosper long-term in Egypt. Well, that is until there are too many of them and a new Pharaoh sees an opportunity to enslave and even kill off some of the Hebrews for his own purposes.

It is at this point that the Biblical book of Genesis ends and the book of Exodus begins with the story of Moses, the self-discovery of his Hebrew roots and *"I Am"* speaks to him. God leads Moses and the Israelites out of the land of Egypt, but at a significant cost to Pharaoh and the Egyptian people.

One can only imagine, but after hundreds of years in a foreign pagan land, the Jews picked up the local bad habits of worshiping idols and other gods. Moses later discovered that the worship of idols and other gods was a major problem on the journey to the promised land. To this regard, it is often said in theological circles, *"You can lead the people out of Egypt, but you can't get Egypt out of the people!"*

Symbolically, the entire Genesis-Joseph-to-Egypt-to-Exodus story is repeated in the life of Christ. Likewise, Egypt in both the Old and New Testaments plays a key role in the plan of God. Bu how so? What are the parallels?

In Exodus chapter one, Pharaoh, the King of Egypt orders the killing of all newborns, *"So the king commanded all his people, 'Every time a boy is born to the Hebrews, you must throw him into the Nile River, but let all the girl babies live.'"* (Exodus 1:22) In Matthew chapter two, King Herod also orders the killing of babies, *"When Herod saw that the wise men had tricked him, he was furious. So he gave an order to kill all the baby boys in Bethlehem and in the surrounding area who were two years old or younger."* (Matthew 2:16)

If destiny would have had it, Moses was to become a victim of the murderous king's edict, that's until he was rescued by "Egypt" herself. It was the Pharaoh's very own daughter who was the one to secretly rescue Moses, *"A woman conceived* (of the house of Levi) *and bore a son; and when she saw that he was beautiful, she hid him for three months. But when she could hide him no longer, she got him a wicker basket and covered it over with tar and pitch. Then she put the child into it and set it among the reeds by the bank of the Nile. His sister stood at a distance to find out what would happen to him. The daughter of Pharaoh came down to bathe at the Nile, with her maidens walking alongside; and she saw the basket among the reeds and sent her maid, and she brought it to her. When she opened it, she saw the child, and behold; the boy was crying. And she had pity on him."* (Exodus 2:2-6) Interestingly, Jesus was to become a victim of King Herod's murderous edict, that is until he is rescued by "Egypt" as well. Coincidental? *"Now when they had gone, behold, an angel of the Lord appeared to Joseph in a dream and said, 'Get up! Take the Child and His mother and flee to Egypt, and remain there until I tell you; for Herod is going to search for the Child to destroy Him.' So Joseph got up and took the Child and His mother while it was still night, and left for Egypt. He remained there until the death of Herod."* (Matthew 2:14-15)

It was in Genesis that God called the Hebrews into Egypt through Joseph and the famine, but it is in Exodus that God then called Moses and the people out of Egypt. *"The Lord said, 'I have surely seen the affliction of My people who are in Egypt, and have given heed to their cry because of their taskmasters, for I am aware of their sufferings. So I have come down to deliver them from the power of the Egyptians, and to bring them up from that land to a good and spacious land, to a land flowing with milk and honey, to the place of the Canaanite and the Hittite and the Amorite and the Perizzite and the Hivite and the Jebusite. Now, behold, the cry of the sons of Israel has come to Me; furthermore, I have seen the oppression with which the Egyptians are oppressing them. Therefore, come now, and I will send you to Pharaoh, so that you may bring My people, the sons of Israel, out of Egypt.'"* (Exodus 3:7-10) Quite similarly, in Matthew chapter two, Joseph, Mary, and Jesus were called into Egypt. There is a Joseph in this story as well. Coincidental? In Matthew chapter two the apostle implies that like Moses, Jesus is also called out of Egypt. *"This was to fulfill what had been spoken by the Lord through the prophet: 'Out of Egypt I called My Son.'"* (Matthew 2:15)

And so there you have it, Egypt! In a few short pages a summary of a long-standing love-hate relationship between the country, its people and the mission and purpose of God throughout the world. Beside the land of Israel, there may not be a more important piece of real estate on the entire planet more central to God's plan. May we always remember to pray for our Egyptian Coptic Christian brothers and sisters and especially the young people who are trying to grasp and hold on to their faith in Christ.

Chapter Fifteen

Heaven and Hell

Intuitively, most people know that the material things we have on this earth have their limits. Our riches and wealthy possessions are all wearing down, rusting, aging and passing away. There is a well-known saying that illustrates what I'm saying. It is often said as a joke! Here is how it goes *"You have never seen a Brinks truck at a funeral have you?"*

In this next journal entry, the Lord expresses a particular concern for people that should know better and yet continue to pray for the perishable things of this world rather than praying for the imperishable wealth and riches of heaven – mercy, kindness, faith, love, forgiveness, hope, charity and compassion.

On Sunday, February 12, 2008, the word of the Lord came just before awakening. This is what he said, *"I have heard all of my people's prayers, and many of them weary me. Numerous kneel in my house to pray and all the while asking for things you should not have. You pray for earthly things in exchange for the riches of heaven. You pray to gamble with your wealth and life and all the while you do not fear the Lord. My house shall be called a house of prayer, and my judgment is upon you. Don't gamble with your life before the Lord. Pray for the riches of my Son; his humility, mercy, and kindness. This is the wealth you should pray for."*

Apparently, the Lord in this message is repackaging and underscoring something he had already said to the apostles and the first disciples during his public ministry. He told them, *"Do not lay up for yourselves treasures on earth, where moth and rust consume and where thieves break in and steal, but lay up for yourselves treasures in heaven, where neither moth nor rust consumes and where thieves do not break in and steal. For where your treasure is, there will your heart be also."* Matthew 6:19-21

Besides Jesus himself, probably no one modeled more than Saint Francis a total abandonment to earthly riches and joyfully wrapped himself all up like with a blanket in a life of self-denial, frugality, emptiness and suffering. Francis deliberately embraced poverty on earth with a blessed assurance to gain the wealth of heaven. He took the words of Jesus literally when he said, *"If anyone would like to become my disciple, let him take up his cross, deny himself and follow me."* Matthew 16:24

On Wednesday, August 4, 2010, I had been reading the book, *"Little Flowers of Saint Francis"* on and off for about a week. Just before awakening the Lord spoke and said, *"Saint Francis was promised the wealth of heaven, only after he had paid the price in silver and gold here on earth."*

Of course, as the story goes, Francis came from wealth. His father was a well-to-do dealer of fabrics, silk, linens and expensive clothing, accessories and other fine apparel. In an instant, Francis gave it all up and never looked back. It seems as though Francis' journey to heaven was thus strategically patterned after the Bible story of the "Rich Young Man;" an account he had read, heard preached in church and knew all too well. Here is how the Gospel of Mark records the incident - a true story about a wealthy young man that has a perchance encounter with Jesus.

Saint Mark states, "And as he was setting out on his journey, a man ran up and knelt before him and asked him, *'Good Teacher, what must I do to inherit eternal life?'* And Jesus said to him, *'Why do you call me good? No one is good except God alone. You know the commandments: 'Do not murder, Do not commit adultery, Do not steal, Do not bear false witness, Do not defraud, Honor your father and mother.'* And he said to him, *'Teacher, all these I have kept from my youth.'* And Jesus, looking at him, loved him, and said to him, *'You lack one thing: go, sell all that you have and give to the poor, and you will have treasure in heaven; and come, follow me.'* Disheartened by the saying, he went away sorrowful, for he had great possessions. And Jesus looked around and said to his disciples, *'How difficult it will be for those who have wealth to enter the kingdom of God!'* And the disciples were amazed at his words. But Jesus said to them again, *'Children, how difficult it is to enter the kingdom of God! It is easier for a camel to go through the eye of a needle than for a rich person to enter the kingdom of God.'"* Mark 10:17-25

Heaven and 911

When someone's life is cut short by war, disaster, terrorism and natural disasters, God takes into consideration their extraordinary suffering (i.e. D-Day or 911). These painful situations account for much - opening wide the gates of heaven in the eyes of God for all the victims. Here is a message from the Lord regarding those who lost their lives in 911.

On Sunday, February 6, 2011, Lord, you granted while I was praying an interior locution regarding those who lost their lives on 911. You revealed how you immediately welcomed the victims to heaven; that is after you gave each upon their death a complete awareness of what had just happened to them, how they died and who was responsible. Lord, an opportunity to know the truth was in order so that each person could reach a personal mindset of forgiveness. However, at this present moment in time, a few individuals have not yet gone to heaven, but are resting comfortably. Why, I asked. You have mercifully and graciously given each person the time they need to reach a state of forgiveness. And so Lord, you yourself have shown us by your own example that heaven is for those who forgive even their enemies. In your last breath on the cross, a victim yourself, you cried out, *"Father forgive them for they do not know what they are doing!"* Luke 23:24

And so the message is given here in my journal notes about heaven, forgiveness, and 911 is also a commentary on the "Lord's Prayer." Jesus himself taught us how to forgive and then pray.

THE LORD'S PRAYER

Our Father, Who art in heaven
Hallowed be Thy Name;
Thy kingdom come,
Thy will be done,
on earth as it is in heaven.
Give us this day our daily bread,
and forgive us our trespasses,
as we forgive those who trespass against us;
and lead us not into temptation,
but deliver us from evil. Amen. C.f. Matthew 6:9-13

Lastly, Jesus sums it all up after teaching the new prayer we now call the "Our Father." He states, *"For if you forgive men their trespasses, your heavenly Father also will forgive you; but if you do not forgive men their trespasses, neither will your Father forgive your trespasses."* Matthew 6:14-15

Similarly, in January 2015 the Lord also spoke in regards to those individuals who lost their lives in Paris, France during the terror attacks on Charlie Hebdo offices and their employees.

On Saturday, January 10, 2015, Lord, in a dream you spoke and said the following, *"I would not drown a victim."* Your words are comforting for victims everywhere, especially for those many persons who have been kidnapped, killed and even the targets of terrorism in Paris this past week. All are welcomed into heaven because of your loving mercy and grace.

Football, Tatoos, and Guys Asking About Heaven

Men, given their propensity to participating in gangs, illegal substances, partying with alcohol and engaging in extracurricular sex; ultimately, they always seem interested in spiritual things at one point or another, especially the older they get. It has been my experience that eventually they become interested in Jesus, repentance, conversion, salvation, heaven and hell. Typically, many a young man's story is similar and as old as, well the Bible. In the New Testament Jesus tells the tale of the young man who moves out of the house and spends all his money on wine, women and partying. C.f. Luke 15:11-32 It could have been written today, it's that contemporary!

On Tuesday, December 23, 2008, in a dream, Lord, you spoke concerning the last judgment, salvation, heaven, and hell. In the vision, I was sitting in the family room of a huge house with a large group of men watching a soccer game. They were ordinary guys filled with lots of exaggerated talk, jokes, and laughter. By-and-large they were middle-aged, and all of them had sewn some serious wild oats in their younger years. Interestingly, it was a diverse group too. Some were black and Hispanic, others were gay, and yet others were former thugs and gangsters still displaying their aging tattoos. All had one thing in common. They were unabashedly self-proclaimed sinners.

At one point, a strong heavy-set man walked over to the television set and turned off the game. The men had decided that they wanted to talk about the moment of death, the presence of God, His final judgment, heaven, and hell.

Here is what I said to this group of jokesters, that all of a sudden got quite serious, *"When you die, first and foremost, God, immediately looks at the whole picture of your life in much the same way as when you yourself watch a football game. You look at the entire game and judge it accordingly as to whether a player or a team played a good or bad game, don't you? After an immediate general assessment of your life, next God passes two judgments about your life in this order and in this priority..."*

THE TWO JUDGMENTS

1 In the first judgment, God, asks the question, *"Did you live a life in which you offered acts of mercy, compassion, and forgiveness to others?"* Conversely, God, will also ask, *"Were you the type of person that for the most part was negative, unforgiving, judgmental, vindictive and unkind to family and friends; never reaching out to the homeless, sick, broken and the unloved that lived around you?"* In order to document your response to these questions, God will also show you scenes from your life; extracts that will actually make you feel as though you are there. If you were a selfish person,

He will show you scenes where you possibly walked by a homeless person or a beggar, and you were indifferent, completely paying no attention and being judgmental. After seeing slices of your life, you will know without a doubt that His coming verdict will be both just and true. God's sentence is also final. One will have no say in the matter. He will judge harshly those who have shown no mercy in their lifetime; evaluating lightly those who have shown mercy. If hell is in the picture for those who are controlling, spiteful and hateful, His final judgment at that very moment will be terrifying for that person, and like I said, final and irreversible.

2 In the second judgment which takes place immediately after the first, God also judges our moral failures. These are the things we do just because we are human. What's the bottom line here? Well, God knows we are *all* part of a fallen race. In fact, in our lifetime, in order to neutralize pride and foster humility, God permits all humans, including the religious, pastors, priests and even future saints to continue in sins of lusts, disorderly desires, theft, perjury and more. God knows that to error is human. However, there is good news in all this burdensome cloak of tainted humanity! The second judgment is of lesser importance and less consequential to the soul if the person has passed the first judgment of mercy. Remember that the one who has been baptized has Jesus as their Advocate (C.f. Hebrews 4:14-16). They will find that through the intercession of Christ, God will judge ever so lightly the ones who have lived a

life of mercy. You can count on it! Jesus, your Advocate, will stand by his word, *"Blessed are the merciful, they shall obtain mercy."* (C.f. Matthew 5:7) Although, one may have been chronic lustful, a prostitute or a thief on a cross; the sins of the law such as passion, desire and the like, all will be forgiven. However, *"Judgment will be without mercy for those who have shown no mercy."* (C.f. James 2:13) This person essentially has two strikes against them. They have been bitter, controlling, spiteful, hateful and unmerciful as well as a normal human, who like all humans is a violator of the law. This person will want mercy (Who doesn't?) but refused to go out and give it to others. But there is more good news for the merciful! The message of mercy is universal and applicable to all. All humans that live a sincere life of mercy whether Christian or not, will find the mercy of God on the other side. Being baptized Christian gives one the added advantage that Jesus, at the time of your death will be there standing before God the Father as your Advocate and Lawyer. It "pays" to be baptized in this life, but if you don't receive the sacrament, in some cases, all will not be lost. Those who have been loving and merciful in this life, but were not baptized will be given an opportunity to accept Christ as their savior during the initial moments when they arrive on the other side. So lastly, in the dream, I do recall that the men were surprised by the message of mercy and how the final judgment works. Some rejoice, but many were troubled by what they had discovered. Numerous guys openly reflected upon how harsh they have been thus far in their lifetimes. Notably, they confessed being unkind and unmerciful towards their girlfriends, wives, moms, dads, co-workers and their children.

Upon awakening, almost immediately supporting scriptures came to mind, *"Above all hold unfailing your love for one another, since love covers a multitude of sins."* (1 Peter 4:8) Most importantly, Jesus himself documented the last judgment, heaven, hell and even Purgatory in the parable of the "Wicked Servant" . . .

"Then Peter came to Jesus and asked, *'Lord, how many times shall I forgive my brother when he sins against me?* Up to seven times?' Jesus answered, *'I tell you, not seven times, but seventy-seven times.'* Therefore, the kingdom of heaven is like a king who wanted to settle accounts with his servants. As he began the settlement, a man who owed him ten thousand talents [approximately 7.5 billion dollars in present-day money] was brought to him. Since he was not able to pay, the master ordered that he and his wife and his children, and all that he had, be sold to repay the debt. The servant fell on his knees before him. *'Be patient with me,'* he begged, *'and I will pay back everything.'* The servant's master took pity on him, canceled the debt and let him go.

"But when that servant went out, he found one of his fellow servants who owed him a hundred denarii [approximately 13,000 dollars in present-day money]. He grabbed him and began to choke him. *'Pay back what you owe me!'* he demanded. His fellow servant fell to his knees and begged him, *'Be patient with me, and I will pay you back.'* But he refused. Instead, he went off and had the man thrown into prison until he could pay the debt. When the other servants saw what had happened, they were greatly distressed and went and told their master everything that had happened.

"Then the master called the servant in. *'You wicked servant,'* he said, *'I canceled all that debt of yours because you begged me to. Shouldn't you have had mercy on your fellow servant just as I had on you?'* In anger, his master turned him over to the jailers to be tortured until he should pay back all he owed." [Jesus then said] *'This is how my heavenly Father will treat each of you unless you forgive your brother from your heart.'"* Matthew 18:21-35

After having had the vision of the men who were interested in the final judgment, heaven, and hell; it also became apparent that many people are interested in the state of their souls. They would like clarity and help in order to make an accurate self-assessment as to what God looks for in His children. So, a few years ago I decided to create a self-assessment tool called *"The Heaven and Risk of Hell Calculator."*

The tool alone is not so unusual. A little research reveals that online there are many self-assessment tools for almost everything, ranging from stroke and heart attack risk to driving patterns and automobile fuel efficiency and even compatibility and romance. Introduced below is the first-ever, *"Heaven and Risk of Hell Calculator."* Go and get yourself a piece of paper, a pen or pencil and answer the following 50 questions as spontaneously and as honestly as you can. In an unscientific but pragmatic way, it will help you to roughly determine which direction you may be headed if you were to die today. Of course, we humbly acknowledge that God has the final decision in these matters. At the end of the quiz, there will be instructions to self-score and to receive an explanation of your results. God bless you!

1. How often do you attend church on Sundays?
   A. Every Sunday
   B. Occasionally
   C. Holidays

2. How often do you listen to or read the Bible?
   A. Daily
   B. Occasionally
   C. Almost never

3. How many spiritual books a year do you read?
   A. More than one
   B. One
   C. None

4. Describe your prayer life.
   A. A few minutes each morning, noon and night
   B. A few minutes here and there throughout the week
   C. None

5. How often do you give thanks before meals?
   A. All the time
   B. When I remember
   C. On holidays

6. How often do you give thanks after meals?
   A. All the time
   B. When I remember
   C. Never

7. How often do you give thanks to God for all He has done, both big and small?
   A. Nightly/daily
   B. Weekly
   C. Not often

8. Do you make time for an overnight spiritual retreat?
   A. At least once a year
   B. Once every few years
   C. Never, but occasionally go on vacations

9. Do you take a few moments of time here and there for "mini retreats;" go for a walk or a drive to relax and pray?

   A. Weekly

   B. Monthly

   C. No, not usually

10. How often do you connect with the "family of God" around you to serve, pray, break bread and share together?

    A. Weekly

    B. Monthly

    C. Rarely

11. Have you received water baptism?

    A. Yes

    B. Not sure, but I think so

    C. No

12. Have you received Confirmation and the anointing of the Holy Spirit?

    A. Yes

    B. Not sure, but I think so

    C. No

13. How often do you humble yourself by admitting and confessing to others your failures and wrongdoings?

    A. Frequently

    B. Rarely

    C. Never

14. Do you have a "spiritual" friend, clergy member or advisor that you can talk about spiritual things?

    A. Yes

    B. Occasionally

    C. No

15. Do you generously share your gifts and talents in service to the Body of Christ, the Church?

    A. Yes, weekly

    B. Yes, occasionally

    C. No, I'm just too busy

16. In a typical year, I am inclined to visit the sick – my family, friends, and co-workers in the hospital or nursing home.

    A. Often

    B. Occasionally

    C. Not usually

17. Typically, when I see a homeless person, I am inclined to help in some way, remembering not to judge.

    A. Frequently

    B. Occasionally

    C. Not usually

18. I've been known to stop in a nursing home to visit family, friends and even people I don't know to share some cheer especially at Christmastime and other holidays.

    A. Often

    B. Sometimes

    C. Never

19. When I hear an approaching ambulance or see a car accident, this is how I usually respond.

    A. Pray for those involved

    B. Respectfully drive by

    C. Quickly get around it and try to make up time

20. When we have or go to parties and host get-togethers, I enjoy having the children around.

    A. All the time

    B. Sometimes

    C. Never

21. When I see someone cut me off or disobey the laws of the road, I have a few choice words for them either to my passengers or inside my head, for instance, "You idiot!"

    A. Never

    B. Sometimes

    C. All the time

22. I have little patience for food servers that get the order wrong; I'm inclined to speak up and get it done correctly.

    A. Never

    B. Sometimes

    C. All the time

23. When I give and give to someone, either at work or in my family; and they don't show appreciation or say "thank you," I am inclined to bring it to their attention.

    A. Never

    B. Sometimes

    C. Usually

24. Homeless people become homeless because they are lazy; why don't they just go out and get a job like the rest of us?

    A. I disagree

    B. I somewhat agree

    C. I totally agree

25. Thanks be to God, everyone likes me. I go to church on Sunday and keep up a nice house, don't smoke or drink too much and give a little money to the collection each week. I'm confident this is the kind of person that is on the way to heaven.

    A. I disagree

    B. I somewhat agree

    C. I totally agree

26. Having the latest phone, computer or clothing style is important to me.

    A. Not at all

    B. Sometimes

    C. All the time

27. I tend to see the glass half empty. I can quickly assess problems and tell others the way it should be.

    A. Not at all

    B. Sometimes

    C. All the time

28 The tax collector Zacchaeus promised to give 50% of all he owned. Jesus commanded the rich young ruler give 100%. But I give to the Lord . . .

    A. 50%

    B. 10%

    C. Less than 10%

29. Thanks be to God that he loves me because I am straight. I check out porn every now and again or entertain occasional bad thoughts; but those gay people, prostitutes, drug addicts and abortionists are headed straight for hell.

    A. I disagree

    B. I somewhat agree

    C. I totally agree

30. I have a motto that works for me, "I don't get mad, I get even."

    A. Not true

    B. Somewhat true

    C. Definitely

31. I am hard on myself when I make mistakes and tend to get anxiety after my failures while striving for even more perfection and attention.

    A. False

    B. Somewhat true

    C. True

32. Many workers and colleagues are idiots and incompetent. Why don't they study, work hard and perform more intelligently like me?

    A. I disagree

    B. I somewhat agree

    C. I totally agree.

33. Jesus told us never to judge, but in all reality, you do have to judge others from time to time.

    A. False

    B. Somewhat true

    C. True

34. Jesus told us to infinitely forgive, 70 X 70, but this is unrealistic, I have my limits.

A. I disagree, we should always forgive

B. I somewhat agree

C. I agree, but we all have limits, and I'm not a doormat!

35. When someone becomes verbally aggressive, it prompts the following reaction from me.

A. I am slow to speak and walk away

B. I put in my two cents and walk away

C. I stay and argue and battle it out

36. If Jesus came today, would the Master find me so doing work for Him?

A. Yes, I am always actively serving the Lord with my life.

B. Yes, I am serving the Lord, but not always consistent.

C. No he would not find me doing a lot for him because I work very hard in my career and I'm very busy all the time, I hope he understands.

37. My style is to have a nice long talk with someone over an issue, especially when my reputation is on the line.
    A. False, they can think and do what they want, but for me, remaining silent is the best thing.
    B. I prefer to remain silent in these situations, however, if they push hard enough I will respond.
    C. Stick up for yourself, speak up, don't let others push you around and let them know you are not going to tolerate this.

38. Lately, I find myself forgiving and praying for my enemies just like Jesus said to do.
    A. Daily
    B. Weekly
    C. Never

39. I prefer to include and stay close to family members and coworkers that are "odd" and may not have the personal gifts, intelligence, good looks or friends that others have.
    A. All the time
    B. Some of the time
    C. I prefer to be with my own crowd

40. I work hard at home and on the job to be kind, compassionate, giving and helpful, but all I get in return is gossip, accusations, misinterpretation of my actions and more.

A. Often

B. From time to time

C. Not usually

41. When someone gets on my bad side, I am inclined to do little things behind the scenes to make their life miserable, just to let them know I am mad and in control.

A. Never

B. Sometimes

C. Often

42. I have been known to use texting or email to vent and speak my mind to someone.

A. Never

B. Sometimes

C. Often

43. Sharing gossip, especially getting it out there about those who have wronged me is nothing more than sharing public knowledge, and it's a good way to get even.

    A. I refrain from doing this no matter how tempting

    B. I do this sometimes

    C. I do this all the time

44. I admit I'm a sinner and in need of a savior. I accept the fact that I am no better off than the people in prison; the only difference being is they have gotten caught.

    A. Strongly agree

    B. Somewhat agree

    C. Strongly disagree

45. When I do good for the poor, the sick and for others, a little thanks and recognition along the way is important to me and inspires me to keep up the good deeds.

    A. I do it and expect nothing in return

    B. Recognition makes me feel good, but I don't wait for it

    C. If in time I don't receive thanks and recognition, I am disappointed

46. When I give my hard earned money to a charity, I at least expect the people there to listen to me and to please understand that I pay their bills, show a little respect by doing things my way.

    A. I donate my money with no strings attached

    B. When I donate, I hope for a little consideration

    C. As my donations begin to add up, the more power and control is natural

47. How often to you confess your failures, shortcomings, and sins to God in prayer?

    A. Daily

    B. When I remember

    C. I don't remember the last time

48. I can confidently say that my personal walk with the God has had a positive effect on inspiring family members and friends to follow the Lord too.

    A. Yes, most definitely

    B. Somewhat

    C. Not sure

49. How would others - pastors, family, and friends rate your spiritual life on a scale of 1 – 10, 10 being the most solid.

    A. 8-10

    B. 5-7

    C. 1-4

50. How would you rate your spiritual life on a scale of 1 – 10, 10 being the most solid.

    A. 8-10

    B. 5-7

    C. 1-4

HOW TO SCORE YOUR SELF-ASSESSMENT

Okay, you are ready to score your responses. Give yourself 2 points for every letter "A." Give yourself 1 point for every letter "B." Give yourself 0 points for every letter "C." Now go ahead, total up all your A, B, C into one final composite score. How did you do?

Heaven Bound 75 – 100

This fifty-question, self-assessment has focused on both the obvious and not so obvious Bible-based spiritual expectations of Christians. More than likely you scored high points in the foundations of our faith like baptism, the sacraments, prayer, thanksgiving, and service. However, you also seem to be aware that those things are not the only determiners in order to be heaven bound. Jesus said, *"Not everyone who says to me, 'Lord, Lord,' will enter the kingdom of heaven."* (Matthew 7:21)

So you also scored strongly in the not so obvious and weightier matters of the law such as mercy, compassion, giving, humility, love and forgiveness. These are complex virtues that are not often easily understood or integrated into a Christian's daily life. Overall, your dedication to frequent prayer and acts of mercy will keep you on the right track until you are called home. May God always bless and continue to strengthen your Christian witness.

Homeward Bound 60 – 74

You do a lot of things right, most probably the basics like prayer and church attendance. By increasing your almsgiving, charitable acts, works of mercy and willingness to forgive, you will be well on your way to heaven. Don't stop now; you are on a good course that just needs a burst of more spiritual determination and a little more polishing, drive, sacrifices of unconditional love and forgiveness of others.

Homeless Bound 50 – 59

The good news is that you know and understand the basics of your faith. The bad news is that you are probably a borderline Christian and possibly lukewarm in your faith. There is nothing less satisfying than a swig of lukewarm water from a water bottle sitting too long in the car on a warm day. Think about it. More than likely you have commitment and dedication issues with daily prayer, church attendance, regular Bible reading and more. You probably have problems with others when it comes to compassion, kindness, mercy, forgiveness and almsgiving.

Remember, Jesus said, *"Blessed are the merciful, they shall obtain mercy."* (Matthew 5:7) You are in need of mercy, and the best way to receive it upon your death is to give it now, while you are still here living this life. People who die with unresolved issues, frequently become homeless in a place called Purgatory. Often they remain there, homeless in desolate and confining spaces for years. Some saints estimate billions of homeless souls are still in Purgatory. Let's be real, even if you die with your faith, but also die with unforgiveness, anger, hate and other unmerciful issues, you will not go directly to heaven, but most wonderfully, thanks be to God, may not go to hell either. Even if you don't believe in Purgatory, you may still be headed there. Increase your prayer life, church going, receiving the sacraments, confession, works of mercy, compassion and forgiveness and you can turn your life around in order to be heaven-bound.

Hell Bound 1 – 49

Well, let's be real. You were willing to take this assessment, so you are not worthy of this preliminary report. You deserve better than this. You should be on your way to heaven. Yes, you may be too busy with your career, your hectic life, acquiring possessions, car, and family but that is no excuse for losing eternal life. Jesus said, *"What good will it be for someone to gain the whole world, yet lose their soul?"* (Matthew 16:26)

Please resolve today to do <u>three</u> things immediately for yourself and for those who love you. Do not delay!

1 Meet with a pastor, religious or church confidant and discuss your spiritual situation. You can use the results of this assessment as a springboard for your initial discussion.

2 Begin today to read the Bible a little bit each morning or night. If you do not have a Bible, please go to a bookstore or order online the *New American Bible* or *New Revised Standard Version*.

3 Begin to pray each day the "Our Father" (page 245) as well as other written prayers (page 185-190) along with your own spontaneous conversation with God. Here's a tip, pray in the car on the way to and from work and listen to spiritual books in the car too. Talk to the Lord openly and honestly about your spiritual situation. Go to the church of your choice this Sunday. May God bless you! I will be praying for you.

Chapter Sixteen

Angels and Demons

The Power of Angels

As you may remember from book one (chapter one, page 12), my first "encounter" with angels was simultaneous to my encounter with God the Father at the time of my NDE. He shielded His white, brilliant "glory light" by remaining protected behind a thin gray screen. However, bursts of His splendor ripped through the mesh overwhelming me to the core. Dazed, all I could think of was the angelic hymn sung at the birth of Christ. So in solidarity with the angels I spontaneously joined in their chorus, repeating over and over . . . *"Glory to God in the highest and peace to His people on earth!"* Needless to say, after this near-death-experience, I most definitely became a believer in angels! Something similar occurred December 2007.

On Monday, December 31, 2007, Lord, thank you for the peaceful vision throughout the night of Sunday into Monday morning. I had been in the hospital's ER because of more heart arrhythmia problems. You comforted me with angelic voices while I slept on a gurney in the hallway. The angels sang over and over, *"Glory to God in the highest and peace to*

His people on earth." I heard the beautiful hymn the entire night in what was a peaceful, angelic chorus singing your praises.

In chapter four (page 53), you may remember that an "earthly" angel came to help me with my dad. Her name is Angelina - a rescue mission supervisor that had seen my father Jim visiting while I was in my office one day helping the homeless in downtown Los Angeles, "city of angels." It is no coincidence that Angelina's name comes from the Italian diminutive of the Greek "Angela" meaning angel or messenger. God uses angels, both human and supernatural beings to accomplish His will.

In Paul's letter to the Hebrews, he addresses the reality of angles by saying, *"Are not all angels ministering spirits sent to serve those who will inherit salvation?"* (Hebrews 1:14) In hindsight, this makes a lot of sense. On page 56 I described an encounter with an angel that was ministering to my dad while he was "homeless" in Purgatory in 2005, just two years after his death. His guardian angel was tranquil, had a soft glow emanating from his face and nodded to me indicating everything was under control. Here is another encounter with angels from my journal.

On Friday, October 27, 2006, Lord, when I awoke in the night, you had filled the room with your presence, as if it were the "Holy of Holies," the inner chamber of the sanctuary where you reside. A pure white fog and a snowy heavenly haze had descended upon my bedroom. The air was peaceful, calm and softly lit by a heavenly light. Lord, your presence, pure and holy filled every fabric of the space. Time seemed to have been suspended. I heard an angelic choir singing a song by Paul Oakley… *"Jesus, lover of my soul. All consuming fire is in Your gaze. Jesus, I want You to know, I will follow You all my days… Alpha and Omega, You have loved me. And I will spend eternity with You… You alone are God, and I surrender, to Your ways."*

On another occasion, I had just left a breakfast café with a friend, Tim. We were just out of seminary for the day and out on an errand. Suddenly, we encountered an angel undercover!

On Saturday, January 27, 2007, I met a homeless woman in a car park where we had left our vehicle while visiting a neighborhood breakfast café. As we got ready to get in and go, she looked up at us from the front of the car, as if appearing out of nowhere and began to speak. But being in a hurry, I quickly offered her some money to help with her needs being that she was homeless and all. She did not want the money and politely refused a handful of one dollar bills. Then she looked at me with piercing eyes and spoke the following words, *"One of you is very energetic"* and then pointed at me. *"You are on a mission,"* she said. I was puzzled and wondered, "How does *she know this? Who sent her?"* But after some thought, it became apparent we had encountered a messenger, an angel in disguise. A scripture comes to mind, *"Be not forgetful to entertain strangers: for thereby some have entertained angels unawares."* (Hebrews 13:2)

In 2008 our team, *Servants of the Father of Mercy* was a relatively new group in the Archdiocese of Los Angeles. By 2012, in just four years we had our share of haters and attackers ranging from local churchgoers to a few priests, deacons, and even some local atheists. One gentleman, in particular, had caused so much trouble, he had launched a hostile takeover so he could personally take control of our name, ministry, California corporation, and IRS 501 (c) 3 tax-exempt status; all very valuable items to those who want to use these things for their own gain. However, in 2008 God had forewarned us in a vision. He cautioned through an angel that a troublemaker was coming and an angel named him by name.

On Friday, November 21, 2008, in the night while I slept you granted a vision. In it Lord, you said, *"Mother Mary is not harsh or condemning in any way toward the people living in the world today. However, she does lovingly admonish everyone to wake up from error, wake up from sin, wake up from sleep and to follow me, her Son."*

Next, I left my body, and I was transported in spirit by the hand of an angel to a tall and beautiful office building. At first, at the front of the building, we had to hide behind a pillar while a couple of people exited the main doors. As we went through the doors there appeared a holy water fountain strategically placed on the right for us to use. The angel blessed himself, and I did the same. Then we went to an upper floor, and the angel left me in the corridor of the main offices. I noticed two workers in a break room preparing lunch for someone in an adjacent office. All the doors were open. The office workers did not see me listening, standing or observing them. One of the workers referred to the person in the main office as "Mike." Then the angel returned and said, *"Mike is responsible for great cunning and evil. Be wary of him."* In a flash, I was placed back in my body which was still asleep in the night in my bedroom.

Flash ahead now seven years. In the twelve months of 2015 and spilling over into January 2016, the vision was confirmed. A man by the name of "Mike" who also works in an office building in the Southern California region had quietly and persistently tried many subtle ways to take over the *Servants of the Father of Mercy*. But having been alerted, "Mike" and his efforts were therefore resisted. *"Blessed be the Lord, who has not given us as prey to his teeth."* (Psalm 124:6) By February 2016, "Mike," getting nowhere, voluntarily left the ministry.

A must-see movie is *"Angel in the House."* I highly recommend it. Briefly, a little boy "Eli" appears at the front door of a couple's house one day, walking all the way from a local foster home. He's totally unexpected and unannounced. You can't but fall in love with an eight-year-old kid that reads the *Wall Street Journal*, orders the best Chinese takeout in town, takes taxis home from grade school and hangs out with homeless people in the neighborhood park. Later in the movie, it is discovered that one his homeless friends is actually an angel working with him undercover. Well, sometimes homeless people are actually chronic angels visiting from the other side with an ongoing mission and purpose on earth. Following is an exact case of that from my journal.

On Friday, May 6, 2011, while exiting the freeway in Ventura County, California, I discovered a homeless man by the name of Dave living among the bushes in the gully. Dave and I first met in 2006 at St. Peter's Church daily food line in Chinatown, Los Angeles, California. At that time, he had not taken a shower in 10-15 years, looked like a mountain man, had a distinct odor and was unable to speak well or communicate his thoughts clearly. In 2007, one day we went to evening Mass together at 5:15 pm and sat in the back of the church so as not to disturb any parishioners with his disheveled presence. Never-the-less, after Mass, we received some feedback that his attendance was unwelcomed. It had gone over like a lead balloon, so we never did that again!

But what was Dave doing 55 miles north of Los Angeles sleeping in a ravine off the side of a freeway? How did he get here? Did he walk all the way from Los Angeles? As we spoke, it was deciphered that over the past four years he had ambled his way along the roadside, gradually making it to Ventura County, California. Was he completely out of touch with reality as usual? But on this day, May 6, 2011, after repeated bear hugs, he pushed me away, pointed his finger at me and said as clear as day, *"You are starting a monastery. God is going to bless you! You are a saint, my brother."* Surprise! That is information Dave did not have. Even if he did, historically he never had the ability to verbalize full coherent sentences. Yet Dave was able to walk 55 miles for four years for a chance rendezvous in order to deliver that message at a transient place and time. It's 2016 as I wrap up his story and I have never seen Dave again.

In book one, my mother encountered the homeless angel "Billy." That story is located on page 67. Similarly, after her death in May 2010, I was visiting a *Carl's Junior* in the late spring having lunch on the road near Santa Barbara, California. As I was dining at a small side-table, a very tall thin young man with long blonde hair walked into the restaurant, looked at me, made eye contact and exited the back door. He did not order food and was only passing through. Flash ahead a few minutes to my departure, as I closed the car door and placed the key in the ignition, the same young man suddenly appeared at the front passenger side. He smiled and looked at me as I rolled down the window. He gracefully pointed his index finger at me and said, *"I am going to pray for you!"* Suddenly, everything around me became calm, peaceful and otherworldly. While caught up in the tranquility of what seemed like "seventh heaven," I spontaneously responded, *"Please pray for my enemies, that God will bless them!"* He laughed while I looked out the front windshield. I turned back to say goodbye. He was gone. He literally had disappeared into thin air!

August of 2014 had been an unusually hot summer for coastal California. It was the worst time to have a broken automobile air conditioner as well as insufficient AC in our homeless supplies warehouse that is made of heat conducting tin roof and walls. Daytime interior temperatures were in the 90s. Long story short, by the end of August the heat took its toll, and I ended up suffering fever, lower back pain, dehydration, reduced kidney function and kidney stones.

One morning I was seen by the doctor at 9 am and was told there is not much that can be done but increase fluids, drink cranberry juice and stay out of the heat. As I drove back to the warehouse, my fever was still 101, and I was looking forward to getting some rest and increasing fluids. But just as I turned the corner to park the car, I noticed a homeless man lying on the side of the road collapsed in the hot sun.

I thought to myself that he looked just like the man lying on the side of the road in Jesus' story of the *"Good Samaritan."* But in this case, I felt legitimately sick, so I did not think it was my responsibility to reach out to him. Someone else will stop I surmised.

However, when I arrived in the warehouse, I was compelled to make a plastic sack filled with treats out of the refrigerator, cold oranges, fresh apples, juice and cold water and deliver it all to the man on the side of the road. I thought how he must be much worse off than I am. Sweating, dehydrating and delirious he sat up, ate and drank his fill. Eventually, he was able to stand and say goodbye. Upon arriving back at the warehouse my fever instantly left, my energy was reinstated as if I had never been sick and for weeks after I was permanently made well and healed from a situation the doctors offered little help.

May we all find the strength to join Jesus every day of our lives remembering to live the parable of the *"Good Samaritan."*

The Parable of the Good Samaritan

And behold, a lawyer stood up to put him to the test, saying, *"Teacher, what shall I do to inherit eternal life?"* He said to him, *"What is written in the law? How do you read?"* And he answered, *"You shall love the Lord your God with all your heart, and with all your soul, and with all your strength, and with all your mind; and your neighbor as yourself."* And he said to him, *"You have answered right; do this, and you will live."*

But he, desiring to justify himself, said to Jesus, *"And who is my neighbor?"* Jesus replied, *"A man was going down from Jerusalem to Jericho, and he fell among robbers, who stripped him and beat him, and departed, leaving him half dead. Now by chance, a priest was going down that road; and when he saw him, he passed by on the other side. So likewise a Levite, when he came to the place and saw him, passed by on the other side. But a Samaritan, as he journeyed, came to where he was; and when he saw him, he had compassion, and went to him and bound up his wounds, pouring on oil and wine; then he set him on his own beast and brought him to an inn, and took care of him. And the next day he took out two denarii * and gave them to the innkeeper, saying, 'Take care of him; and whatever more you spend, I will repay you when I come back.' Which of these three, do you think, proved neighbor to the man who fell among the robbers?"* He said, *"The one who showed mercy on him."* And Jesus said to him, *"Go and do likewise."* (Luke 10:25-37) * The two denarii were a day's wage for a laborer at that time.

Remember that an encounter with a homeless stranger may be a test from God. Paul in his letter to Hebrews said, *"Do not forget or neglect or refuse to extend hospitality to strangers in brotherhood. Be friendly, cordial, and gracious, sharing the comforts of your home with strangers and doing your part generously. For by doing so, some have entertained angels without knowing it."* Hebrews 13:2

The Weakness of Demons

In the first section of this chapter, angels are described as strong and powerful messengers of God. Conversely, we can assume therefore that demons are weak. That's good news because in their feebleness they primarily utilize tactics such as smoke and mirrors to try and scare or disrupt our lives. So, there is nothing to fear from these ones that are so pathetic and feeble. Here is the case of one demonic encounter that I recorded in my journal about ten years ago.

On Tuesday, July 11, 2006, I am finally ready to journal about a chance meeting with the enemy I had in the early hours of the morning, around 3:00 am a week or so ago. At the time, I was sitting up in bed with the night light on and praying the rosary. I was just enjoying the quiet of the evening while living in a church rectory in downtown Los Angeles. Well, without warning, a man in a nicely tailored gray suit and wearing a matching gray t-shirt walked through the closed-door entrance of my bedroom. I was not frightened, but it was evident that he did not need to open the door to get in. He walked right through it as if he were a ghost. At first, he appeared tall, well-groomed and with a short military-style haircut. He stood at my bedside and looked down at me as if he were a physician attending the bedside of a patient in a hospital room.

Calmly, in a liminal and peaceful state of mind I made eye contact with him and spoke first setting ground rules for his visit, *"You are not welcome here unless you say 'Jesus is Lord.'"* He stared at me with piercing eyes and stated in a gruff Darth Vader voice, *"Jesus is okay."* Persistent, I spoke again, *"No that is not good enough. You must say 'Jesus is Lord' if you wish to stay here."* Quickly he retorted sarcastically, *"Look, I have no problem with Jesus."* Determined, I calmly I spoke a third time and said, *"You cannot stay here unless you say Jesus is Lord."* He gruffly whispered once again quite rapidly, slurring his speech, saying, *"Jesus is lardy!"* He was hoping that I would not hear his clever corruption of the word "Lord" to "lardy." Immediately I noticed his fraud and replied, *"No! That is not good enough."* With that said, he immediately began to morph into a werewolf – from the top of his head to his neck and then on down to his feet. What I remember most were his evil eyes flashing veins of yellow, orange and green. After he finished morphing, he instantly disappeared. In the aftermath, there was an awful smell as if someone was smoking crack cocaine or "cooking drugs." The horrible Sulphur underworld stench permeated my room, mainly around 3:00 am, and that continued for many months afterward.

After having had a week to reflect on the incident and before recording it in my journal, I remember initially feeling a sense of joy and exhilaration because the Lord had given us authority over demons through the authority of His Name. However, it was also later I recalled from the Scriptures that we are not to rejoice in having power over the enemy, but to rejoice because one's name is written in the *Book of Life*. These sorts of attacks are actually indications that one's name has been registered in heaven and so we give thanks when they happen. Jesus said, *"Do not rejoice that the spirits submit to you, but rejoice that your names are written in heaven."* (Luke 10:20)

Some people dismiss stories of demons as a figment of human imagination. But the Bible tells us to, *"Put on the full armor of God, so that you can take your stand against the devil's schemes. For our struggle is not against flesh and blood, but against the rulers, against the authorities, against the powers of this dark world and against the spiritual forces of evil in the heavenly realms."* – Ephesians 6:11-12 We are also advised, *"Be sober-minded; be watchful. Your adversary, the devil, prowls like a roaring lion, seeking someone to devour."* – 1 Peter 5:8 The spiritual world is real, and there is a battle going on.

Though Satan and his demons rarely reveal themselves to ordinary people, when it comes to those who are strong in the Lord and winning souls for Christ through their life, work and testimony, demons apparently sometimes make open attacks. John Vianney, priest and saint is one such case.

In early 1800s France, soon after St. John Vianney had opened his parsonage as a refuge for the poor, the strangest noises began to disturb his rest at night, and to trouble the quiet of his home. His own account of the origin of these persecutions is as follows: "It was about nine o'clock at night, I was just going to bed when the demon came to torment me for the first time. Three heavy blows were leveled at the door of my courtyard: you would have thought someone was trying to break it open by force. I opened my window, and asked *'Who is there?'* but I saw nothing, and commending myself to God, I quietly retired to rest. I had not, however, gone to sleep, before I was again startled by three still louder knocks, not now at the outer door, but at that on the staircase, which led to my chamber. I rose up, and cried out a second time, *'Who is there?'* No one replied. At the first commencement of these noises at night, I imagined that they were caused by robbers, and fearing lest the beautiful ornaments of the church might be in danger of being carried off, I thought it well to take precautions. Accordingly, I had two courageous men to sleep in the house, who were ready to assist me if needed. They came several nights successively. They heard the noise, but discovering nothing, they were convinced that it proceeded from other causes than the malice of men. I myself soon came to the same conclusion; for one night in the midst of winter, three violent knocks were heard. I rose quickly from my bed, and went down into the courtyard, expecting to see the intruders making their escape, and intending to call for help; but, to my astonishment, I saw nothing, I heard nothing, and, what is more, I discovered no traces of footprints upon the snow. I resigned myself to God's will, praying Him to be my guard and protector, and surround me with angels if my enemy should return to torment me." www.CatholicHarborofFaithandMorals.com

---

On Thursday, January 6, 2011, Lord, I had just woke for the day at 6:00 am in my apartment in California and was transported out of the body to the small, but the historically notorious ghost-filled town, Charleston, SC. I found myself walking at the top of a tree-lined side street near the city's historic section when a woman stopped me and said, *"Please hurry, go down the block, on the left to house number 711. The people there are under attack by the enemy, and they need your help."* I walked past rows of historic Victorian homeless and waves of Spanish moss carpeting the trees making it into a well-shaded, dark and eerie street. Through the sheets of green moss, I could hear faint shrills and screams in the distance. Getting ready for spiritual battle, I kept repeating out loud, "Jesus is Lord! Jesus is the King of Kings. Jesus is Lord!" I kept affirming that the devil has no authority over me. When I arrived, it was a big old three-story Victorian home. I heard strange animal noises pouring out onto the street. People were screaming. From the street, I opened the black iron rod garden gate and wandered on a brick path to the front of the house. I climbed the creaking porch steps and rang the doorbell.

The attack going on in the house was loud and all out spiritual warfare. They could not hear the doorbell. So I backed away from the porch and walked to the side of the house. Looking up, I saw a man who had opened a rounded window in the stairwell and was hanging out shouting for help. He feared for his life. The man was contorted and distorted in appearance.

While I was talking to the man, suddenly two large dogs leaped out of the second story window at me, apparently demons in disguise. While they were jumping, I made the sign of the cross on myself. Next, I blessed the dogs and the entire yard with the sign of the cross, repeatedly saying, *"Jesus is Lord!"* I continued and said, *"Jesus is Lord of all!*

Jesus is Lord with the Holy Spirit, Jesus is Lord with God the Father, Jesus is the Lord of Lords." I stood firm with my authority and showed no fear. As a result, the screams, the animal noises, and smoke had all disappeared. Peace had come to the house.

To my surprise, three men walked out the front door, onto the porch and down the front steps no longer under the influence of demons. They ultimately had regained their sanity and were very grateful that the siege was over. Before departing from them and returning back to my body that was still lying in a bed in California, I encouraged each man to pray a prayer of dedication to Jesus Christ, *"Repeat after me,"* I said. *"O God, I give you my heart, my life, my soul."* (Repeat) *"Come enter into me now."* (Repeat) *"I give you all that I am."* (Repeat) *"I am sorry for my sins and ask you for your forgiveness."* (Repeat) *"Jesus, come and be the Lord of my life."* (Repeat) *Amen!* Each prayed that prayer and then they pointed to one of the men and said, *"He goes to Church every Sunday."* I responded, *"All of you must go to Church every Sunday - under pain of mortal sin if you do not go." "Yes, we will go,"* they replied enthusiastically.

Having had this first-hand combat with the enemy, I've come to think of it this way. Picture yourself being safely inside a big old house. The blinds are drawn, the doors locked, windows secured and overall the three floors of your large house are securely protected. That is what happens to your soul when God takes control of it. You are encased, enclosed, protected and guarded, from top to bottom, by the most sophisticated, 24-hour security alarm system this side of heaven. The apostle Paul said, *"Put on the whole armor of God that you may be able to stand against the wiles of the devil. For we are not contending against flesh and blood, but against principalities, against the powers, against the world rulers of this present darkness. Stand therefore having girded your loins with truth, and having put on the breastplate of righteousness, and having shod your feet with the equipment of the Gospel of peace; above all taking the shield of faith, the helmet of salvation and sword of the spirit which is the word of God."* (Ephesians 6:10-18)

But some people ignore the importance of putting on God-protection or worse, others actually open doors for the devil, actually inviting him to come into their life. A few years ago, I was asked to pray with a man, his girlfriend and teenage stepson who had been suffering from bad school performance, extreme anxiety, depression, self-mutilation, sleep disturbance and more. There was no peace in the home or the lives of the individuals involved. First I spoke with the guardians. They loved the boy very much, taking him to doctors and counseling, but nothing seemed to work. After praying together, it became apparent through the Holy Spirit that the son and the house were under demonic attack. Eventually, they described how the son saw spirits of demons who had come through the window next to his bed at night. The nocturnal apparitions were unnerving and added to his anxiety. I asked the boy if he had any images of Satan in his room. He said no. The parents were asked the same question. They said no. I was not convinced, so we went to see the room where he sleeps. He opened the closet door. Immediately, it was exposed that the boy had an enormous, almost uncountable collection of murder, death, war, mutilation and other violent video games. The door of the devil had been opened wide by his involvement in violence-oriented game media. The door to the devil was also opened by the family's weak faith and inability to establish daily prayers and attend church on Sundays. As a result, they did not put on the armor of God which comes through the reading of the word of God, praying together, attending church on Sundays and filling one's life with the good works of charity. Unfortunately, there is no in-between while putting on the armor of God. It's all or nothing!

Lastly, there has been a lot of speculation about the person of the antichrist. Just as Jesus is the embodiment of Good, so the antichrist is the embodiment of all that is evil. Over the years, there have been conspiracy theories and Sunday armchair quarterbacks who have claimed to have had the antichrist all figured out. In the past, some have insisted that Henry Kissinger and then after him, Barack Obama was the antichrist. Not long ago, the Lord spoke and gave the following indication as to how to identify the antichrist!

On Friday, July 18, 2014, there was an attack of the enemy in a dream. Lord, you spoke in the night, *"The mark of the coming antichrist is that it will be all about him."* You then said, *"This is how to recognize him when he comes."*

Chapter Seventeen

The Second Coming of Christ

UFO of Love

In 1992, what later became to be the *Weather Channel's* senior hurricane expert Bryan Norcross; in the early 90s, he was just achieving stardom for the expert coverage of *Hurricane Andrew.* A life-long Florida resident, Bryan had been working at WPLG, Channel 10 and after his strong coverage of Hurricane Andrew moved to the Miami-based NBC owned station WTVJ, Channel 6 as their Chief Meteorologist. We both shared two things in common in those years. First, in 1992 we were residents of an ultra-modern high-rise built facing Biscayne Bay built by *Carnival Cruise Lines,* Mickey and Ted Arison. Along with *Carnival Cruise Lines, Inc.,* they had also founded the *Hamilton Corporation* which was responsible for the ownership, construction, and operation of a 28-story signature Miami skyline luxury condominium called *"Hamilton on the Bay."* I lived on the 14th floor facing east overlooking *Biscayne Bay.* Bryan Norcross was living on a higher floor, facing east as well. We both had a view of the bay, then off in the distance Miami Beach, and a bit further out the Atlantic Ocean. One balmy evening in the summer of 1992 at about 11 o'clock we both were eye witnesses to a huge, eerie ball of amber light spinning and spiraling across the sky from the ocean, over the bay and nearly crashing into our building. From the wraparound balcony, I could see the object as it passed overhead. Its fiery light projected an enormous shadow of *Hamilton on the Bay* onto the high-rise next door, the *Charter Club*.

After calling *Miami International Airport* tower, the FAA and others in the neighborhood, at that point apparently, no one had seen this enormous and glorious phenomenon but me. However, that is until I called WPLG, Channel 10 at 11:00 pm. My call was answered during their broadcast of the nightly news. The producers answered the phone and revealed they had just received a call from their own Bryan Norcross who was living in the same building, *The Hamilton on the Bay*. He had been an eye-witness to the mysterious object as well. When it traversed overhead, Bryan had observed it on a higher floor from the same vantage point. Right after this strange and eerie event, I began to receive dreams, visions, and warnings about the soon second coming of Christ within our lifetime for many of us who are alive on the earth today. So, regarding this spectacle which some would call a rare encounter with the phenomenon of "ball lightning," I wrote the following message from the Lord in my journal some fifteen years later.

On Thursday, November 15, 2007, the Lord spoke in a vision regarding the strange event that I actually witnessed in the summer night's sky of 1993. He said, *"UFO of Love."* And so, Lord, these signs we see in the heavens that appear to all of us from time to time are postcards from you, letters and messages of love for humankind. Lord, you brought to mind the Scriptures, *"And there will be strange signs in the sun, moon, and stars. And here on earth, the nations will be in turmoil, perplexed by the roaring seas and strange tides."* Luke 21:25

Not many years later, in 1998 I received the first direct message from the Lord in a nighttime vision. At this time, I was extremely busy, as are most professionals working in the business world. I was not thinking about spiritual things at all. In fact, there was no time to do much else but work. Some may relate to my predicament and trap that many career-oriented people find themselves in. Yet, it was at this "unearned" and very unexpected moment in time that Jesus took time from his busy schedule running the universe to appear and speak to me about his soon coming. Here is what he said, "I will return *within* two generations from now."

According to the Bible, historians, collective wisdom and even *Ancestry.com* – in general, we think of a generation being about 25 years from the birth of a parent to the birth of a child. It is also generally accepted that in the Bible the length of a generation in these earlier periods of history was closer to 20 years when humans mated younger, and life expectancies were shorter. Based on this information I began to understand the meaning of the Lord's visitation that night in 1998 and arrive at a "season" for his return, but not knowing the day or the hour. In that regard it is clearly stated by Christ himself, *"However, no one knows the day or hour when these things will happen, not even the angels in heaven or the Son himself. Only the Father knows."* Matthew 24:36

With that said, the key word in the message from 1998 is *"within."* At some point within the time span of 1998 to 2038, forty years later, the Lord will return as king to rule the earth. The prophet Ezekiel famously speaks about that exact coming moment in time when Jesus will physically return to the earth.

"I will take the Israelites out of the nations where they have gone [For they were dispersed throughout the world in 70 A.D. because of a brutal Roman conquest]. I will gather them from all around the world and bring them back into their own land [This actually took place on May 14, 1948, right after WWII when six million Jews had just been exterminated by Hitler and Nazism – Israel became an official nation for the first time since its destruction in 70 A.D.]. I will make them one nation in the land, on the mountains of Israel. There will be one king over all of them, and they will never again be two nations or be divided into two kingdoms. They will no longer defile themselves with their idols and vile images or with any of their offenses, for I will save them from all their sinful backsliding, and I will cleanse them. They will be my people, and I will be their God.

"My servant David will be king over them [This is code for Jesus Christ whom the Gospels have placed his genealogy as being a descendant of the house of David.], and they will all have one shepherd [Jesus said, *"I am the good shepherd."* John 10:11 and 10:14]. They will follow my laws and be careful to keep my decrees. They will live in the land I gave to my servant Jacob, the land where your ancestors lived. They and their children and their children's children will live there forever, and David my servant will be their prince forever. I will make a covenant of peace with them; it will be an everlasting covenant. I will establish them and increase their numbers, and I will put my sanctuary among them forever. My dwelling place will be with them; I will be their God, and they will be my people. Then the nations will know that I the Lord make Israel holy, when my sanctuary is among them forever." Ezekiel 37:21-28

In this chapter, while writing about the two final generations that will most definitely be alive for the return of Christ between the years 1998 and 2038, we also discover that the Blessed Mother is the key person responsible for delivering Jesus the Christ to these two generations. Her responsibilities began at the birth of Christ and were never taken away from her. Once God gives a gift, he does not take it back! Forever this is Mary's gift, her calling, and her vocation; which is to deliver the gift of Christ to each new generation. The Gospel writers tell us that Mary is quoted as saying, *"For he has looked with favor upon his lowly servant. For behold, from this day all generations will call me blessed. The Almighty has done great things for me and holy is his name."* Luke 1:48

On Monday morning, January 7, 2008, Lord, I thank you for this morning's locution where in it, you spoke so simply and yet so profoundly, *"All generations will call her blessed."* Then interiorly, separate from the locution you gave the intimate understanding that *"all generations will call Mary blessed, including the last two generations, the ones living right prior to Jesus Christ's return."*

What makes Mary so unique for the people and times leading up to the return of Christ is not necessarily her "chosenness," although that is in itself quite spectacular! But the most striking fact of all is Mary's response to the angel's proclamation. She does not as Moses did attempt to exempt herself from God's call. She does not ask Him to choose someone else. She wholeheartedly accepts the word of the Angel. She says "Yes!" Mary is blessed above all other women because she reacts in humble obedience: "Behold, I am the handmaid of the Lord; let it be done unto me according to thy word" (Luke 1:38).

So, in a time where living on this earth means to be consumed with "yes" to iPhone, "yes" to chat and messenger and on and on and on until there is no time to say "yes" to God; to proclaim, "yes I will get ready for your second coming!" The two last generations that are alive right now – the Millennials and Generations X/Y will want to reach out to Mary and let her "yes" become their role model and guide in order to be adequately prepared for the Second Coming of Christ.

On Saturday, November 19, 2005, I am notating in my journal that today is my first birthday since encountering the Lord this past September 27th after having had an NDE. This morning while still asleep, I had an out-of-body experience (OBE). Without notice, I found myself in what some would call astral travel while having an OBE. Flying with no effort whatsoever, I crossed the North American continent and navigated the Atlantic Ocean with 747 sky-high views in the time span and flash of only a few seconds. My feet softly touched down in a hallway outside the door of the Sistine Chapel at the Vatican in Rome, Italy. Ever so gently and quietly, I pulled the door open a few inches and observed what appeared to be a global emergency meeting of both Catholic and Protestant leaders. They were in one accord while speaking, collaborating and working in harmony together. This group was not the Catholics and Protestants we remember that were incensed with hate 500 years ago at the time of the Reformation. The pastors and ministers met with the current Pope to discuss an enormous persecution of Christians and their martyrdom that was now rampant throughout the world right prior to Christ's return. It seemed as though the Christian world was in dire straits and they were united to work on solutions together. After getting a better understanding of their meeting and mission, a reverse OBE took place. In the span of only a few seconds, I was once again peacefully at rest in my body which was still lying in bed right where I had left it.

To believe in the physical return of Christ, is not at all so very unusual. The Holy Spirit has been at work educating on the subject both Catholics and Protestants and building awareness ever since the Charismatic Renewal spontaneously erupted like a volcano in 1966 on the campus of Duquesne University in Pittsburgh, Pennsylvania. With that said, Catholics have always proclaimed the Second Coming of Christ each and every day at Mass. Spoken or sung during the Liturgy of the Eucharist, it is affirmed by the congregation, *"We proclaim Your Death, O Lord, and profess Your Resurrection until You come again."* Protestants as well believe. In fact, some groups have even popularized it with bestselling movies and books such as *"Left Behind"* by Dr. Tim LaHaye and Jerry Jenkins. Dr. LaHaye's quick ascension from relative obscurity in the 1980s reflects the remarkable growth in the market for Christian books about this subject over the last 30 years. But for *Bantam Dell* who pays LaHaye "John-Grisham-size" advances, it's also a bet that Dr. LaHaye will grow a larger readership interested in the end times.

In this regard, on the eve of Pope Benedict XIV retirement, right prior to his final day of work I had received a vision in the night about the "end times." Here is what I recorded in my journal.

At about 8:00 am Wednesday, February 27, 2013, right before awakening for the day, Lord you spoke. *"The next pope to be elected in just a few days from now will be under great attack by the enemy. When you see him flee from office and go into hiding, the end will be near."* Then you said, *"I do not know the day or the hour when this will occur, only the Father knows. It could be in a few months or within ten years."*

Again, in March of 2013, another similar message was noted in my journal.

On Monday, March 25, 2013, Lord you spoke at around 1:00 pm as I rested in the afternoon after a long weekend of traveling and serving the homeless. You said, *"The new pope [Francis] must be concerned with two things: First, prayer and second, the Cardinals."* Next, you underscored what you shared previously, this past February, by stating, *"When Pope Francis goes into hiding, the trials of the end-time will unfold rapidly, and then the Christ will return."*

"The Cardinals!" That may surprise you. But, as it was in Jesus' day, there will always be some religious leaders that in their pride, self-righteousness, and power, they will uphold the law over mercy. At this very moment in time, there is a gathering storm in the Church, fueled by conservative cardinals that are challenging Pope Francis over teachings on the family. On Monday, November 14, 2016, Reuters' Vatican writer, Philip Pullella reported, *"four conservative Roman Catholic cardinals made a rare public challenge to Pope Francis over some of his teachings in a major document on the family, accusing him of sowing confusion on important moral issues."* At issue are some of the Francis' teachings in a 260-page treatise called *"Amoris Laetitia"* (*The Joy of Love*), a cornerstone document the pope wrote in an attempt to make the 1.2 billion-member Church more inclusive and less condemning.

In the document, issued in April 2016, he called for a Church that was less strict and more merciful and compassionate towards any *"imperfect"* members, such as those who divorced and remarried, saying *"no one can be condemned forever."* The cardinals are Raymond Leo Burke, an American who was demoted from a senior Vatican position in 2014 and who has often and openly criticized Pope Francis, Germans - Walter Brandmuller and Joachim Meisner, and an Italian Carlo Caffarra.

In their letter, they officially asked the pope to take a stand on five "doubts" they have about some of his pronouncements.

The season of Christ's return has come. We just don't know the day or the hour. That is why he has warned us to be ready. (C.f. *"Therefore you also must be ready, for the Son of Man is coming at an unexpected hour."* Matthew 24:44) As mentioned on page 287, I had received notice that Christ had indicated in a dream his second coming between the years 1998 and 2038. He has always said he does not know the day and the hour, but he does know the season. (C.f. Jesus said: *"From the fig tree learn its lesson: as soon as its branch becomes tender and puts forth its leaves, you know that summer is near. So also, when you see all these things, you know that he is near, at the very gates."* Matthew 24:32-33) However, it was in 2011 that I noted in my journal that although thirteen years had passed, the Lord was now saying that time is imminently winding down. Here is what I wrote.

It's Monday, December 26, 2011. Lord, thank you for the locution in the night. You succinctly said, *"You are half way there."* Then you gave the internal realization that all of time is winding down. The time of human tragedies of WWI, WWII, the holocaust and other calamities is almost over. You will return very soon!

On Monday, October 29, 2012, Hurricane Sandy made landfall on the East Coast just after sunset. According to CNN reports and Encyclopedia Britannica, the historic hurricane caused $62 billion in damage, killing more than 125 people in the U.S. alone and making it the nation's most expensive storm. At its greatest extent, the storm measured more than 900 miles (about 1,450 km) in diameter. Coincidentally, a full moon made high tides 20 percent higher than normal and amplified Sandy's storm surge. At 6:00 am, just eleven hours before Sandy's impact, history was made as part of a "perfect storm" of world events defining the end of times, I had the following dream.

Monday, October 29, 2012, Lord, in a dream right before awakening this morning you showed me a wrist watch that someone had lost, then another watch lost, and another and so on and so forth. Then you gave me to know that the dream was meant to be interpreted as "mankind is at a loss of time." We have reached the proverbial, "end of our rope." There is nothing left. I then prayed you would be merciful and help us to prepare for your soon return by equipping your people with good works and charity for the poor, broken and homeless. This dream took place on the same day Hurricane Sandy, the storm of the century made landfall on the East Coast in the early evening.

The soon return of Christ to the earth is not just for Christians. It's good news for everyone, the entire human race, especially the Jews! Rabbi Simeon bar Yochai (140 CE) was a 2nd-century sage in ancient Israel, said to be active after the destruction of the Second Temple in 70 CE. According to ancient writings, he asks the questions, *"Why was Israel likened to a vineyard? Where* [in Scripture] *is Israel called a vineyard?"* He identifies the verse, *"For the vineyard of the Lord of Hosts is the House of Israel, and the seedlings he lovingly tends are the people of Judah."* Isaiah 5:7

On Thursday, December 5, 2013, during the season of Hanukkah, Lord, you granted a vision in the night of a large gathering of Jews in a huge, modern auditorium. They were singing, clapping and celebrating in their tradition the songs and hymns of Israel. Next, interiorly you gave me to know that *"their eyes will suddenly be opened!"* In these end-times, the Jews will reach a pivotal moment immediately understand that Jesus is the true Messiah. Suddenly, the music stopped! A female reader came forward to the podium and addressed the crowd. She read from the New Testament, Mark chapter 12, the parable of the vineyard.

Jesus began to speak to them in parables: "A man planted a vineyard and put a wall around it, and dug a vat under the wine press and built a tower, and rented it out to vine-growers and went on a journey. At the harvest time, he sent a slave to the vine-growers, in order to receive some of the produce of the vineyard from the vine-growers. They took him, and beat him and sent him away empty-handed. Again, he sent them another slave, and they wounded him in the head and treated him shamefully. And he sent another, and that one they killed; and so, with many others, beating some and killing others. He had one more to send, a beloved son; he sent him last of all to them, saying, *'They will respect my son.'* But those vine-growers said to one another, *'This is the heir; come, let us kill him, and the inheritance will be ours!'* They took him, and killed him and threw him out of the vineyard.

What will the owner of the vineyard do? He will come and destroy the vine-growers and will give the vineyard to others. Have you not read the Scripture?

'The stone which the builders rejected,
This became the chief corner stone;
This came about from the Lord,
And it is marvelous in our eyes.' [Psalm 118:22]

"And they were seeking to seize Him, and yet they feared the people, for they understood that He spoke the parable against them. And so, they left Him and went away." Mark 12:1-12

Next, in my vision, there was a bit of laughter coming from an all-Jewish audience that had just heard how Jesus had confronted the self-righteous Jewish leaders of his day and how he annoyed them, their pride and authority.

What we probably see here when Jesus tells the parable of the vineyard in the Gospel of Mark chapter 12 is an expansion of Isaiah 5:7; a prophetic passage describing Israel as God's vineyard. The workers in the vineyard are in fact the leadership of Israel, the elders who are in charge of the spiritual well-being of God's people. The parable has angered the establishment and is clearly aimed at the leadership of the Jews that have questioned Jesus authority. Now, in these last days, there will come the point in time when his authority will no longer be challenged. There will be the lifting of a two-thousand-year-old veil, eyes are going to be opened, and Jesus will be suddenly recognized as the long-awaited Messiah prophesied 44 times in the writings of the Old Testament.

On Monday, September 21, 2015, Lord you granted an afternoon locution stating, *"Deep down inside, await* [prepare for] *the coming of the Bridegroom."* You left me with an internal sense that your coming is very soon. We are to plan on it and get ready by doing good works of charity for others. Your soon coming coincides with the 100 year anniversary of the Blessed Mother's appearance to the children in Fatima, Portugal (May 1917 – May 2017. Millions of Catholics, Church leaders and Christians are in anticipation of *"Great spiritual events to take place on the earth at the time period of the 100 years' anniversary."*

On Tuesday, May 3, 2016, Lord you granted the following announcement while I was in a twilight liminal state and resting for a brief moment in the early afternoon. You spoke, *"The leader will land on earth* [soon]."

Lastly, for as focused Pope Francis has been on the centrality of the person of God himself – namely his love, mercy, compassion, care for the poor, the broken and homeless; many don't get it. As it was in Jesus' day, today, certain influential leaders, Cardinals, Bishops, Priests, Deacons, and parishioners continue to elevate the law, church rubrics and even the Latin Mass over the giving and living of mercy and love.

Jesus spoke out against this, and it is for this reason he was crucified. The dark original sin of pride promotes interior rhetoric that makes many of us unloving and liable for hellfire: *"I am proud I go to Mass every day, pray the rosary and kneel when I am told, etc., etc. I do everything perfectly. What about all those losers that don't kneel, cheat on their spouse (more than me), support women deacons and go to guitar Mass. How shameful!"* Here is what angered the staunch traditionalists when Jesus spoke in his day.

Then Jesus said to the crowds and to his disciples: "The teachers of the law and the Pharisees sit in Moses' seat. So, you must be careful to do everything they tell you. But do not do what they do, for they do not practice what they preach. They tie up heavy, cumbersome loads and put them on other people's shoulders, but they themselves are not willing to lift a finger to move them.

"Everything they do is done for people to see: They make their phylacteries wide and the tassels on their garments long; they love the place of honor at banquets and the most important seats in the synagogues; they love to be greeted with respect in the marketplaces and to be called 'Rabbi' by others . . . The greatest among you will be your servant. For those who exalt themselves will be humbled, and those who humble themselves will be exalted." Matthew 23:1-12

On Saturday, February 8, 2014, Lord you gave me to know that the Vatican under the leadership of Pope Francis is on the verge of initiating major reforms. Particularly, there will be more of a focus on elevating women into ministry. You indicated that whatever the reforms are, they will radically challenge traditionalists and rock the Catholic Church with the equivalent of a major earthquake. You then spoke, *"When this time comes, the Pope will go into hiding, and the end will be soon after."*

The Bible tells us, "First of all you must understand this, that scoffers will come in the last days with scoffing, following their own passions and saying, *'Where is the promise of his coming? For ever since the fathers fell asleep, all things have continued as they were from the beginning of creation.'"* 2 Peter 3:3-4 Also, in the book of Jude a similar admonishment is made saying, "But you must remember, beloved, the predictions of the apostles of our Lord Jesus Christ; they said to you, *'In the last time there will be scoffers, following their own ungodly passions.'* It is these who set up divisions, worldly people, devoid of the Holy Spirit. But you, beloved, build yourselves up on your most holy faith; pray in the Holy Spirit; keep yourselves in the love of God; wait for the mercy of our Lord Jesus Christ and for eternal life. Convince some, who doubt; save others, by snatching them out of the fire; on some show mercy . . ." 1:17-23

On Thursday, January 24, 2008, Lord you spoke in the night while I slept and you said, *"There will be scoffers."* You gifted an inner awareness that in these last days many people will mock and scoff at any announcement and anyone who sounds the warning alarm of your soon return to earth. It was said by an angel standing on the mountain at the time of your ascension to heaven, *"Men of Galilee, why do you stand looking into heaven? This Jesus, who was taken up from you into heaven, will come in the same way as you saw him go up into heaven."* Acts 1:11 Yet, Lord, many will not be ready! Your Word tells us, "But as to the times and the seasons, brethren, you have no need to have anything written to you. For you, yourselves know well that the day of the Lord will come like a thief in the night. When people say, *'There is peace and security,'* then sudden destruction will come upon them as travail comes upon a woman with child, and there will be no escape. But you are not in darkness, brethren, for that day to surprise you like a thief. For you are all sons of light and sons of the day; we are not of the night or of darkness. So, then let us not sleep, as others do, but let us keep awake and be sober. 1 Thessalonians 5:1-6

In conclusion, this is all so not unusual. The people laughed at Noah too! He built a Royal Caribbean supersized ocean liner, but even odder, he built the ship in a place that had no water. He sounded the alarm in a time and place where there was no physical evidence or indicators to support his claim. It took faith! Unfortunately, only Noah and his family believed.

Now, there is a necessity to embrace watchfulness by all those who call themselves "Christian" and be willing to exercise their faith in Christ. In fact, Jesus asks his followers at all times and in all ages to be awake and vigilant for his soon return. He said, "But of that day and hour no one knows, not even the angels of heaven, nor the Son, but the Father only. But, as it was in the days of Noah, so it will be at the coming of the Son of man. For as in those days before the flood they were eating and drinking, marrying and giving in marriage, until the day when Noah entered the ark, and they did not know until the flood came and swept them all away, so will be the coming of the Son of man." Matthew 24:36-39

Looking to the future, many wonder what will happen immediately after the Lord's return to earth. In that regard, a message was given.

On Saturday, September 13, 2008, Lord, in a vision and locution you revealed that upon your return to earth the martyred saints who labored in particular cities and regions, because of their sacrifice, they will now govern with you the same areas all across the globe where they had been murdered. Also, you stated those on earth at the time of your coming would be "transformed instantly into resurrected bodies." You said, "Miraculously, it will be done smoothly!" Interiorly, you gave me to know that the resurrection process and our new bodies will feel smooth, natural and not shocking or confusing.

Lord, this is reminiscent of the book of Revelation: "Then I saw thrones, and seated on them were those to whom judgment was committed. Also, I saw the souls of those who had been beheaded for their testimony to Jesus and for the word of God, and who had not worshiped the beast or its image and had not received its mark on their foreheads or their hands. They came to life and reigned with Christ a thousand years. The rest of the dead did not come to life until the thousand years were ended. This is the first resurrection. Blessed and holy is he who shares in the first resurrection! Over such the second death has no power, but they shall be priests of God and of Christ, and they shall reign with him a thousand years." Revelation 20:4-6

Chapter Eighteen

Sharing My Story in Photos

Fall 2006, St. John's Seminary, Priest Formation Class Outing

Mother Antonia, the *"Prison Angel"* Speaking at our Retreat, May 2013, Five Months Before She Died and After 30 Years of Prison Ministry in Tijuana, MX

USA Hockey Coach and Referee Certification, Winter 2003

Manager 1982 – 1986
Employee-owned PEOPLExpress Airlines

Fall 1998 Teaching at Penn State University,
State College, PA

New York City, 1994 with Natalee Rosenstein, Senior V.P. Penguin/Putnam/Berkley Launching My Newest Book

Our Struggling and Poor Italian Immigrant Family circa 1920

Grandfather Allessandro Working in a Brickyard Near Pittsburgh, PA circa the early 1900s

Founding Member & Author of *This Bible Talks!*
Pam Fischer

Bishop Kicanas (Diocese of Tucson, AZ) Shares Copies of *This Bible Talks!* From a Grant by *Our Sunday Visitor* (OSV)

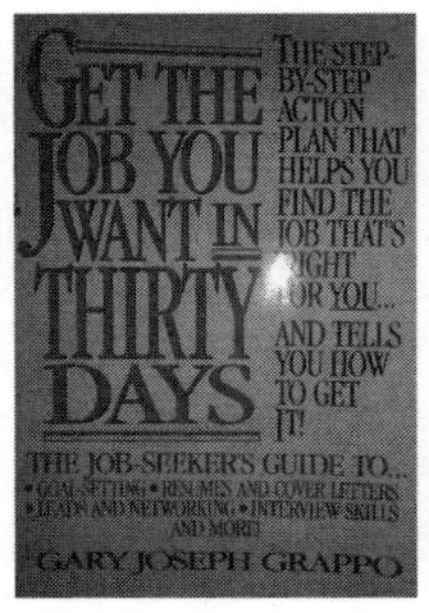

My First Book, *"Get the Job You Want in Thirty Days"* was a Career Bestseller, Published by Penguin/Putnam/Berkley and Republished in Other Languages & Countries

At the *Barron's Educational Books,* I Coauthored the Million + Career Bestseller, *"How to Write Better Resumes."*

Many Career & Business Books were Publishver the Years

Performing Street Theater for las Posadas
December 2006

Worship Leader for a Homeless Prayer Group
December 2007

"Pepper" a Dear Homeless Man We First Served in 2001

Ignacio Lives Under a Los Angeles Bridge Receiving Our Monthly Deliveries of Food, Water, Rosaries, Hygiene Kits & Clothing Since 2001

Since 2008 We Deliver Love, Hugs, Handmade Crafts, and Gifts to the "Homeless" Old Folks in area Nursing Facilities

For Valentine's Day, Our Youth & Families Handcraft *"Love Bugs"* as Gifts for Old Folks in area Care Facilities

In the Fall, Pinecones are Decorated by Our Youth & Families as Gifts for the Elderly and Homeless Fundraisers

Fr. John Neiman our Spiritual Director Standing in front of the Team's New Toyota, Tundra Homeless Supplies Delivery Truck

In July 2016, *Servants of the Father of Mercy* Started to Deliver Bottled Ice Water, Food, Clothing, Rosaries and Hygiene Kits to the Homeless Living in 120 Heat of Desert Palm Springs, CA

"A Homeless Person Without a Bottle of Water in His Hand is a Dead Homeless Person!" Bro. Gary Joseph

Rebecca, Diego, their Parents Enrique and Yanira Involve the Whole Family Serving 80,000 + Homeless in the So Cal Area

The First Edition of *Proof of the Afterlife* was 194 Pages and Published in November of 2010. There were a Number of Printings Over the Years Until it went Out of Print, June 2016. This Second Expanded Edition with 406 Pages Replaced the First and was Published in May of 2017. (Cover design by Kristine Cotterman, *Exodus Design*, Apple Valley, MN)

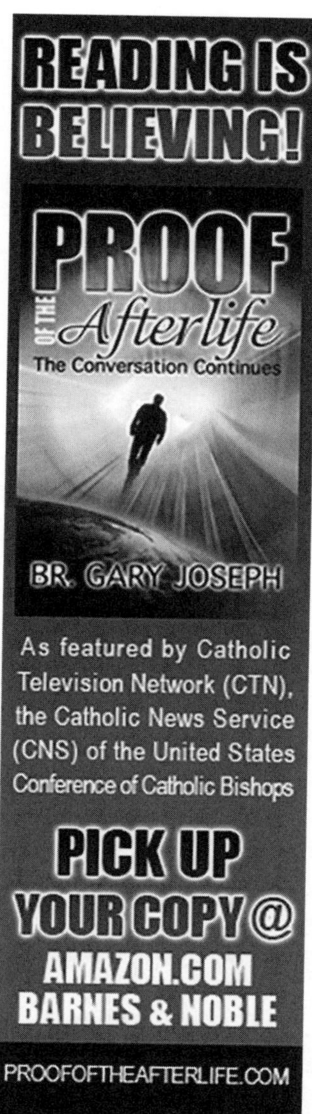

Sample Ad that was Published Over the Years in *Our Sunday Visitor* (OSV), *Priest Magazine, Catechist Magazine* and Many Others.

Our Annual Team Retreat,
Memorial Day Weekend, May 2016

A Homeless "Family" We Serve that Lives Remotely Under a Bridge in Calcutta-like Conditions in Los Angeles

Chapter Nineteen

Dreams, Defeats, Tales and Triumphs

September 26, 2005 NDE "A-FIB!"

The medical doctors had been confused as to why I had the cardiac event that left me thirty minutes dead just weeks after routine thyroid surgery in August of 2005 at Cedars-Sinai, Los Angeles, CA, one of the top hospitals in the country. Now, because of my NDE, I can live to tell the tale. Scientific explanations have been slowly emerging eleven years later. Especially after nearly fifty ER visits over the years in California, South Carolina and Georgia and hundreds of follow-up doctor appointments.

As one ER doctor told me at 3:00 am in the morning in August of 2016 at St. John's Hospital, Camarillo, CA, he said, *"Brother, you have every coronary risk known to man!"* In 2010, endocrinologist, Dr. Nissar Shah, through his compassion, care, and dedicated research, he began to unravel the mystery of my ongoing heart palpitations and arrhythmias that began the night of the NDE, September 26, 2005.

A leading physician on his team, Dr. Leonard-Love discovered first and foremost I had been here-to-for undiagnosed with extremely low vitamin D levels and systemic complications from severe deficiency. This was not something that would ever have been easily discovered in hospitals even after 100s of ER visits. Months later, the vitamin D condition was identified as being the result of having *Secondary Hyperparathyroidism*.

Then in 2014, Dr. Shah had been tracking the remaining left thyroid gland levels and discovered I should have been placed on Synthroid back in August 2005 after the surgeon performed a right-side thyroidectomy. Unknown to everyone, I had been living years with an underactive thyroid known as *Hypothyroidism* which causes a lot of negative bodily and cardiac symptoms. It becomes even worse when combined with *Secondary Hyperparathyroidism.* Of course, truth be told, this is after years of many other physicians like Dr. X and Dr. Y of the Santa Paula, CA clinic who from 2005-2010 insisted it was all in my head. So, at that time there was little to no follow-up of the primary core health issues.

But, thanks be to God for Dr. Shah who in 2013 identified the mounting symptoms and weight gain issues as a result of untreated *Hypothyroidism*. Being overweight escalated into two other conditions making matters worse. Dr. Shah identified *Type II Diabetes and High Blood Pressure.*

In 2015, my primary care physician, Dr. Shawram Fatemi of *St. John's Dignity Healthcare* aggressively pursued my symptoms of full-body joint pain, muscle weakness, burning lower back and hip pain. I could not walk from the parking lot to the door of a grocery store without sitting down on someone's car bumper! However, it had all been sacked for years by Doctors X and Y. In their mind, it was just a little routine osteoarthritis. But, after Dr. Fatemi took over, he rescued my overall care from a stall and sent me forward to see a rheumatologist. The doctor initiated blood tests and lower back/hip x-rays which identified moderate bone loss and fusion of the spine, better known as *Ankylosing Spondylitis*. Seeing the rheumatologist for a few years now, she said it would not be surprising if we eventually uncover other issues at play, probably *Rheumatoid Arthritis, Chronic Fatigue Syndrome* and/or *Fibro Myalgia*.

In 2005, it was not absolutely clear to me, my doctors and for that matter, some of the book readers, how a person could have a heart attack just a few weeks after a routine thyroidectomy. Well, providentially, *Loyola University Medical Center* published a study regarding this exact question on May 19, 2015, and is available at Medicalxpress.com. Through their research, they discovered that after any surgery, atrial fibrillation increases, including the risk of heart attacks and strokes. Up to 12 percent of patients undergoing major, non-cardiac surgery experience an irregular heartbeat called atrial fibrillation within the first 12 months of surgery.

Postoperative atrial fibrillation (POAF) often is dismissed by doctors as a transient phenomenon. But a *Loyola University Medical Center* study has found that POAF can significantly increase the risk of heart attack or stroke during the first year.

The *Loyola University Medical Center* study issued a firm warning about the phenomenon that I had experienced the night of September 26, 2005. Unfortunately for me, it was discovered and announced ten years after my NDE experience. The writers of the study state, *"Physicians should be vigilant in assessing postoperative atrial fibrillation, even when transient, and establish appropriate follow-up, given the increased risk of cardiovascular morbidity,"* (First author Robert Blackwell, MD, senior author Gopal Gupta, MD, and colleagues.)

In hindsight, my NDE experience was triggered by what is now known as atrial fibrillation, also known as A-fib, (so, pun intended, as some naysayers have indicated, my NDE testimony is *not* "A FIB!") which is an irregular and often rapid heartbeat that can cause poor blood flow to the heart and entire body. In my case, it came on suddenly and as I had stated before there was no time to call 911.

Along with the scientific and medical evidence all supporting my NDE, the subsequent events that followed are substantial and corroborate a genuine God-encounter. We know for a fact the Bible teaches us that "God is Love." Therefore, anyone who has had a genuine encounter with God should be inspired by loving qualities. Certainly, that is what happened in my situation. A ministry to the homeless was born out of my NDE along with serving elderly in nursing facilities, children, youth, and families. Here is what the Bible has to say about people who claim to know God.

"Beloved, let us love one another, for love is from God, and whoever loves has been born of God and knows God. Anyone who does not love does not know God, because God is love. In this, the love of God was made manifest among us, that God sent his only Son into the world so that we might live through him. In this is love, not that we have loved God but that he loved us and sent his Son to be the propitiation for our sins. Beloved, if God so loved us, we also ought to love one another. No one has ever seen God; if we love one another, God abides in us and is perfect in us.

"By this, we know that we abide in him and he in us because he has given us of his Spirit. And we have seen and testify that the Father has sent his Son to be the Savior of the world. Whoever confesses that Jesus is the Son of God, God abides in him, and he in God. So, we have come to know and to believe the love that God has for us. God is love, and whoever abides in love abides in God, and God abides in him. By this is love perfected with us, so that we may have confidence for the day of judgment, because as he is so also are we in this world. There is no fear in love, but perfect love casts out fear. For fear has to do with punishment, and whoever fears has not been perfected in love. We love because he first loved us. If anyone says, *'I love God,'* and hates his brother, he is a liar; for he who does not love his brother whom he has seen cannot love God whom he has not seen. And this commandment we have from him: whoever loves God must also love his brother." 1 John 4:7-21

Therefore, if my testimony is real, authentic and genuine, then the message of this book is that the Church and its individual members need to be less of a courtroom of judges and more of a hospital filled with compassionate doctors and nurses. Leave the judging up to God; we ought to be serving one another and doing nothing else.

Brother Mel and Brother Mic

In April and May of 2008, I was a part-time volunteer helping Brother Mel and Brother Mic (not their real names) host various types of church-related meetings, lunches, dinners and guests at their "home" in Los Angeles. For being a volunteer, the job was demanding at times. The brothers ran a tight ship, and that was to be admired and respected. They never had any complaints about my quality of work ranging from gardening and pool maintenance to meals preparation and cleanup. One day while working on a large packing project in the house, Brother Mel asked if I could bring over extra volunteer helpers. The next day I arrived with two friends who were seniors but able-bodied. At 11:00 am we took Brother Mel in our car to do some shopping. My two friends asked if we could also stop a moment at CVS to pick up their prescriptions, roughly in the same neighborhood. Brother Mel emphatically said, "No!" He insisted, *"I want to go home right now."* Two minutes later, without saying a word, I turned the car into the CVS parking lot. My friends went in for their prescriptions. Well, if looks could kill, Brother Mel was fuming. With the car windows rolled up, he went into a tirade saying, *"All you think about is yourself! You don't care about what I want.* (It looked like he was going to have a heart attack.) *I want to go home right now, and I hope I never see you again."* I guess at this point receiving a *"thank you"* for all the volunteering I had done, was out of the question. So, remaining silent, (the Bible tells us *"Jesus remained silent."* Matthew 26:63) I drove Brother Mel home and never saw him again. That is until the following God-smack took place about thirty days later.

On Friday, June 27, 2008, I had been visiting my mom in Myrtle Beach, SC for nearly a month. At the beginning of June, a road-trip had taken me from Los Angeles, Santa Monica Beach on the Pacific coast, across I-10 to Birmingham, Alabama and then north to Myrtle Beach along the Atlantic coast. However, today, sadly our visit is over. It's time to begin the long drive back to Los Angeles. Initially, I had intercepted I-40 near the U.S. Navy base in Wilmington, North Carolina and drove across east toward Ashville, North Carolina and on to Knoxville and Memphis, Tennessee. On Saturday and Sunday, I passed through Little Rock, Arkansas, Oklahoma City, Oklahoma and on to Texas. Then on Monday morning, I left a motel in Amarillo, Texas unusually early. The drive began at 7:00 am sharp with no time for a shower or to even indulge in a cup of coffee or some Texas French toast. Later, in need of fuel and coffee; at about 8:00 am I had decided to stop at a small gas station nestled in the middle of nowhere in the tumbleweeds of western Texas.

First things first, after parking the car, I knocked on a locked men's bathroom door in the gift shop. A man gruffly shouted through the door, *"Can't you see there's someone in here!"* So, whiling away the minutes, I browsed through the station's dusty shelves filled with miniature teepees, quartz rocks, fool's gold and country humor refrigerator magnets. Then, I heard the toilet flush a few times. Thanks, be to God, my turn was coming! But, when the men's room door opened, I nearly peed my pants right there standing in the gift shop. Out walked Brother Mel, all the way from Los Angeles, zipping up his pants in the middle of nowhere-USA. He looked as though he had seen a ghost too. Brother

Mic walked into the gas station at the very same moment. After exchanging brief pleasantries, I went into the bathroom and locked the door. I thought to myself, *"What just happened here? What is God saying? What are the possibilities of this encounter?"* My mind raced, *"After driving nearly 8,000 across the United States, I run into the same two brothers from Los Angeles. It's like a Star Trek sci-fi moment. These two men have suddenly beamed down and are here to torment me in the tumbleweeds of Texas! How could this happen?"* Soon, disbelief turned to belief. I had to have faith and then said to myself, *"There is a God!"*

Photos Taken Monday, June 30, 2008,
8:30 am at a Remote Highway Exit in Texas where
Unexpectedly I Rendezvoused with
Los Angeles-based Brothers Mel and Mic

What is the lesson here? In hindsight, remaining quiet in the car at CVS when berated for doing good for others is for me a constant reminder that "suffering in silence" makes way for the justice of God, in due time, to speak loudly. A teaching written by the apostle Peter comes to mind that substantiates this is difficult for us mortal humans, but never-the-less an important spiritual principle for all to learn and follow. Peter states, *"But if when you do right and suffer for it, you take it patiently, you have God's approval. For to this, you have been called, because Christ also suffered for you, leaving you an example, that you should follow in his steps. He committed no sin; no guile was found on his lips. When he was reviled, he did not revile in return; when he suffered, he did not threaten; but he trusted to him who judges justly."* 1 Peter 2:20-23

Therefore, let us always be inspired by the fact Jesus suffered in silence. He left us the example speaking no words is better than many words. *"In a multitude of words, you shall not avoid sin."* Proverbs 10:19 *"Let every man be swift to hear and slow to speak."* James 1:19 *"Of every idle word a man speaks, he shall give an account on the day of judgment."* Matthew 12:36

Sundry Dreams, Visions & Locutions

Lord, on Thursday, September 13, 2007, you spoke during the night, *"I will be faithful to those who show mercy."* Thank you Lord for the promise of support and faithfulness toward all those Christian and non-Christian who are genuinely merciful toward others – the sick, weak and dying.

On Friday, December 21, 2007, Lord, you spoke in the morning right before I woke up saying, *"The end of all things is at hand."*

Lord, on Tuesday, March 4, 2008, you spoke in the morning hours just before I awoke and said, *"Everything I am telling you will happen in your lifetime."* Interiorly, you gave me to know that the many messages you have spoken regarding your return will take place soon.

Monday, August 26, 2008, at about 7:00 am, you spoke in your own voice and said, *"both at once the shortest and the tallest building in the world."* Next, you granted a vision of a small open cave at the top of a very high mountain. Thus, it is both at once the shortest and the tallest building in the world. Interiorly, you gave me to know and understand the meaning of the riddle. What is both the shortest and tallest building in the world? It is humility! Through humility, we become both the smallest and tallest temples of the Holy Spirit in the world.

Thursday, September 11, 2008, Lord you spoke in the early morning hours saying the most amazing words, *"The King loves the poor."*

On Saturday, October 11, 2008, Lord, throughout the night, over and over I heard a single word, "Gibbs." (For many years I waited. There seemed to be no clue as to what it meant.) [Now, in hindsight as I write the book, *Proof of the Afterlife 2,* I realize "Gibbs" is a prophesy granted six years ago predicting what we do now – namely, we have been serving weekly hot meals, snacks and water since January 2014 – 2017, helping a ten-year chronically homeless father and son, Rick and Cody Gibbs (photos). We immediately met them while they slept out in a late-model truck upon moving into our ministry's new warehouse in Ventura, CA, February 2014.]

Rick Gibbs (above), and son Cody Celebrating a Newborn Daughter, Brook Lynn Gibbs in May 2016

On Monday, October 27, 2008 the Lord spoke in the early hours of the morning and said, *"First Christian unity, and then the end."*

Thursday, May 7, 2009, Lord, you spoke in the night with

an admonishment, *"Just serve the poor!"* You gave an interior awareness that we are to concentrate on serving the poor homeless. Avoid distractions and diversions. Stay focused!

The Lord spoke the following on Tuesday, June 24, 2009, saying, *"The sign of the Son of Man will be seen all over the earth."* Then, he granted a strong interior awareness that the sign is the cross and it will appear in the sky for many days so that everyone on the earth will see it. Yet, some hearts will be so hard and cold that they will deny its image and implications. Lord, in your Word you spoke, *"And I, if I am lifted up from the earth, I will draw all men to Myself."* John 12:32

Monday, November 9, 2009, Lord, you spoke in the morning right before awakening and said, *"I associated with misfits, and I would like you to go and do the same. Go, associate with misfits."* Fr. F. my spiritual director today also confirmed this message. He suggested that I meditate on the fact that Jesus indeed did associate with misfits. Examples would be *"the woman at the well"* (C.f. John 4:7) who was a Samaritan and had five 5 husbands, *"the adulterous woman"* (C.f. John 8:1) who was nearly stoned to death for her extramarital affairs, Zacchaeus, a midget (C.f. Luke 19:1), Matthew, a tax collector (C.f. Matthew 9:9) and Peter, an uneducated fisherman (C.f. Matthew 4:18), just to mention a few.

Ben Affleck

In October of 2009, on a Sunday, apparently, I was seated right next to Ben Affleck working incognito in Ventura, California, Starbucks on Main Street in downtown. I was working for the homeless ministry on my laptop at a café that I had never visited before. It was very crowded in the early afternoon. There was almost nowhere to sit. However, this man right next to me had a ski hat pulled down low, nearly to the nose. He was crafting some sort of movie script with a paper pad and pen. Every now and again he would look over at me, check out the Christian cross and shield on my t-shirt and offer a brief nod, hello or smile. I went home and prayed for him the next couple of days. It definitely looked like Ben Affleck. But that was not the end of that encounter.

On Friday, December 11, 2009, Lord, you came to me this morning and reminded me of the encounter I had one Sunday in October and the apparent serendipitous meeting with Ben Affleck. This morning before waking you said, *"Ben left Hollywood that day and came to a Ventura café because he was looking to be around 'regular' people."* Lord, you also said, *"deep in his heart Ben is looking for the truth."* Luckily, when he glanced over at me that day, he saw the cross and shield, a testimony to the person who said, *"I am the way, the truth and the life."* C.f. John 14:6 Now praying for him since that time.

Snowmageddon

On Sunday, June 6, 2010, and in the heat of summer, the Lord granted a prophecy in the night. He spoke the words, *"Blizzard of the Century [is coming]!"* Interiorly, he gave me to know that the snow storm will be catastrophic and will descend well into Atlanta, the deep South and parts of California too. (Six months later in December 2010 as well as bridging over to January and February of 2011, the northeast was hit with blizzards and snow accumulation, the most ever known since records began to be kept more than one hundred years ago. Atlanta and other parts of the South received record cold and snow, typically unknown and extremely rare for the region.

In hindsight, the media reported the December 2010 North American blizzard was a significant nor'easter and historic snowfall affecting the Contiguous United States and portions of Canada from December 5–29, 2010. From January 4–15, the system was known as Windstorm Benjamin in Europe. It was the first significant winter storm of the 2010–11 North American winter storm season and the fifth North American blizzard of 2010. The storm system affected the northeast megalopolis, which includes major cities such as Norfolk, Philadelphia, Newark, New York City, Hartford, Providence, and Boston. The storm brought between 12 to 32 inches (30 and 81 cm) of snow in many of these areas.

To add insult to injury, the summertime prophecy was fulfilled a second time when on January 25–27, 2011 a North American blizzard was a major Mid-Atlantic nor'easter and winter storm, and a New England blizzard that affected many parts of the northeastern United States and Canada. The storm came just two weeks after a previous major blizzard had already affected most of the same areas earlier in the same month of January. The storm also came just one month after a previous major blizzard that affected the entire area after Christmas in December 2010. This storm was the third significant snowstorm to affect the region during the 2010–11 North American winter storm season. It was followed a few days later by another massive storm that also blanketed much of the United States and Canada. The infamous "Snowmageddon" was part of this season with the total of U.S. damages in the billions of dollars.

Are we saved by grace, by faith, by works or by all three? If anyone can answer that one, Martin Luther would roll over in his grave! That is what this next God-encounter speaks about - shared in the first book but worth repeating!

Saturday, July 10, 2010, Lord, thank you for the vision this morning where in it I saw a perfect large circle drawn on a parking lot. At the top of the circle were written the words, *"salvation by faith."* Then I heard the Lord say, *"Go! Walk around the circle with your works of mercy, compassion, and kindness."* He then inquired, *"Where does it bring you back to?"* Jesus responded, *"It brings you back to 'salvation by faith' doesn't it?"* Lord, you illustrated quite simply your complete plan for our salvation. It's a reminder and confirmation of similar lessons from the letter of James when he states, *"You see that a person is justified by what he does and not by faith alone."* James 2:24

Book Reader Having a Heart Attack

With the Lord, he is always full of surprises, and one never knows in his infinite wisdom what is going to happen next. One such surprise took place the night of Thursday, February 24, 2011, when a man appeared to me in my bedroom at around 4:00 am. He identified himself by saying, *"I am one of the first book readers."* With that information, I assumed he was from the time period of when *"Proof of the Afterlife"* was initially published and launched in November 2010. The man needed prayer! He spoke and said, *"I am in the hospital's ER and having a heart attack."* My response was, *"I will pray for you!"* Miraculously, the spirit took over, and I began to pray for him in my sleep. The following morning and in the days that followed, we offered more prayers for him at the *Servants of the Father of Mercy* team prayer chapel.

Servants of the Father of Mercy Team Prayer Chapel, September 30, 2016

On Friday, March 18, 2011, Jesus, you spoke in the night about the book, *"Proof of the Afterlife."* In a soft voice filled with intrigue, you sweetly said, *"The book you wrote, it's odd, but it sure is beautiful!"* Lord, thank you for the encouragement!

Ian's Story

People are always in need of prayer. That is why the Bible tells us to "pray without ceasing." C.f. 1 Thessalonians On Thursday, April 14, 2011, at approximately 8:00 am an ambulance siren startled me awake. Sitting up in bed, the emergency vehicle was quickly getting ready to pass just feet from my bedroom window in what is usually a very quiet and peaceful residential neighborhood. What happened next is even more astonishing. In an instant, a voice filled the bedroom, and I could see and feel as if I was sitting in the back of the ambulance as part of the crew. The patient was a young boy, and the paramedics were tending to him. Next, I heard the lead technician address the child. He said, *"Ian, the doctor is waiting for you. He will see you immediately when we arrive."* Next, the ambulance's siren blasted by the house and up the street until gradually fading in the morning's light. Quite naturally, my body and presence returned to focus inside the four walls of my bedroom. Without delay, I began to pray for a little boy urgently on his way to the hospital by the name of Ian.

Glitter and Gold

On Good Friday, April 21, 2011, at about 4:30 am, the Lord once again reminded us that the actual gold in our life is our works of charity for the poor, homeless, sick and dying. When he was here on earth, he told his disciples, *"Do not lay up for yourselves treasures on earth, where moth and rust consume and where thieves break in and steal, but lay up for yourselves treasures in heaven, where neither moth nor rust consumes and where thieves do not break in and steal. For where your treasure is, there will your heart be also."* Matthew 6:19-21

So, on this particular morning, the Lord made it his mission to talk more about "true gold." First, he woke me up out of a dead sleep and gave me a BIG hug. There was an interior bathing, and a saturation of his immense love that seemed to say, *"I accept you as you are and don't care about your failures or weaknesses."* There is only one person that can make you feel that way. Immediately, I knew who was in my room hugging me! Hugging him back, I said, *"Jesus, I trust in you! Only you and the Father can heal me. Jesus, I trust in you."* Then quite spontaneously and humorously the Lord responded back and said, *"You are loved way more than you are a stick [in the mud]."* I laughed, smiled while filled with his joy and peace. The Lord repeatedly kissed and hugged me.

But just when I thought he was getting ready to depart and take leave from this surprise magical gift encounter, he had a message. But let me back up a minute. Just four months ago from around Thanksgiving in 2010 when the first book was published through to Christmastime, perfect strangers, adults and children alike began to make odd comments to me about seeing gold glitter on my face and hands. I had never heard of this phenomenon before. I had no idea what they were talking about. However, one day in

December, a woman took her handkerchief and wiped my face showing the gold on the cloth. We then noticed it was on the hands too. Others observed strange signs at the November 2010 book signing that had eighty guests in attendance. A young child seated in the front and a teenager seated near the back, children that do not know each other had told their parents about seeing a blinding light from behind as I spoke on the auditorium stage while giving a one-hour presentation of the book's testimony.

So, now it is Good Friday, April 21, 2011, and I've just been awakened by the Lord. But, right before leaving he said, *"Remember the gold glitter that lightly filled your hands at Christmastime?"* I replied, *"Yes Lord, I remember."* He then sweetly and romantically inquired, *"Guess who put it there?"* Enthusiastically, like getting the right answer on Jeopardy, I responded, *"You!"* He smiled. In an instant, he was gone, but before departing, he said, *"Look now at your hands now! They are filled with the gold glitter [of charity]."* It was at this time that the *Servants of the Father of Mercy,* which was born out of my near-death experience was rapidly growing. We were expanding beyond serving the homeless in Los Angeles. New team members like Mark Burke, Michael Valencia, and Craig Palm began to help coordinate care for 80,000 + homeless in the region focusing on the Anaheim/Disneyland area and other team members like Angela and Henry Chavez organized helping the homeless in Ventura County.

Yves

Similar to the "Gibbs" revelation mentioned earlier in this chapter, a parallel event happened on Thursday, July 28, 2011. While sleeping in the night, many times over I heard the name, *"Yves."* Upon awakening, I had no idea whatsoever what it meant. However, there is a St. Yves of Kermartin (October 17, 1253 – May 19, 1303) who was known for his extraordinary care and concern for the poor and who is also the patron saint of abandoned children. I thought, okay, possibly this is the meaning since we also serve the poor homeless. The "Yves" event was recorded in my journal, and I never thought much more about it. Like "Gibbs" I had to learn to accept the unknown and for many years at that! Similarly, the Bible tells us, *"Mary pondered all these things in her heart."* Luke 2:19

Then, in the winter/spring of 2013, I was contacted by Petra and Hans Kusters-Verstraten in Venlo, Holland, the adult children of the Verstraten family that my dad and other American troops had liberated their southern region from the Nazis in World War II. Since 1945 our families have affectionately grown up together. The Verstratens are called, "our Dutch family." Petra and Hans wanted me to know that their teenage son Yves will be in the U.S. for a few months at *Bowling Green University* participating in an English studies and engineering internship. He was planning to come to California to meet me, his "American family" at the end of May. Immediately, I thought to myself, *"Is this the 'Yves' spoken of in my journal?"* It did not seem to make sense, so I dismissed it again. That is until the day Yves arrived. After taking some delays with college friends while driving across the U.S. and stopping in Las Vegas, he revised our meeting date a few times. The actual day he drove into town and we finally met for the first time was May 19, 2013, the feast of St. Yves! So, now because of Divine intervention, I have adopted Yves, another family member onto my prayer list.

Yves Kusters-Verstraten Ski Holidays in Switzerland with His Girlfriend, December 2015

Tuesday, November 8, 2011, Lord, thank you for the vision right before waking this morning. In it, I saw a person kneeling at communion time. With all remorse and sincerity, he said, *"Lord I am not worthy to receive you, but only say the word, and I shall be healed."* Then, you said, *"The kingdom of heaven is not about being perfect but about humility."* I understand that it is your will that we learn to put aside human pride, acknowledge our sin and the actual reality of our broken condition. Sadly, you said, *"Some people refuse to say this prayer at communion because they disagree with it."* Lord, many believe now in our modern culture of high self-esteem, to be proud of one's accomplishments and they think this prayer of humility is obsolete. The contemporary goal is to instill pride, self-worth, and self-acceptance in our children and all our lives. Your Word has said, *"So you also, when you have done everything you were told to do, should say, 'We are unworthy servants; we have only done our duty.'"* Luke 17: 10 And again it says, *"For in sacrifice you take no delight, burnt offering from me you would refuse, my sacrifice, a contrite spirit. A humbled, contrite heart you will not spurn."* Psalm 51: 16-17

Maquerading as a Homless Person

Not all dreams and visions are from the Lord. There is a famous story about St. Padre Pio in this regard. One day he returned to his monastery cell after saying the morning Mass. When he opened the bedroom door, his spiritual director was seated in a chair next to the window. Padre Pio, utilizing the gift of discernment of spirits, realized he has never met with his spiritual advisor in this part of the monastery. He asked the man to speak. Declare, *"Jesus is Lord!"* said Padre Pio. He refused and then disappeared. Clearly, the enemy can and has masqueraded as others, including Jesus and the Blessed Mother.

In the early morning hours of Wednesday, January 18, 2012, the Lord granted the gift of discernment of spirits. A man appeared to me lying on the floor of my bedroom completely wrapped in a dirty blanket from head to toe, looking exactly like a poor, tattered and destitute homeless person. *I said to him, "Let's take the blanket off your face so we can see who you are."* I was suspicious because he wrestled to keep his face covered. After struggling to get the blanket off, it was clearly apparent that he was the enemy posing as a homeless person. I always keep a small bottle of holy water in the bedroom. Taking the water in hand, I exclaimed, *"Here let's anoint your head, your face and your hands with the sign of the cross!"* Then devoutly I said, *"I bless you in the name of the Father, the Son, and the Holy Spirit. Amen."* At that pronouncement, he twisted, turned, squirmed and resisted the unwanted holy shower. He immediately disappeared.

Shark Attack

Another unwanted attack by the enemy took place on Wednesday, March 14, 2012. At about 4:00 am I was alarmed by a dream featuring an aggressive animal with a blood-thirsty jaw and teeth was after me. However, instead of running, I boldly flipped the tables on the aggressor. Turning around, I confronted the animal right to its face, saying, *"In the name of Jesus" you must stop!"* Now the evil one was placed on the defensive. But the closer I got to his face, the more he would back away. Then, in an unexpected turn of events, he took off his animal mask and said to me, *"Brother Gary, this is Mike Applebee* (not real name), *an attorney from Ventura, California."* In shock, I replied, *"Who are you?"* Then I demanded, *"Spell it! Spell your last name."* He mumbled, *"A-p-p-l-e-b-e-e."* I then responded, *"Why were you haunting me like this?"* His reply was classic. He exclaimed, *"The devil made me do it!"* Mike continued, *"Just so you know, someone came to the legal offices of Mike Applebee recently and wanted to sue you. I refused because it was frivolous. Also, there was no money in it."* I replied, *"Mike, thank you for not doing it."* Then, I placed my arm around him and told this shark of an attorney Mike Applebee the following and totally unexpected words, *"Look, Mike, I love you very much. You are my brother in Christ. I am going to pray for you to find peace in the Lord."*

The rest of the night as I slept, I made a note in my head of how to spell this attorney's last name – over and over, *"A-p-p-l-e-b-e-e."* Upon awakening, the first order of business was to check and see if there is in actuality an attorney by the name of Mike Applebee working in Ventura, California. To my amazement there absolutely is an attorney with a law office operating here under that name. He has been practicing law in the region for more than ten years.

On Tuesday, March 15, 2012, in the morning, right before awakening, I received a dream where in it the Blessed Mother appeared. She is amazingly beautiful! Her hair is golden brown, and she had clear and beautiful skin. She looked about thirty to thirty-five years old. The Blessed Mother is so very kind, personal and caring. Meeting her was if she had known me forever. As she held me in her arms, we prayed the "Hail Mary" together. After praying, she said, *"I never noticed before the two chains you are wearing around your neck."* She inquired, *"When did you start wearing those?"* I explained that all my life I never really liked to wear things around my neck. Then, recently, I said, *"At the time of my mom's funeral in February of 2010."* The Blessed

Mother interjected, *"Yes I was there. It was so very beautiful."* I replied, *"I tried to make it beautiful."* Then I continued by saying, *"It was at that time that mom wanted to be buried with this cross, the one that I am wearing now. As you can see, it is gold and with a few small diamonds in it. However, she had been wearing it every day since the 1960s. I thought it would be an excellent memory for me to have and wear it."* She nodded with approval. Then I said, *"My mom is wearing my cross."* As the Blessed Mother held me, we prayed one more "Hail Mary" together and then the dream was over. The other chain that I was wearing but did not have a chance to tell her about was my dad's. It's a small medallion of just the face of the crucified Christ that he had worn on D-Day at Normandy, France and subsequently all through World War II.

Ten-Foot-Angel

On Tuesday, March 20, 2012, at about 9:00 pm I had set out for the grocery store dressed super casual – wearing black sweatpants, a black t-shirt, and sneakers. With not many people around, it was a quiet evening at our neighborhood Albertsons (recently merged with Safeway/Vons). After quickly and smoothly checking out at the full-service lane, I slowly walked to the front doors carrying two bags of groceries. Suddenly, I see a middle-aged woman hurriedly walking toward me from the baking aisle located in the middle of the store. She is smiling, waving her hand and shouting, *"Wait! Wait!"* I think to myself, *"Who is this lady? I've never met her before."* What she says next has me pondering her words for years to come. The woman exclaims, *"Don't leave yet! You have an angel following behind you. He's ten feet tall!"* Caught by surprise, I laughed and said to her with astonishment, *"Thank you for sharing that!"*

For whatever reasons, she was given a gift to see the supernatural. She can see spiritual realities that most of us, myself included do not have access to, especially in mundane places like a grocery store.

Hosanna in the Highest

While reflecting on Palm Sunday at Mass and during prayer time today, April 1, 2012, the people's cry, *"Hosanna in the Highest!"* rang out in my head all day long. Obviously, "Hosanna!" expressed the joy they felt for Jesus, the one who would soon become their earthly king. In their minds, Jesus, with all his miracles, power and charisma had the authority and control to free the people from the Roman Empire's occupation, brutality, and tyranny.

Yet, Jesus disappointed the people a few days later when he walked the road to suffering and execution. He did not have the right stuff, so they deserted him, shouting "Crucify him!" But, who knew that the road to power was through brokenness, humility, and crucifixion. They did know it. We do not know it. It is no human in our thinking. Yes, the Lord was lifted up as a prophet, but exalted on a cross? How queer! It was certainly a different type of kingship, a different way of being high and mighty. Jesus' way is totally unlike the kings, royals and influential people of the world.

And so, the thoughts of kingship continue Easter Sunday, April 8, 2012. The original sin of pride was sold by the serpent in the Garden of Eden to Adam and Eve. In *"De Civitate Dei,"* St. Augustine's view of this evil act of disobedience was preceded by an evil will be derived from pride, a craving for "undue exultation." The book of Genesis gives us this account of how the evil will of human pride entered our race. In fact, the same pride that made the angels fall from heaven got passed on to us. The Bible says in Genesis.

"Now the serpent was craftier than any of the wild animals the Lord God had made. He said to the woman, *"Did God really say, 'You must not eat from any tree in the garden?'* The woman said to the serpent, *'We may eat fruit from the trees in the garden, but God did say, 'You must not eat fruit from the tree that is in the middle of the garden, and you must not touch it, or you will die.'"*

"'You will not certainly die,' the serpent said to the woman. 'For God knows that when you eat from it, your eyes will be opened, and you will be like God, knowing good and evil.'" Genesis 3:1-5

And so, the Lord turned the original sin of pride upside-down and inside out by exemplifying humility in his suffering, passion, death and resurrection. Jesus showed us that the power of humbleness is the cure for the perceived power of pride. Christ, singlehandedly redeemed all of humankind from the sin of pride, haughtiness, and arrogance which had separated us from God and from each other. It had made us enemies of one another and enemies of God.

Because Jesus took the low road when he did not have to, therefore, God has highly exalted him and bestowed on him the name that is above every other name. C.f. Philippians 2:9-11 Through his life, death, and resurrection, the Lord Jesus defined a new power. He showed that supremacy does not come from muscle and brawn, but is born out of love, servitude, humility and brokenness.

On Sunday, January 13, 2013, at about 4:00 am, Lord, you granted a vision of my cousin Mike, Kim's (see chapter 6, *"Cousin Kim"*) brother who is still alive, came to me while I slept and said, *"My brother Bob has had a somewhat sedentary lifestyle lately. More than likely he has clogged arteries and is at risk of having a heart attack."* Mike then asked, *"Would you please pray for him?"* In January of 2013, I began to pray for my cousin Bob as requested. Then, on the afternoon of March 1, 2016, at his own home, Bob suddenly died of a heart attack, just as his brother Mike had alerted, requesting prayers for him in the vision granted on January 13, 2013.

Also on the same day as above, Sunday, January 13, 2013, Lord, in a dream this morning, suddenly I felt as though with your help I could fly. Indeed, that is what happened. I leaped from the ground, and I was flying high above churches, buildings and the people that witnessed it were jealous. Then Lord, you said apologetically for my gift, "It's the law of mercy!" It was here that you reminded me that the "law of mercy" is the "law of freedom." (*"Speak and act as those who are going to be judged by the law of freedom, because judgment without mercy will be shown to anyone who has not been merciful. Yet, mercy triumphs over judgment."* James 2:12-13)

Catherine de Hueck Doherty (1896-1985) is a Russian-born aristocrat who has recently been proposed for canonization. She emigrated to North America and was a Roman Catholic social worker and foundress of the Madonna House Apostolate, a community serving the poor. Here is a short story she is famous for telling about the "law of mercy."

The Butler Announced, *"Christ is at the Door!"*

by Catherine de Hueck Doherty

"When I was growing up in Russia, my father was a diplomat. One time he and my mother gave a big, fancy tea party at our home for several hundred ambassadors and dignitaries. We were in the middle of having formal tea, with everyone using nice china and so forth. I was about nine years old at the time, and I was allowed to be there, all dressed up and carrying little cakes and being polite. Suddenly, the butler opened the door and announced to my father, *"Christ is at the door."* Well, the French ambassador's wife dropped her expensive teacup on the rug. She was not used to such interruptions!

"Father excused himself, mother excused herself and off they went. And whom did they welcome? A hobo who had come to the door begging. And what did they do? My mother and father served him themselves, even though we had fourteen servants in the house. My mother laid out the best linen, the most expensive silver and our best china and so forth, and she served a hobo. My father did likewise. I saw all of this, and I wanted to help the hobo too, but mother said, *'Oh no. You were not obedient last week; you cannot serve Christ unless you are obedient.'* So, in my little mind, to serve the poor was a great honor and a great joy.

"Now that's Christianity. You don't have to have catechism lessons when you see that sort of thing. That was how my parents treated the poor, so that was what my brother and I learned from growing up in that kind of household, thanks be to God.

"Of course, I was like any other kid too. I would say, *'Well, do we live in a monastery or something like that?'* My parents would say, *'No. We live in a family, of which Christ is the head.'* So, in the end, it all seemed quite natural to me to serve the poor. Christ was in the poor, and we must serve him."

It was on Wednesday, February 27, 2013, at about 4:00 am, Lord, you granted the song, *"Where charity and love prevail, there God is ever found; brought here together by Christ's love, by love are we thus bound."* Afterward, you spoke about how charity and our finances are linked. You said, "Do not pray for money." Rather you requested, *"Pray for an increase in charity."* Lord, thank you for explaining and showing us the difference between praying for money and praying for charity. This revelation is a gift from you. In the end, you said, *"Pray for charity! Then, I will also open the doors for an increase in finances."*

WHY IS THERE SUFFERING?

The Bible tells us that Christ would have to suffer and die for us. *"But this is how God fulfilled what he had foretold through all the prophets, saying that his Christ would suffer."* Acts 3:18 Why all the suffering in the world? Why do you, me, our family and friends have to suffer? If God is good, why does he allow suffering?

There may be many explanations for the problem of suffering by various, sundry thinkers and Bible experts. But simply put, I like to say that, *"Suffering is the universal sign of achievement."*

Those few words explain it all, doesn't it? Essentially, we know that winners are always identified by their suffering. Likewise, losers can be identified by how they curse difficulties and run from pain. The whiners, complainers and slothful are never winners.

Dr. Denis Waitley, a bestselling American business writer, and consultant to the Apollo moon mission has stated something very similar when presenting his *Psychology of Winning* series at conferences and seminars. He states, *"Winners do what is difficult and necessary, while losers do what is quick and easy."* Ed Foreman who once served in the House of Representatives said something analogous, *"Winners are those people who make a habit of doing the difficult things losers are uncomfortable doing."*

Anything valuable, anything worth achieving, the hallmark of such success is suffering. I'll say it again, *"Suffering is the universal sign of achievement."* How profound! How does an athlete get crowned? *"No pain, no gain!"* he would say. How does common ore become pure gold? Burning fire! How does mom deliver a newborn? A child arrives through labor pains. How does a scholar graduate? After years of blood, sweat, and tears. How are sparkling diamonds formed from black coal? Suffering years of enormous pressure. How did Jesus arrive at the extraordinary brilliance of the resurrection? He agonized through the scourging at the pillar, many insults, and a brutal crucifixion. The New Testament corroborates my point about the why of suffering:

"Let the same mind be in you that was in Christ Jesus, who, though he was in the form of God, did not deem equality with God as something to be grasped at. But rather, he emptied himself, taking the form of a slave, being born in human likeness. And being found in human form, he humbled himself and became obedient to the point of death—even death on a cross. Therefore, God has also highly exalted him and gave him the name that is above every other name, so that at the name of Jesus every knee should bend, in the heavens and on earth and under the earth, and every tongue confess that Jesus Christ is Lord, to the glory of God the Father." Philippians 2:5-7

In accordance with the above Scripture, Jesus becomes poor although he was rich. He divested himself of his heavenly glory and was born homeless, in a manger. How many people in Beverly Hills would leave their mansion one day and move into a barn? How many would then live homeless in the heat- forsaken dry dust and sands of the Egyptian desert for three years? Jesus said, *"The poor will be with you always."* Matthew 14:7 Jesus is both poor and eternal. Therefore, in Jesus, poverty will always be with us, forever. Again, the Bible states, *"There will always be poor people in the land. Therefore, I command you to be openhanded toward your fellow Israelites who are poor and needy in your land."* Deuteronomy 15:11

It was noted earlier in book 2 that pride is the original sin and how St. Augustine taught it was at first human pride that disordered our will. We wanted "to become like God, " and that attitude weakened us to commit many other sins. I'm always praising God when I find a Christian who gets it, especially, a dear Baptist brother like Mark McKeen. He earned a Bachelor of Theology degree from *New Brunswick Bible Institute* in 2009 and attends *West Rockport Baptist Church* in West Rockport, ME. Regarding pride he states:

The Distortion Made by Pride, the Original Sin by Mark McKeen

"For thus says the High and Lofty One who inhabits eternity, whose name is Holy: 'I dwell in the holy place, with him who has a contrite and humble spirit, to revive the spirit of the humble, and to revive the heart of the contrite ones.'" – Isaiah 57:15

"Pride, our big egos give us a false view of reality. Pride is like wearing a pair of glasses with magnifying lenses. It distorts how we see the world and how we see ourselves. Let me show you: The proud man lifts himself up. He has an elevated view of himself. He considers himself more important and more prestigious than his peers. In fact, the proud man is higher, in his own mind, than anyone else on the earth. He needs no one's help. He desires to have no equal and definitely desires no superior. But the reality is this throne of pride that he has put himself upon is lower than any position on earth. The reality is that pride has drained the very life from him.

"If pride is the pair of glasses that distorts our vision, then humility is the pair of glasses with the correct prescription. Humility sharpens our view of reality. Humility helps us to see ourselves in the light of who God is. Isaiah proves this to us. Just look at his description of the Lord—look at this glimpse of reality: God is the High and Lofty one. God inhabits eternity. His name is Holy. He dwells in a high and holy place. Indeed, our God is great than any other. He is what we could never be. He does what we could never do. He dwells where? In a humble manger, a carpenter's shop, nailed to the wood of a tree, and laid in a borrowed tomb. Places that human pride would protect most of us from going."

So, pride is a slippery slope for all of us! A person who does good works for the poor can gradually be overcome by the sin of pride. One could say, *"Too bad others don't care about the poor the way I do!"* A person that prays frequently or goes to daily Mass and communion can be overcome by the grave sin of pride too. He or she might say, *"No one makes the time anymore the way I do, no one cares about the Lord but me."* All humans fall prey to pride. *"I always kneel after receiving communion, too bad the others have lost that respect,"* some might say. We often comment, *"If it was me, I would never have done it like that."* Yet others have said, *"I can't believe she did not send a thank you note. I would never do such a thing; I was taught better!"* The list of our pride statements goes on and on.

On Thursday, October 23, 2014, the Lord granted a live reenactment of the story, *"The Good Samaritan."* C.f. Luke 10:25–37 This morning at about 9:00 am, the doctor's appointment was unable to offer me much in the way of a solution for back pain, apparently caused by kidney trouble that's coupled with chills and fever. Arriving home at about 10:30 am and going straight to bed seemed like the best thing. However, just like in the story of *"The Good Samaritan,"* there was a homeless man collapsed (photo page 358) on the side of the road, laying in the hot sun just a block from *Servants of the Father of Mercy*. Cars driving by, no one stopped to help him. Then Lord, you spoke, *"He is suffering more than you."* Upon arriving home, I quickly discovered some cold water, refreshing juices, and fresh fruits to bring the man. As I sat down on the curb, I woke him up and surprised him with the care package. Within an hour the fever left, the back pain was permanently gone, and it never returned, thanks be to God! After being healed, I remembered the Bible has this to say about those who help the poor:

"How blessed is he who considers the poor;
The Lord will deliver him in the day of trouble.
The Lord will protect him and keep him alive,
And he shall be called blessed upon the earth;
And will not be given over to the desire of his enemies.
The Lord will sustain him upon his sickbed;
In his illness, the Lord will restore him to health."
Psalm 41:1-2

Homeless Man Collapsed in the Desert's 115 Degree Heat

Every now and again I discover that a coming world event is being warned about from the other side. That was the case earlier in this book 2 while sharing the story of the earthquake in Japan that also had a severe impact on a nuclear power generator. In this next locution, granted twice during the month of March 2015, a warning was given about a yet-unknown "star," meteor or asteroid that will impact the earth. As you will see, the information does not include time, date or location, so we have to pray for the world!

On Monday, March 2, 2015, I received a locution in the morning hours while I was asleep. A voice, like that of an angel, spoke loudly and urgently said, *"DEFCON 1 – DEATH STAR 1!"* I did not know what DEFCON meant.

After a little research, I discovered that according to the U.S military, the DEFCON system was developed by the *Joint Chiefs of Staff* by unifying and specifying combat commands. It prescribes five graduated levels of readiness (or states of alert) for the U.S. military. It increases in severity from DEFCON 5 (least severe) to DEFCON 1 (most severe) to match varying military situations. During the Cuban Missile Crisis and 911, the military was ordered to DEFCON 3, a heightened state of readiness. DEFCON 1 indicates nuclear war is imminent.

Then, Thursday, March 19, 2015, on the feast of Saint Joseph, while taking a brief afternoon rest, I was abruptly awakened by a brilliant flash of light. I witnessed a sudden explosion in the sky. The detonation sound wave was deafening. Quickly, everything became calm and peaceful again.

On Tuesday, June 30, 2015, at about 6:00 pm during a brief rest, the Lord spoke about the nature and comprehension of the Trinity. He said, *"The Trinity may be better imagined and explained as being very similar to a tripod."* Just as a tripod has three distinct parts but becomes one, so is the Trinity.

Chapter Twenty

God Chooses the Weak to Confound the Wise

Reading, Writing, & Arithmetic

You may remember in the first book reading a lot about different types of abuse the young children suffered in our family, myself included that continued well into our teen and early adult years. The various exploitations took a physical and psychological toll on developing children and manifested itself in many ways. In my case, I received poor grades in school stirring up more friction, physical and emotional abuse. It all started in the first grade when I had a difficult time focusing on homework. We were often required to come home from school, jump in the family car and go with our parents to paint, repair and clean many fixer-upper rental units they had invested in over the years. During summer break each year, the entire vacation was often dedicated to a forty-hour work week. We scraped and painted old Victorian-era homes inside and out, getting up at 6:00 am and returning home around 6:00 pm on most days.

By the time I reached high school, the parental and family abuse along with their internal and external raging conflicts damaged my ability to focus, think, comprehend and study. In the seventh grade, I had to repeat mathematics in summer school. In the ninth grade, I was placed into a particular high school class for slow students needing better reading, writing and study skills. The class was a big help, and by senior year I was voted editor of our twice monthly high school paper, *"The Cardinal"* and even had my own column. I also attended summer classes at the Billy Graham Christian writing institute at the BGEA headquarters, Hennepin Plaza, Minneapolis/St. Paul, MN, June of 1972.

Senior year in high school I began to notice other spiritual gifts in my life. At this time, I was the music director of the Saturday, 6:00 pm vigil Mass at *St. Dominic's Church*. I was also volunteering as guitar worship leader for Sunday evening gathering of the *"Jesus Movement"* people at *Pleasant Valley Evangelical Church*. Along with music, worship, and writing - I had begun to notice the gift of prophecy in my life as well.

Between junior and senior year, whenever students were given 5 minutes to rest at the end of a period before the bell rang, I frequently began to have visions. Usually, with my head down on the desk, I would vividly see forthcoming airline crashes. The loss of life triggered my compassion and prayer, but then they would still take place within a week or two of a revelation. I was never given time, date or place. In particular, I can remember early in December of 1972 being warned in advance of the impending crash of a large plane accompanied by a fireball and loss of life. On

December 29, 1972 – *Eastern Air Lines* Flight 401, a Lockheed L-1011 TriStar, crashed into the Florida Everglades, killing 103 of 176 people on board. The crew was distracted by a faulty gear-down light, resulting in a controlled flight into the terrain. This was the first crash of a widebody aircraft and the first loss of a Lockheed Tristar. I questioned this gift. Why me?

Too Stupid!

During senior year, I had applied to Providence College, a private Dominican, Roman Catholic university located about two miles west of downtown Providence, Rhode Island. I was inspired to move forward with the inspiration, a calling deep down inside to go into full-time church ministry as a priest. In May of senior year, the college sent a letter back in regards to my application. The priest said they look for students with 3.8-grade point averages and that I would not be qualified to enter school at their institution. Not taking the rejection any further, I had enough. I was already quite aware from attending special education classes in grade school and high school that I was not the *"brightest bulb on the tree!"*

The Love Pastor, Rev. Leonard Evans

Over at *Pleasant Valley Evangelical Church* where I was Sunday night guitar worship leader. The church pastor was Rev. Leonard Evans. He had a Ph.D. from *Princeton Theological Seminary*, Princeton, New Jersey. We discussed my high school low grade-point-average, and he offered a suggestion that I could apply to a Bible college. More than likely I will find Bible school welcoming to anyone that wants to serve God with their life. I had never heard of a Bible college. Heretofore, I was distraught and had thought that the Dominicans were pretty much speaking for everyone. I was just backward and naïve in this regard. But Rev. Evans had good news for dummies!

Interestingly, Rev. Leonard Evans (portrait below) became well known among Catholics and evangelicals as the *"Love Pastor."* His testimony was that he had cried out to God to show him "true religion" after receiving the heady knowledge of the Bible while attending *Princeton Theological Seminary*. God answered his prayer and taught him the *"Love Message"* in the Scriptures. C.f. *"This is my commandment that you love one another as I have loved you."* John 15:12 Rev. Evans found the *"Love Message"* everywhere in Scripture, preached on it every Sunday, but angered a lot of staunch conservatives, self-righteous, and Bible thumpers. Yet, thanks be to God, he became my mentor throughout undergraduate and graduate theological studies. I was blessed!

Reverend Leonard Evans, a.k.a. the "Love Pastor"

Just a year before graduation from a Bachelors degree in Theology, I met with Pastor Evans privately at a Chinese restaurant near *Pleasant Valley Church.* We ordered *Moo Goo Gai Pan,* his favorite dish. Somewhere between the egg roll, the soup, and the main dish, I apparently let pride get in the way and tried to impress Leonard with my knowledge of hermeneutics, Biblical exegesis, Old Testament archaeology, and eschatology. I was now getting As and Bs in college and proud of it! But, before leaving the restaurant that day, Leonard looked over at me from across the table and gently said, *"You've become so heavenly minded, you're no earthly good!"*

Well, God sure has a way of keeping us humble. His last words to me at the end of lunch kept ringing in my ears for months, if not years. Knowing the source, it cut like a sword. When I returned to my dorm room in Anaheim, California, I repeatedly cried out to God to make me holy as he is holy. I had no idea at age nineteen-years-old what that meant, *"to be holy as he is holy."* But I wanted it. One holiday weekend, in particular, the dorm mates were all gone on break. I took the weekend as a time to make a personal retreat, pray, reflect and ask God to make me holy. Be careful what you pray for!

Shortly after that weekend, the first thing I noticed in answer to my fervent prayer was absolutely nothing. Nothing happened. It was the same old, same old. I was waiting and waiting for some type of transformation that included preaching like Bishop Sheen or even Billy Graham. I was hoping my faith would heal the sick, raise the dead and convert sinners. But nothing like this ever happened. I was just the same old me.

In hindsight, something very significant did happen when I was nineteen. In that same year of crying out to God for holiness, I had received an intense and vivid dream and vision. In it, I had become a well-known writer. I was told by someone from the other side that I am going to write books and they will be published by Penguin – Putnam. Well, I told priests, pastors, teachers and Rev. Evans. Everyone thought I was crazy. To me, the vision seemed so intensely real. I did not mind being chastised, corrected, laughed at and admonished for even talking about such things.

Penguin Putnam Books

In the 1980s, the decade began with doing doctoral studies in Roman Catholic *Moral Law and Ethics* at *Duquesne University* in Pittsburgh, Pennsylvania. Out of Pittsburgh I was interviewed and recruited to be an owner and start-up manager for PEOPLExpress Airlines and had to transfer to the New York area. By 1989, PEOPLExpress Airlines was sold to *Continental Airlines.* Career assessment and job searching became a necessity. I wrote my first book, *"Get the Job You Want in Thirty Days."* Miraculously, the book was bought by *Berkley Books* in New York. But, I mentioned to the Lord, you were right about me publishing a book in a vision at age nineteen, but what happened to the *Penguin Putnam* part? That bugged me. The dream got the book right, but not the publisher. Then in 1993 my editor, Natalee Rosenstein sent a letter to *Berkley* authors notifying us that they have merged with *Penguin Putnam.* Mystery solved!

After publishing multiple business and career books with

major publishers like *Penguin Putnam Berkley Books* over the years, I had thought it odd that the Lord went through all this setup since 1974. He took the time to reveal that a slow learner, who was unable to read and write correctly is going to write and publish books. Like Moses who could not speak well, it did not make any sense. But God chooses the weak in the world to confound the wise! That is so evident in the selection of David by God to be king of Israel. C.f. Samuel 16 Brought before the Lord by Samuel are all the sleek, tall, handsome and powerful sons. Then they remember there is an uneducated, short, homeless and smelly sheepherder out in the fields. They have for good reason excluded from the lineup. Once brought in, he is exactly the candidate God tells Samuel, *"Go ahead, anoint this one."* Here is what Paul has to say about the foolish, stupid and weak.

"But we preach Christ crucified: a stumbling block to Jews and foolishness to Gentiles, but to those whom God has called, both Jews and Greeks, Christ the power of God and the wisdom of God. For the foolishness of God is wiser than human wisdom, and the weakness of God is stronger than human strength.

Brothers and sisters, think of what you were when you were called. Not many of you were wise by human standards; not many were influential; not many were of noble birth. But God chose the foolish things of the world to shame the wise; God chose the weak things of the world to shame the strong. God chose the lowly things of this world and the despised things—and the things that are not—to nullify the things that are, so that no one may boast before him. It is because of him that you are in Christ Jesus, who has become for us wisdom from God—that is, our righteousness, holiness, and redemption. Therefore, as it is written: *'Let the one who boasts boast in the Lord.'"* 1 Corinthians 1:23-31

And so, little did I realize that all my writing experience throughout the 90s and into the new millennium was all leading up to one thing: Journaling, writing and publishing a near-death-experience God-encounter that was to take place on the night of September 26 and in the early morning hours of September 27, 2005. Indeed, God has chosen what is weak and despised in the world to accomplish his will in this matter. Now, assuredly, I have nothing to boast in but to boast in the Lord for using his extraordinary well-developed writing talent, myself to tell the tale of an astonishing story, a human encounter with God himself.

Chapter Twenty-One

Other Near-death Experiences

Howard Storm

Before his near-death experience, Howard Storm, author of *"My Descent into Death"* (www.howardstorm.com) was a professor of art at *Northern Kentucky University*, was not a very pleasant man by his own admission. He was an avowed atheist and was hostile to every form of religion and those who practiced it. He often would use rage to control everyone around him, and he didn't find joy in anything. Anything that wasn't seen, touched or felt, he had no faith in. He knew with certainty that the material world was the full extent of everything that was. He considered all belief systems associated with religion to be fantasies for people to deceive themselves with. Beyond what science said, there was nothing else. But then on June 1, 1985, at the age of 38, Howard Storm had a near-death experience in a Paris hospital while on vacation, due to a perforation of the stomach and his life has since forever changed. His near-death experience is one of the most profound, if not the most significant afterlife experience ever documented. His life was immensely changed after his near-death experience. He resigned as a university professor and devoted his time attending the *United Theological Seminary* to become a *United Church of Christ* pastor. Today, Howard Storm is presently happily married to his wife Marcia and is pastor of the *Covington United Church of Christ* in Covington, Ohio.

While lying in the hospital feeling intense abdominal pain and near death in the middle of the night June 1, 1985, Howard was on a gurney waiting for the doctors to arrive back around 7:00 in the morning. Suddenly he said, *"I discovered voices calling me originating from the doorway. Different voices were calling. I asked who they were, and they said, 'We are here to take care of you. We will fix you up. Come with us.'"*

The truth of the matter was these were dark figures; silhouettes that were gradually pulling him out the door and down the hallway into a fog or haze. *"Pain is bullshit!"* they said. Now things got worse as Howard was forced by a mob of unfriendly and cruel people toward some unknown destination in the darkness. They began shouting and hurling insults. They refused to answer any questions. Finally, Howard insisted, *"I will not go any farther."* Instantly, they changed. They became much more aggressive and insisted he cooperate with them. A number of them began to push and shove Howard, but he responded by hitting back at them. A wild orgy of frenzied taunting, screaming and hitting ensued. All the while it was evident that they were having great fun. It seemed to be, almost a game for them, with Howard as the centerpiece of their amusement. Another's pain became their pleasure.

Howard Storm said, *"Then a most unusual thing happened.*

I heard very clearly, in my own voice, something that I had learned in nursery Sunday School. It was the little song, 'Jesus loves me, this I know!' I don't know why, but all of a sudden I wanted to believe that. Not having anything left, I wanted to cling to that thought. And I, inside, screamed, 'Jesus, please save me.'"

Then, in the distant darkness somewhere, the tiniest little star appeared. Not knowing what it was, Howard assumed it was a comet or a meteor because it was moving rapidly. It was coming directly toward him. It was getting very bright, rapidly. When the light came near, its radiance spilled over. Howard was lifted up from the darkness, fog, and haze. He saw all his wounds, tears and brokenness melt away. Howard states, *"I became whole in this radiance. What I did was to cry uncontrollably. I was crying, not out of sadness, but because I was feeling things that I had never felt before in my life. Another thing happened. Suddenly I knew a whole bunch of things. I was given to know things. I knew that this light, this radiance, knew me. I don't know how to explain to you. As a matter of fact, I understood that it knew me better than my mother or father did. The luminous entity that embraced me knew me intimately and began to communicate a tremendous sense of knowledge. I knew that he knew everything about me and I was unconditionally loved and accepted."*

Then Howard encountered two magnificent illuminated beings that conducted his life review. While watching his life reviewed, he states, *"Most of the time I found that my interactions with other people had been manipulative. During my professional career, for example, I saw myself sitting in my office, playing the college professor, while a student came to me with a personal problem. I sat there looking compassionate, and patient, and loving, while inside I was bored to death. I would check my watch under my desk as I anxiously waited for the student to finish."*

The two beings which Howard calls his friends asked if he had any questions after his life review. Howard asked, *"What about the Bible?"* They said, *"What about it?" "Is it true?"* he said. They told him he has to read it with and open mind and with a spiritual bent. *"Yes, it is true!"* they said. Howard states, *"I asked them, for example, which was the best religion. I was looking for an answer which was like, 'the Presbyterians.' I figured these guys were all Christians. The answer I got was, 'The best religion is the religion that brings you closest to God.'"* Asking them if there was life on other planets, their surprising answer was that the universe is full of life.

Howard asked the two beings about death - what happens when we die? They said that when a loving person dies, angels come down to meet him, and they take him up - gradually, at first, because it would be unbearable for that person to be instantly exposed to God. He also asked about all-out nuclear war. The beings said "no" to that, but there is the possibility that one or two nuclear weapons will go off accidentally.

Lastly, against Howard's better judgment, the beings of light insisted that he return to the earth for his wife, family, and child as well as for his own learning and development. The next thing he knew, he was back in his body in the hospital, pain and all. Howard Storm, *My Descent into Death*, Harmony Books, 2005.

Gloria Polo

Gloria's story begins on May 5, 1995, at the *National University of Bogotá* at 4:30 pm. A dentist, she and her 23-year-old cousin who is also a dentist, were studying in order to get the specialization. On that rainy day, with her husband, they were going to the *Faculty of Dentistry Library* to find some books. Gloria and her cousin walked with a small umbrella while her husband wore a raincoat and walked near the wall of the General Library. As they jumped over a rather large puddle, they were hit by a lightning bolt which left them both burned and their skin badly carbonized.

The cousin died immediately. The lightning bolt entered from behind, burning him inside totally, and came out thru his feet, leaving him intact externally. Notwithstanding his young age, he was a very religious young man. He had a great devotion to Baby Jesus, and he always carried around his neck that image in a quartz medal. The authorities said that it was the quartz that attracted the lightning bolt to her cousin because it entered into the heart burning everything. He died on the spot.

In her own words, Gloria states, *"As for me, the lightning bolt entered from my shoulder, burning the whole body terribly, inside and out. My flesh disappeared including my breasts, especially the left one, leaving a hole. The bolt caused the flesh to disappear off my abdomen, legs, ribs, carbonized the liver, burned the kidneys, lungs, ovaries and exited through the right foot."*

For contraception, she was using a spiral (an intrauterine device in the form of a T), and because of the material with which it is made (copper) it's a good conductor of electricity; the lightning bolt carbonized and pulverized the ovaries which became like two raisins. She remained in cardiac arrest.

There is a good part in her story. She said, *"The good part is that, while my body laid there badly burned and in cardiac arrest, in that same moment I found myself inside a beautiful white tunnel of light, a wonderful light, which made me feel a joy, a peace, a happiness that I do not have words to describe the greatness of that moment. It was true ecstasy! I looked, and at the end of that tunnel, I saw a white light, like a sun, a beautiful light. I say white to tell you a color, but we are talking about colors that cannot be compared to those that exist on the earth. It was a splendid light. I felt from it a source of peace, love, and light. When I went up in this tunnel toward the light, I said to myself, 'Ay Caramba, I'm dead!'"*

Then Gloria was aware of hearing the voice of her husband. He lamented and cried out, *"Gloria! Gloria! Please, do not leave me! Look at your children; your children need you! Gloria, come back! Come back! Do not be a quitter! Return!"* She heard everything and saw him cry with much pain.

She returned back to her body, and after the electrical charges were completely free of the body, she was taken to the hospital and the operating room. It was here, similar to Howard Storm that shadowy figures, demons began to attack her and beckon her into the darkness. After feeling irrevocably lost because of a life of self-centeredness and being highly critical of others, Gloria was rescued by St. Michael the Archangel and plucked up from the abyss. While she was shouting out to be rescued from the gates of hell she could hear others crying, thousands and thousands of persons and even youth. Yes, above all youth! Teens and young adults with so much suffering. She states, *"I perceived that there, in that horrible place of hell, in that quagmire of hate and of suffering, they were gnashing their teeth, with screams and laments, that filled me with compassion that I will never be able to forget."*

Then, in her life review, she declared she was a Catholic. The Lord asked her if she, *"Loved the Lord her God above all other gods?"* She said, *"Yes!"* But the Lord acknowledged that it was only out of times of extreme necessity that she prayed and came to Him. Especially, she would do this when needing money. The Lord spoke, *"You made me promises. You insisted. But you never kept them! Beyond making promises, you never thanked me."* Gloria states, *"With that, I was humbled. I realized I ungratefully saw the Lord as an ATM machine, a bank cash dispenser, and nothing more."*

The Lord took issue with her pride. He said, *"All that you had, it was not given to you because you had asked for it, but it was a blessing that you received from heaven. Instead, you said to others you obtained it all by yourself because you were a hard worker, a fighter! You believed everything you had was conquered with your own hands and by the sheer force of studying long hours. No! Consider how many professionals are in the world that are more qualified than you, who work as much or more than you? I am the one that makes wealth and brings success."*

After receiving judgment on multiple other accounts, Gloria Polo was instructed to return to earth. She now shares her testimony everywhere in the world in many languages. It's on the Internet for free, alerting others to how to live life here on earth, death, dying, judgment, God and the life to come.

For more of Gloria Polo's story, go to
http://testimony-polo.blogspot.com

Gloria Polo was Struck by Lightning May 5, 1995, at the *National University of Bogotá,* Columbia at 4:30 pm

Chapter Twenty-Two

Biography
Bro. Gary Joseph

"One loser showing another loser where to get a meal!"

Bro. Gary Joseph

- Founder, President of *Servants of the Father of Mercy*, Inc.
- Studied Catholic Priesthood at *Saint John's Seminary*, Camarillo, CA
- Studied Doctoral Studies Catholic Moral Law and Ethics at *Duquesne University*
- Studied Master's Degree, Theology, Biblical Studies at *Assemblies of God Theological Seminary*
- Studied B.Th., Bachelor of Theology at Melodyland School of Theology

After having a near-death-experience in September 2005, Brother Gary Joseph is the author of the bestselling, *Proof of the Afterlife - The Conversation Continues* first published in

November 2010. For the past twenty-five years, he has been a business consultant authoring many books and publications for *Penn State University, Breakers of Palm Beach, Super Bowl, Four Seasons* and others. He has written for the *Wall Street Journal, Chicago Tribune, Miami Herald* and has multiple bestselling business books for *Barron's, Penguin/Putnam Berkley Books* and others.

Bro. Joseph has been an avowed brother of the Catholic order since 2007. He is the founder and president of the *Servants of the Father of Mercy,* an association and community of avowed and lay members of the Archdiocese of Los Angeles and an IRS 501 (c) 3 nonprofit, tax-exempt California corporation.

The *Servants of the Father of Mercy* serve homeless men, women, and children, 80,000 + in Southern California alone – delivering food, water, clothing, blankets, jackets, sneakers, socks, hygiene kits, love, hugs, pastoral care and spiritual supplies. Community members follow the Rule of St. Benedict, taking vows of poverty, chastity, and obedience. Lay brothers and sisters of the third order dedicate themselves to practicing basic Catholic spirituality and serving homeless people at least five hours a month.

Although books of private revelation do not need to receive approval from the Catholic church, Br. Joseph's book *Proof of the Afterlife; The Conversation Continues,* has received wide acclaim from leaders of the Catholic church including thank you notes from Archbishop Emeritus of the Archdiocese of Los Angeles, Cardinal Roger Mahony and Bishop Edward Clark as well as reviews from priests and an "Apostolic Blessing" from Pope Francis.

Bro. Gary Joseph has appeared on *"The Archbishop's Hour"* (Archdiocese of San Francisco), *Atlanta Live, Jordan Rich, WBZ Radio,* Boston, MA, *Nite Line,* Greenville, SC., *Literati Scene with Dick Concannon and Smoki Bacon,* Boston, MA, *Catholic Television Network* (CTN) and reviewed by the *Catholic News Service* (CNS) of the *United States Conference of Catholic Bishops* (U.S.C.C.B.), *Priest Magazine, The Catechist and Our Sunday Visitor* (OSV).

Br. Joseph lives in Southern California where he serves a community of 80,000 + homeless. All proceeds from the sale of *Proof of the Afterlife, the Conversation Continues,* go to the *Servants of the Father of Mercy* homeless mission.

Therefore, "There should be no liberals in America,
just the merciful. No conservatives, just the compassionate.
No liberals, just the forgiving. No conservatives, just kindness.
No liberals, just the patient. No conservatives, just love."

Bro. Gary Joseph

Chapter Twenty-Three

Praise for "Proof of the Afterlife"

Since November 30, 2010, hundreds of *Barnes and Noble* and *Amazon.com* reviews have consistently and collectively rated the book 4.9 out of 5 stars. Below, the well-loved and respected *Midwest Book Review* gave *'Proof of the Afterlife'* a five-star review . . .

A Five-Star Review

"For thirty minutes, Gary Joseph was dead. *'Proof of the Afterlife'* is a Christian and devotional tale as Brother Gary Joseph offers his own testimony to the existence of the afterlife, as he relays his story of his death and return to the world of the living, saying that there is something after and to remember that no one is gone for good, that they wait on the other side. Of metaphysical and Christian interest, *'Proof of the Afterlife'* is very much worth considering for anyone looking for tales of real people's brushes with the afterlife."
—*Midwest Book Review*, May 2011

United Stated Conference of Catholic Bishops A Review by the Catholic News Service

"The afterlife is a common topic of discussion for a religious brother in Ventura County, California, since the publication of his book, *'Proof of the Afterlife — The Conversation Continues,'* a book of hope, forgiveness, and mercy.

"People can say, *'Oh that wasn't just a dream.' God was having a conversation with their life,'* said Brother Gary Joseph, founder of the *Servants of the Father of Mercy*, an association of vowed and lay members in the Archdiocese of Los Angeles.

"Brother Gary said he has had encounters with God and been involved in conversations with the afterlife ever since his 'near-death experience' Sept. 27, 2005: At 1:15 am, 'an out of control' heart arrhythmia caused him to collapse and his heart to stop, and he felt the overpowering presence of God.

"In that state, according to his book, he was immersed in the embracing love of Christ and absorbed spiritual messages. When he was resuscitated, Brother Gary said, he awoke and noticed the clock read exactly 1:45 am. *'I had been a dead man, immersed in this encounter for exactly 30 minutes,'* Brother Gary told Catholic News Service in a February 8, 2016, telephone interview.

"A priest guided him to a spiritual director who at the time was planning on doing a film on God-encounters. The spiritual director encouraged Brother Gary to keep a journal and eventually write a book. The manuscript was sent to Los Angeles Cardinal Roger M. Mahony (Archbishop Emeritus of the Archdiocese of Los Angeles) for theological review prior to its publication November 30, 2010.

"When people read his book, it helps them to connect the stories and dreams they have had in their life; Brother Gary told CNS. *'They never knew how to interpret them.'* There was a woman who had told him of her dream about her deceased husband, who was wandering helplessly and in need of her prayers. The book helped her understand the dream, he said.

"Saying people have a fear of death, 'a fear of dying,' and they remain in the dark about it, Brother Gary said he hopes his book will trigger hope for people. *"This (book) shows there is proof of the afterlife and what you do in this life will affect you in the next life,"* he said. In the few months, his book has been out; Brother Gary said he has already seen its effect on families in three cases. One family ordered 16 copies to be handed out to other family members and friends.

"He believes the book can help people who have a terminal illness, referring to his mother and a cousin, who both fought cancer. *'It's a perfect match for those with illness. It can give a lot of hope.'*

"Although the book has been well-received by many, including Cardinal Mahony and the head of the *Eternal Word Television Network,* Brother Gary sometimes worries people will take it the wrong way.

"'I still wonder if people are ready to hear this, that God is talking with us,' he said. When asked by CNS how one can tell if an encounter is from God, one's self or the devil, he offered two basic filters to distinguish the difference. He said the first is that the dream, vision or physical encounter will

inspire greater acts of charity. Secondly, he said, the experience would increase the person's faith.

"Since Christmas 2010, *'Proof of the Afterlife — The Conversation Continues'* ($19.95, softcover) is being sold by *Barnes and Noble* in its stores nationwide and online at Amazon.com.

"'*All proceeds of the book are going to Servants of the Father of Mercy congregation serving homeless men, women, and children in America with food, water, clothing, blankets and spiritual supplies,'* said Brother Gary.

"The *Servants* follow the *Rule of St. Benedict*. The community's religious brothers and sisters take vows of poverty, chastity, and obedience. Its lay members must commit themselves to practicing basic Catholic spirituality and serving homeless people at least five hours a month." — (Emily Lahr) *Catholic News Service, The United States Conference of Catholic Bishops,* February 22, 2011.

Professional Reviews

"Having read 'Proof of the Afterlife,' I would like to order 20 additional copies for our church, St. Mary's. As a priest and psychologist, I can truly relate to your work. Will keep you in prayer." Fr. Joseph M., Pinconning, MI

"I, a Roman Catholic Priest, found this account of Brother Gary's near-death-experience to be compelling. The book is an enjoyable read that can teach virtually anyone something new. Simply enjoy the book with an open heart and let our Lord touch your heart through Gary's experience. It will be something you wish to share with someone else. God bless you." Fr. Joseph D.

"An incredible journey of faith and the proof of the eternal life that awaits us! *Proof of the Afterlife* is a very comforting book, and Brother Joseph is sincere throughout his depictions of his encounters and in his relationship with his family and close friends. This leads me to believe he truly has had all these experiences, as he has written in his book. Soon after his life-after-death experience, Gary started to have apparitions, dreams and other out of this world things happen and continue for many years of his life, which he documented.

"Bro. Joseph was raised in a very dysfunctional family, with a controlling father, an abusive brother and a mother who never stood up for herself. Gary explains about his struggle to understand and forgive his parents and his brother, all who are now deceased. His greatest conflicts were with his father, who even disowned and refused to visit his own son, Gary's brother, while he lay dying. As his father grew older, Gary later tried to get him to have a relationship with God, especially before his father passed on. I found this part of the book to be very emotional and difficult.

"Bro. Joseph chose to write and share about his life and this incredible journey, not only to show how he found peace during the most difficult times in his life but also so others could find comfort in knowing there is life after death. That we may know there is a God who loves us all, even if we think we are not deserving of that love.

"God chose Gary to speak directly to, yet he is just like anyone else on this planet. Bro. Joseph is a sinner like us all, and he makes it a point many times throughout the book. I clearly understand the way, Bro. Joseph explains how God may speak to someone. Whether it be thru a dream, or in our daily thoughts, Gary gives many accounts throughout the book of being in the presence of God and having visits from the other side. All of which I believe are genuine since he always describes them as being peaceful and always giving him guidance and understanding.

"Having studied and read hundreds of accounts of afterlife experiences. It has been well documented by many that do cross over and then coming back to life do keep a spiritual connection to that other side and even continue to have visits and unusual experiences. *Proof of the Afterlife* is a life changing book and one to share with others. This is a very powerful book, and it makes a great read for anyone, atheist, Christian, any believer in God and especially for those who may believe there is no afterlife." *Barnes and Noble, Autumn Blues Reviews*

Book Reader Reviews

"Bro. Gary's book was a wonderful read with so much in it that I am reading it for the second time. Gary has a way of simplifying Our Lord's teachings so that we can put them into practice. Above all else, I believe that mercy and forgiveness is the message of the book, with no exceptions to this. Readers who are already practicing Catholics or Christians of other denominations will find a gentle reminder that charity covers a multitude of sins and that we are not to judge others regarding the state of their souls. Non-Christians will find this a fascinating read which is likely to instill a desire to explore the themes in more depth through other Christian authors. Gary has a way of explaining some of the tenets of our Catholic/Christian faith in a manner that is easy to understand, such as the distinction between body, soul and spirit, and the role of Mother Mary in our lives. I suppose that for those who choose not to believe in the sort of experiences that Gary and others have had, they will never find proof of God or the afterlife unless they have a similar encounter themselves. This is truly sad because there is so much we can learn from the experiences of others." *Amazon.com*, Paul Lisney

"The book, 'Proof of the Afterlife,' was truly amazing! Very inspirational and uplifting. Also, it was so cool to read a Catholics near-death-experience. I have read many Christian experiences as well. But it was really great to read a Catholic's account. Everyone should read this book!" Amazon.com, Daniel Allen.

"'Proof of the Afterlife' was hard to put down! I read the book cover to cover in one sitting. The experience I had was one of the renewal of my faith, increased spirituality, more hope and the true meaning of reconciliation. I enjoyed it so much, each of my adult children received a copy." Barnes and Noble, M. Shafter

Kid's Reviews You Can Trust!

On May 16, 2013, Bro. Joseph spoke for two hours to the fourth-grade children of St. Mary Magdalene Grade School in Camarillo, CA. Because the kids were so highly engaged in the topic of life after death, having lots of questions and comments, a parish priest gifted each student a copy of the book, *'Proof of the Afterlife.'* Here are a few of their reviews.

"Thank you, Brother Gary, for telling that amazing true story. It is so cool to know about that." Love, Isabella

"One of the things that impressed me was when you saw the gigantic cross." Sincerely, Nathan

"Brother, I remember you talking about love, mercy, merited grace and unmerited grace." Thank you! Nathan K.

"Brother Gary, thank you for the speech, it was really cool." Love, Ethan

"Bro. Gary, you were great, you got me into the book. I read it for like 30 minutes. You took me on a journey." Your pal, Keanu

"Dear Brother Gary, thank you for the wonderful book. Yes, like you said, 'If your sister is being mean, go clean her room.' Ha, ha, ha, funny! Thanks to you 1000,000,000,000 times 2000, 000, 000,000 = 3000, 000, 000,000 thank you!" Your fan, Angelina O.

"Dear Bro. Gary, I loved it! I liked it when God talked to you. Your story is inspiring. I love your book!" Love, Sydney S.

"Dear Brother Gary, first of all, the book you made was so good that my family read it. The way you put it in such detail, I felt I was with God and with Jesus. All I have to say is thank you!" Your friend, John

"Dear Brother Gary, thank you so much for visiting our fourth-grade class. My grandma and I are such a big fan of you! I got home I told my parents and my grandma all about your visit!" From, Kaela

"Dear Brother Gary, one of the things that made an impression on me was that you said it was peaceful when you were above your body. I love your book." Love, Paige

"Thank you, Brother Gary; I didn't know your chest could go that high!" Your friend, Stanley

"Brother, thank you! Mercy message made an impression on me. Thank you, you changed the way I look at things." A student, Isaac

"Dear Brother Gary, when you said you were peaceful when you were dead; when I'm dead, I want to feel like that." A student

"Dear Bro. Gary, I remember everything. Thank you for sharing your journey." Love Brandon, P.S. *"I'm the Filipino man."*

"Dear Brother Gary, I remember when you had to trust God through the darkness, it was my favorite part." From William L.

"Brother Gary, Thank you! Thank you for the book. I will never forget you and your story. It was great." God bless, Omari

Chapter Twenty-Four

Final Anecdote

What is an anecdote, you may ask? An anecdote is a short story, usually serving to inspire an audience or readers to laugh or ponder over a topic. Almost always, the anecdote relates well to the subject matter at hand, as it does in this case, the book's "message of mercy."

Before I share my closing story, we must ask; What is the purpose of an anecdote? Why take up the audience's time with what seems like just another tall tale? In general, short stories introduced by a writer or speaker are first and foremost to bring cheer. In our book, it's a great way to end this publication on an up note. An anecdote like the one I will share now can just make people laugh and brighten their mood.

A second benefit is to reminisce. People enjoy talking about the past and reading tales that take them there. Readers can look back favorably on moments in another person's life and share the joy and insights that time had to offer.

Thirdly, an anecdote will in many cases illustrate caution to the participants. The writer is trying to show the audience what can happen if they do not follow a better way. As moms and dads know in raising their children, just laying out rules for individuals is not effective. The parents also need to share stories that can illustrate and help their children to do the right thing. In fact, before I was born, my middle sister Beverly Jean had as a toddler accidentally touched a boiling pot on the stove and spilled berry jam all over herself. Immediately she found herself immersed in a kitchen sink ice bath. So, when I was born, I heard the story about Beverly Jean and the burning hot jam dozens of times. In hindsight, it was shared frequently in order to teach and guide the correct way a child should behave in the kitchen and around the stove.

Fourthly, anecdotal stories are infused, injected and dispersed by a writer in order to possibly persuade and inspire others. Speakers and writers want participants to know that they are there to help, and that they have faced similar struggles. They want the audience members to know that there is the possibility of a brighter future if they put the work into improving their lives.

Lastly, on rare occasions anecdotes do not have to serve any purpose whatsoever. They can just be part of a natural conversation with other people. Recently, a dear acquaintance, Francesco, a young man from Italy joined Fr. John and myself for dinner on his birthday at a German restaurant in Palm Springs, CA. Francesco's one and only anecdotal story began as we walked into the restaurant, continued through placing the menu order and then non-stop shared through the salad plate, main course and desert as Fr. John and I struggled to keep our eyes open. Finally, I spoke up and said, "Francesco, can we change the subject?"

Then more directly I interjected, "We've almost lost Fr. John here a few times!" It was all due to an anecdotal story gone wild and well into overtime!

The Rummage Sale

Some years ago, the Servants of the Father of Mercy mission to deliver supplies to the homeless was in part funded by rummage sale fundraisers. Tia Babe, the owner of Tia Babe's Restaurant had fostered a wonderful and generous helping relationship with our team in order to better serve the homeless in the region. In those years, she was still located at the restaurants original and first location for thirty years, 915 East Harvard Boulevard, at the corner of Tenth Street, Harvard Boulevard and the CA 126 freeway in Santa Paula, CA. Wow! What a great location it was to have a rummage sale out front bright and early on a Saturday morning, long before the restaurant even opened. We had the entire parking lot available to spread out tables, chairs, electronics, furniture and more.

On this particular Saturday, Dudley Davis, the owner of Doright's Plant Growers sent a truck over at 6:00 am filled with flats of perennial flowering plants in 4 inch pots. He was donating them to help the local homeless and our mission. By 7:00 am the early bird junk collectors, hoarders and antique store owners were out in full force. The sale was not scheduled to open until 8:30 am. However, the pressure of this group left us very little time to set up, display and negotiate pricing properly. Visible from the busy intersection was our large selection of bric-a-brac, furniture, electronics and the colorful fresh flowers. The trays and trays of flowers! They were the eyecatchers drawing the people in. Shoppers who were hoping to get a bargain while preparing their homes and flowerbeds for springtime.

Some of the elderly female volunteers whom I affectionately call "the church ladies" and who are aptly named after Dana Carvey's, Saturday Night Live character, "The Church Lady," unknown to me were negotiating with a tall, well-built farmer, a sixty-something man plotting the sale of all the flowers in one fell swoop. It was only 7:00 am and still had more than an hour before we officially opened.

The next thing I know the man was beginning to walk off with all the flower pots packing the flats in his truck. I thought to myself, "how is this possible since we were still setting up?"

"Sir," I said. "What are you doing?" He responded, "Two of your workers sold the flowers to me." "All of them?" I questioned. He abruptly responded, "All of them!" My next question he knew was forthcoming. "Well, how much are you willing to donate for them? You know this is a rummage sale for the homeless. We're trying to help the poor here." I said. He replied, "fifty cents each."

Next, I explained to him that we got caught by surprise at such an early hour with so many guests that we literally did not have time yet to discuss and agree upon the suggested donations for key items, like the trays of flowers. Therefore, I said, "Sir, the grower made it a point to say each pot sells for $3.99 retail at local grocery stores." I also made the point, "We would be willing to accept $1.00 for each 4-inch pot but certainly not 50 cents, especially since the rummage sale had not even begun yet."

Well, the man towering feet above me walked over to where I was standing and became furious. Angrily he responded in a tirade that seemed to go on forever and for everyone to hear for blocks around . . . "You call yourself a Christian? You're despicable! Nothing but a disgusting piece of sh*t." Pointing his finger at me he continued, "You're a loser! You're all fu**ed up and don't care about anyone but yourself.!" And then came silence as all the volunteers and guests gathered around focused on what will happen next.

Filled with the peace, calm and sensibility of Holy Spirit, I simply looked up at this gentleman with lots of love and forgiveness and said, "Sir, how did you know that about me? Every word you just said is true. In fact, my own mother would agree with you. Thank you for being so honest and truthful." Shockingly, that was not the response he was expecting. More than likely he was preparing to do battle. A verbal war of sorts. I then said, "Even though it's all true what you have said about me, you still have to donate $1 for each of the plants, fifty cents is totally unacceptable."

With that, he quickly left the rummage sale area and got in his truck parked at the curb and slammed the door. There was a sigh of relief! Giant troublemaker was gone. Well, gone just for the moment. Next, what the man did surprised everyone, including himself.

He opened the truck's door, got out and came back to where I was standing, the exact spot where the crowd had gathered because of his outburst. Trembling and with tears in his eyes he softly spoke and said to me, "Sir, you have just taught me a very valuable lesson. I am sixty-three years old and it has taken me this long to learn it." Over and over he spoke up repeating himself saying, "Thank you! Thank you very much. Thank you!"

After pulling out a wad of cash from his pocket he proceeded to pull out enough bills until he had donated $1 for every last one of the flower pots. He happily loaded them into his truck and off he went, leaving myself and everyone with a memory and a lesson and ultimately a question, "Exactly, what valuable lesson did he learn here today?"

Archdiocese of Los Angeles

Office of the Regional Bishop (310) 215-0703

Our Lady of the Angels Pastoral Region

5835 West Slauson Avenue Fax (310) 215-0749

Culver City California 90230

27 March 2017

To Whom It May Concern,

Thank you for allowing the Association of the Servants of the Father of Mercy the opportunity to apply for funds to further their evangelization work in the Archdiocese of Los Angeles.

The Association has worked for several years in the greater Los Angeles area of the Archdiocese serving the poor and homeless individuals and families by providing food, clothing and assistance to them.

With the approval of Archbishop Jose Gomez, I am pleased to endorse the efforts of the Association of the Servants of the Father of Mercy and their outreach programs in the Archdiocese of Los Angeles.

Sincerely in Christ Jesus,

Most Reverend Edward Wm. Clark
Auxiliary Bishop of Los Angeles
Our Lady of the Angels Pastoral Region